RETURNING
THE GAZE Essays on
Racism, Feminism and Politics

Edited by Himani Bannerji

ISBN 0-920813-55-0

Canadian Cataloguing in Publication Data
Main entry under title
Returning the Gaze: Essays on Racism, Feminism and Politics

Includes bibliographical references.
ISBN 0-920813-55-0

1.Women, Black - Canada. 2. Native peoples - Canada - Women.*
3. Chinese - Canadian women. 4. Minority women - Canada. 5. Women
immigrants - Canada.   I. Bannerji, Himani

FC104.R48 1993   305.48'89071   C93-093078-0   F1055.R48

Cover Design & Layout: Hazelle Palmer
Editor for the Press: Makeda Silvera
Copy editor: Martha Sharpe
Printed and bound in Canada by union labour.

Published by: **Sister Vision Press**
                       P.O.Box 217
                       Station E
                       Toronto, Ontario
                       Canada M6H 4E2

Published with the assistance of the Canada Council and the Ontario Arts Council

For Audre Lorde — in memoriam
a comrade and a sister

RETURNING THE GAZE Essays on
Racism, Feminism and Politics

Edited by Himani Bannerji

Sister Vision
Black Women and Women of Colour Press

Contents

Talking About Structures   167

RETURNING
THE GAZE Essays on
Racism, Feminism and Politics

Returning the Gaze: An Introduction

The oppression of women knows no ethnic or racial boundaries, true,
but that does not mean it is identical within these differences . . . To
deal with one without even alluding to the other is to distort our
commonality as well as our difference.

Audre Lorde, "Letter to Mary Daly" in *Sister Outsider*

A beginning or a point of departure

This is not *the* book to top all books of critical writings by non-white
women. In fact, it is the beginning book, a small but absolutely urgent
attempt to put together a volume which is entirely composed of critical, not
creative, writings by them. Hopefully, this will be one of many, because even
as I write, Sister Vision Press has put out a call for another such collection.
Maybe other similar plans of publication are in action, unbeknownst to me.
However, it will be a long time before we elbow and out-compete each other,
or before we overturn the demand-supply ratio of the publishing market and
its practices in Canada. At present, we begin from an unimaginable absence
and silencing — note that I do not say "silence" — on the part of non-white
women themselves.

The words "silencing," "absence," "invisibility," "exlusion," and "non-
representation" have come to be considered, in Canadian mainstream femi-

nism, as cliches or the rhetoric of "women of colour" and black feminist politics. But their importance remains undiminished for anyone who has searched for a developed critical voice of non-white women in Canada, and/or tried to put together a course on gender, race and class with Canadian content. Driven by an absence of books, finding only token presences in anthologies otherwise devoted to "women" (the adjective "white" always implicit), and searching through widely scattered ephemeral tracts or rare "theme issues" of women's journals, I undertook the task of compiling a text. The purpose was to show that there are critical voices of non-white women among us, though Canadian publishing companies and editors have not tuned in to the frequency to capture them. This is a necessary intellectual and political task. This anthology is a movement in that direction.

Our first tasks are to counter existing stereotypes and create a critical space. Our research prior to this compilation led us to the conclusion that the dominant public voice of non-white women was mainly a creative one, and some of it extended directly into political-critical writings. The latter consisted of political statements, refutations and polemics. We found some volumes of poetry, short stories and oral histories. The critical writings were to be found mainly in designated theme issues of *Rikka, Fireweed, Resources for Feminist Research, Kinesis, Trivia, Atlantis* and *Candian Woman Studies*, while there were also some isolated chapters in anthologies.

This situation gives rise to a misperception about our critical abilities and politics and intensifies the historical and existing racist common sense which imputes non-intellectuality to Third World peoples in general and women in particular. It matches racist notions about our difference. As brought out in texts such as Frantz Fanon's *The Wretched of the Earth*, Aime Cesaire's *Discourse on Colonialism*, Henry Gates Jr.'s (ed.) *"Race," Writing and Difference*, David Goldberg's (ed.) *Anatomy of Racism*, among numerous others, this perception of our difference equates us with emotionality and physicality, presenting us as being "natural" rather than as endowed with reason. Translated by the popular media this perception casts suspicion upon native self-government, or, as pointed out by Edward Said, it creates myths about Third World people's proneness to terrorism and violence (see *Covering Islam* or *The Question of Palestine*). It also ramifies into projections of non-white women as beasts of burden, mindless nurturers, and seductresses. Works of Angela Y. Davis, bell hooks, Audre Lorde, June Jordan, among others, speak to these distorted representations and powerfully challenge them. As put forward by an issue of *Resources for Feminist Research* on "Transforming Knowledge & Politics" or by the editors and authors of *Unsettling Relations* it also extends into academia, where "race" and racism are seen as mere "issues" and opinions rather than as integral aspects of social theory. Though feminism has elevated itself to a theoretical status for quite some time now, anti-racist feminism simply serves as a marginal sub-theme.

This one-sided visibility as creative writers has actually put us in a double jeopardy. In the first instance, as non-white women, our experiences of "difference" need form and expression. For this reason, creative writings or oral histories are crucial, and make a fundamental demand for change. But this demand calls for a systematic analytical thinking, and this is what needs to be elaborated by us. The lack of this elaboration is not due to any absence of intellectual-critical abilities of non-white women; rather, the intellectual and publishing establishments of Canada, including the universities, have put neither time nor money towards creating any space to promote or support our writings, especially non-fictional. In the U.S. and Britain the situation is a little better, but there, the publishers and teaching establishments have been historically held hostage to Afro-American, Caribbean, Hispanic and South Asian peoples' more vocal and organized politics and protests. In Canada, until recently, even the feminist presses and publications were bereft of our presence. And even now, with the exception of the reorganized Women's Press (Toronto), non-white women and men almost wholly rely on presses and publications of our own communities. Some examples are Williams & Wallace, Sister Vision and the Toronto South Asian Review. Among the established women's journals, occasional efforts are made to put forward theme or community-based issues. Scholarly journals, such as *Resources for Feminist Research*, *Canadian Woman Studies Journal*, and *Atlantis*, are consequently quite tokenist in their approach, while the performance of cultural magazines such as *Paralellogram*, *Canadian Dimension* and *This Magazine*, etc., leave much to be desired. *Fuse* and *Fireweed*, however, have been the most responsive in terms of infusing a race-gender-sexuality analysis throughout their volumes. This situation of racism by omission creates a vicious cycle both in terms of output and image. Less produces less, and reproduces the myths and stereotypes of our uncriticality contributing to the ongoing racism. All in all, this anthology begins from our absence, and derives its rationale for compilation, its organizational principle, and its methodology for social analysis from this very absence itself.

Regaining subjectivities

I should not have to hope, I should not have to care, about the multiplying, white interpretations of me, of Black people. We should have an equal chance to express ourselves directly.

June Jordan, "On Listening: A Good Way to Hear," in *Moving Toward Home*

An absence, then, as much as a presence, is a good point for a beginning. And when any situation is replete with both - where a pervasive absence signifies an absent presence, and a fleeting presence itself signals to a hidden imperative of invisibility, then that is precisely where work of inquiry and description must begin. We begin with what we have - our invisibility.

What I am saying is not a Zen conundrum, a paradox from "the mystic East," though I am from India. Rather, it is a restatement of what I have been saying so far about us non-white women, variously named as "women of colour," "visible minority women," "immigrant women." The invisibility of "visible minority women" in Canada is such that, until recently, readers and scholars residing elsewhere could perhaps justifiably conclude from published evidence that: a) Canada does not or did not have a significant non-white population; or b) if they at all existed, women (or men) among them were/are incapable of writing or not significant enough to be written about; and c) understanding Canadian society is possible without any consideration of colonialism and (sexist) racism. The situation becomes even more puzzling when small signals of other lives erupt in current mainstream (white) feminist texts, which, in hurried anxiety and soft murmurs, speak of entities such as "visible minority women" or "women of colour," or recite the formula of "gender, race and class" without concretely substantiating either the content or the context. One wonders where the impetus for this originates. But suddenly racism and "women of colour" appear as phrases or topics thrown into books as chapters, producing tight little breathless paragraphs or footnotes. If certain themes and peoples are so important, we wonder about their sudden, urgent, yet parenthetical appearance. What part do they play in the Canadian feminist project?

These questions become pressing for the Canadian reader who actually knows something about Canadian history and society — of its past as a white settler colony, the dispossession of its indigenous peoples, for example, or of Canadian labour history marked with indentured labour, "head tax," "selective" immigration policy, and so on. She may well wonder how Canadian history or political economy, being mostly devoid of this content of racism and violence to non-white peoples, can be advanced as responsible academic disciplines. Her question, *our* question, is: what creates such an invisibility while ironically, or paradoxically, handing us the appellation "visible minorities"?

If this is the problem with our absence, then our "presence" confronts us with another. The presence and representation of non-white women moves from the margin to the centre only to be marginalized again. Boxed into an alien agenda in a feminist text as a variation on the theme of "woman", even when the non-white women express themselves, an effect of alienation sets in with the very act itself. Why? Because it is always on the borderline, judged by extrinsic and irrelevant standards, and serves another's cause: for example, as a tribute to pluralism, diversity or a tolerant form of difference. It is always contained within an adjectivized boundary, such as "black" poetry, "visible minority" prose writings, "women of colour" politics, "black" feminism, etc. This situates our "difference" or constructs it, as it were, through the very gestures of "inclusion" and multiculturalism. They become empty references as far as the main issues of racism and exclusion are concerned. The 1989 Autumn issue of *Studies in Political Economy*, for example, expresses a need for articles based on an integrated gender, class and race analysis, and yet contains only one article by D.E. Smith that could substantiate this call. No direct writing was included by any non-white woman, and perhaps that was better, since a single token presence would have an empty and fatuous add-on character to it. It would be just another topic in a long list of woes of different types of women. In no way would it alter or affect the basic character of feminism as present in the journal as a whole.[1]

Our presence so far in the intellectual or academic world has been a token one, a component in ritual references to gender, race and class. Yet that should not be considered as negligible, but rather as having seized a space from the all-obliterating earlier feminist essentialism. Not found in numbers as authors of critical texts, or in refereed journals, lacking "scholarly" respectability, defying established norms and forms of criticism as well as literary and artistic canons, the writings of non-white women echo the same struggle which threw a challenge to the International Women's Day Committee (1986) and bring it into academia and the intellectual world.

The last six years in particular have seen a growing momentum in critical, albeit polemical, writing among non-white women which maps out a complex terrain of analyses, discourses, descriptions and inventions. At once critical, creative and political, these ventures echo with a multiplicity of political/ideological and critical strategies. They point to radically divergent political possiblities and directions, as well as their "common difference" and politics of solidarity. But this enterprise of writing as a whole is fraught with dilemmas produced by context, restricted space and otherizing forms of difference. Trinh T. Minh-ha, for example, speaks eloquently of this in *Woman, Native, Other*. In her essay "Commitment from the Mirror-Writing Box," she comments on the "conflicting identities" that this current "colonial" situation puts non-white women writers into. She is torn in three ways with regards to her standpoint, self-situation and construction by others. Is she a "writer of colour," a "woman writer" or a "woman-of-colour writer"? She sees that even an inclusion in the mainstream culture attributes her creativity with "race and sex and cheapness." But this very problem, she notes, is also capable of being turned on its head because the contradictions themselves involve a "specification of the writer as a historical subject," showing her that "writing itself as a practice is located at the intersection of subject and history — a literary practice that involves the possible knowledge (linguistic and ideological) of itself as such."[2] From the realization of this contradiction it is possible to hope for change.

The method and the difference: A situated critique

> *Women's liberationists did not invite a holistic analysis of women's status in society that would take into consideration the varied aspects of our experience. In their eagerness to promote the idea of sisterhood, they ignored the complexity of women's experiences.*
>
> bell hooks in *Ain't I A Woman?*

The essays in this book provide a very different notion of visibility than the one we spoke of earlier. They rest on a politicized notion of representation rather than the liberal notion of visibility which structures the discursive practices of multiculturalism and ethnic and race relations. Beginning from the specificities of our different subjectivities, shaped by different forms of colonial and neo-colonial imperialist histories and political economies, both the content and the arrangement of the anthology provide initial grounds for critical thought unindentured to this or that theory. The essays are to be read as separate pieces but also as a unified whole. The arrangement or sequencing of the essays expresses a method of inquiry based on historical and cultural materialism, which links social and literary analysis with politics and experience, even though each essay may not perform that exact task. The idea expressed by the overall organization is to show how subjectivity and agency link with the institutions and structures within which they arise and subsist. Grounded in an analysis of class and patriarchy, this form of feminist marxist analysis is projected from the standpoint of anti-racism or anti-imperialism. The project, to echo D.E. Smith, is to work towards an

> *alternative, reflexive and materialist method of developing a systematic consciousness of our own society through which we can become conscious both of the social organization and relations of the objectified knowledge of the ruling institutions. . . .*[3]

The point of departure for this materialist, integrative method, however, is not from within another theoretical domain, but the daily lived relations and experiences of non-white women.

The essays compiled here are embodiments of consciously and critically experienced relations between non-white women and mainstream Canadian publishing and culture, bourgeois (white) feminism, and a "race" and ethnicity implicated political economy. These texts, therefore, begin from what D.E. Smith has called a "rift" or a "fissure," from a disjunction between what we know ourselves to be and what the social and intellectual environment where we are "raced" tells us.[4] Thus, we begin from an experiencing and knowing historical self and move to a critique of an ideological, dominant version of history and knowledge. Here, social forms of being and social relations of ruling known as "race," gender and class are deeply implied in creating forms of knowing as well. There would be no critique if we did not begin from our actual lives.

Thus, the enterprise is not simply representational in the sense of liberal politics, just to become central from having been marginal, or to seek representation or inclusivity within the existing realm of opportunities currently restricted to white middle-class women. The point is to shift the centre itself from the mainstream to the so-called margin. By understanding "representation" to mean re-presentation of our realities, from a foundationally critical/revolutionary perspective, there can emerge the possibility of making our very marginality itself the epicentre for change. This has always been the principle of any fundamentally revolutionary or critical perspective. After all, all relations of ruling become better visible where they converge most fully: for example, in the structures of the daily lives of non-white women, particularly if they are working class, and, I would add, lesbian. It is from the theorized experience of the most oppressed, as Marx would have said, that the possibility of most knowledge arises. This does not mean endowing each non-white woman individually with a preternatural and spontaneous insight into social reality, but rather, that the social relations which structure her locality and her experience hold clues to the entire society's organization, and that her experiences offer critical entry points into it.

It is important to speak here of June Jordan's crafted essays in *Moving Towards Home* on knowledge and social being of the everyday lives of Afro-Americans. Jordan does not equate being with knowing in any simple/direct fashion. Herself a teacher and a creative writer, she is not fostering the notion that black people have access to knowledge simply through their social being or spontaneity, and thus need no formal education or training in critical thought. But rather, she makes the historicity and experiences of that social being itself the entry point and object of knowledge. June Jordan, similar to Frantz Fanon, for example, claims that the social being of the colonized or oppressed is none other than a historical, existential intersection of all the relations of domination and resistance.[5] A revolutionary-critical thinking would be the conscious unravelling and reworking of those relations of ruling. It is only through this materialist, reflexive epistemology that the concept of the subject can be articulated to that of a revolutionary agency.

This topic of agency requires an extended discussion, but for our purpose, a few basic points must be made here. As with the notion of "difference," that of "agency" also has a variety of uses, and changes with regard to what it is articulated to, what it is motivated by. If agency is articulated to the notion of "diversity" as power-neutral multiplicity of cultural coexistences, the result is quite different from agency's articulation with a powered set of social relations as proposed by Chandra Mohanty, for example, in her introduction to *Third World Women and the Politics of Feminism*.[6] Whereas Roberta Hamilton, in the introduction to her *Politics of Diversity*, sees "power" as an accidental social circumstance messing up the relations between women of different classes, cultures and sexual orientations,[7] Mohanty sees "power" as historical and socio-cultural. She views social relations of power or ruling as organizing that difference, power itself intrinsically as the central pivot of domination. Using D.E. Smith's notion of social relations of ruling and historicizing them as colonialism and imperialism, Mohanty offers us concrete social versions of power and difference.[8] Agency, in this context, is one of revolutionary feminist anti-imperialism rather than a plea for pluralism or liberal tolerance. For, at best, the latter can be radicalized to the extent of thinking in terms of civil rights. This agentic proposal is derived from the notion of "diversity" as coherent with the political economy of a welfare state.

The writers of *Returning the Gaze*, as I do myself, deploy the notion of agency in Mohanty's sense, which goes far beyond the liberal notions of civil rights and voluntary participation. We query the very content of this participation, asking what it comes attached with. We want to know what we are agents for, and where we stand, particularly with regard to the state and its insitutional production of political names or appellations for us. Brand and Carty, for example, reveal the pitfalls of acting as agents in the name of the state category "visible minority" women. In an essay commenting on the origin and function of the Coalition of Visible Minority Women, they cast a critical look on Canada's practice of creating agencies among non-white women, which serves to construct and confer subjectivities that delete fundamental contradictions of race and class while seemingly rejecting difference. To be active at the behest of political-ideological schemas of the state or ruling categories which are structured by the state to contain and manage difference only promotes the elaboration of state power. The agents which are constructed through these ideological devices are social and political subjects, not for themselves, but for an interest alien to themselves. It goes without saying that this form of agency is a co-opted one, and subjectivities so constructed are fundamentally passive. The attempt of *Returning the Gaze* is to critique these co-opted subjectivities while putting in place reflections, analyses and agencies that propose genuinely oppositional possibilities.

The first section of the book begins with self-explorations and reflections which are critical, open-ended and dialogical. While May Yee speaks of herself as a forming subject, posing questions and creations by inhabiting the dual spaces of Canada and China, Amita Handa and Anita Sheth engage in a debate-dialogue, exploring the different meanings of being Indian, which is in turn commented on by Sherene Razack and Himani Bannerji. May Yee's essay, which is a collage, slides from factual statements and memories to criticism and reflective poetry. She is present throughout her text as a changing subject and a subject of change looking at herself in Canada and in her ancestors' world in China, a world where she is also presently embodied. The text moves through a complex interweaving of different stages and states of being, at once and in historical succession, and moves the notion of "identity" from a static, self-enclosed concept, to an always-already-there basis for actions and decisions.

The witty, acerbic, almost scrappy tone of the Anita-Amita dialogue/ debate, critically relfected upon by two other South Asian women, is tonally and formally quite different from May Yee's. The topic is identity, the nebulous notion of being Indian women, as understood by two women presently living in Canada, one of whom has grown up here, while the other spent up to her post-adolescent years in India. Of the commentators, one grew up in India and the other in Trinidad. Here, faced with four different possibilities, the topic of identity leaves behind its usual rigidity, its closed character of fixed cultural values and forms. Everyday life in many of its aspects are debated, discussed back and forth, and commented upon. The result is one of scuttling any settled identity, definition or stereotype of being "South Asian" or "Indian," and instead foregrounding the issue of racism, which, in the end, turns out to be the key reason for wanting a fixed identity in the first place.

Sherene Razack's essay on "Storytelling" or narrativizing selves might be seen as a way of reflecting on the very processes of social self-explorations that are found in the more directly experiential essays. She helps to high-light the critical and interpretive nature of these or any autobiographical exercises, extending the notion of experience from that of private to an incor-poration of the social in every individual's life-version. Self-representation is shown to be a re-presentation of an experienced, embodied social reality.

The next section of the anthology, entitled "Mirrored in the World," speaks further to the politics of representation, establishing the polarities between sexist-racist objectification and authentic self-expression and politi-cal agency. In the general context of culture, these essays in cultural criti-cism draw our attention to what Antonio Gramsci would have called, and Erol Lawrence following him does call, common sense racism. Ranging through a criticism of different ways of signifying non-white women, of how they are made "visible" in ideological-imagistic ways, essays by Aruna Srivastava, Lee Maracle, Arun Mukherjee and Himani Bannerji, collectively show that culture is deeply social. Arun Mukherjee's essay in particular is important in showing how even so-called oppositional stances of feminist criticism are deeply embedded in the social culture of racism. Overall, these essays accomplish the task of feminist, anti-racist/imperialist criticism, and widen the problematic of culture and politics by showing the materiality of history and ideology in mediating and constructing moments and images of oppression and ruling. Cecilia Greene's reflections on Angela Y. Davis's *Women, Race and Class* further highlight the relationship between consciousness and history, with particular emphasis on class.

The third section, "Talking About Structures," grounds our political-cultural critique in the social organizations, structures and institutions whose reflective, mediatory forms they are. Our analysis of "race" and racism, and the experiential critique offered by our descriptions are here joined with an analysis of political economy and the state. This is well displayed in Brand and Carty's work, while Silvera speaks to the particular issue of the state's role in organizing patriarchal oppression of class in the cases of non-white domestic workers, especially of Caribbean and Guyanese origins. These institutions and structures of liberal democracy, exampled through Canada, are shown at work in organizing exploitation and ruling on the bases of race, sex, and class. In this section, then, politics and economics are explored topically. Canadian history, the development of forms of ruling, its capitalism and the stages of state formation are all queried from an anti-racist/colonial/imperialist feminist stance. For example, Roxana Ng's essay on colonialism and nationalism uncovers the fundamental racism of Canadian nationalism. In the perspective of the Canadian government's stance against the indigenous people at Oka (Summer of 1990), her essay becomes even more relevant. The authors of these texts show a double expertise. They have an insider's understanding of being dominated by those structures and institutions of ruling which they describe, while they also possess the critical and analytical expertise to deconstruct them.

The last section brings us full circle to the very beginning of the book, where experience offered us the door through which to enter our world, a door which in the end proves to be an integrated part of the world we inhabit. In short, the private and the public lose their boundaries, creating a mediatory and formative relation between experience, subjectivity, social organization and history. If the personal, as the liberal women's movement claimed, is truly political, we may perform a reflexive double turn through our anti-racist/anti-imperialist feminism and add that the political is personal as well.

Returning the gaze

The history which bears and determines us has the form of a war rather than that of a language: relations of power, not relations of meaning.
Michel Foucault, "Truth and Power," in *Power and Knowledge*

In conclusion, I want to point out that the authors in this anthology share a common perspective of an anti-racist/imperialist feminism, though they have adopted different narrative and analytical strategies for elaboration and exploration of their concerns. One may have used the deconstructive apparatus of post-colonial critique (Srivastava or Razack) while another engages a more directly marxist method of analysis (Mukherjee or Brand and Carty), but there is a common acknowledgement of capital (colonial to imperialist), class, race and gender as analytical counters or naming devices for powered difference. The essays on history, state and economy reveal this stance most directly, while the personal reflections signal and implicate them more indirectly. The anthology as a whole, from the introduction to the last piece, displays a political and epistemological focus.

Step by step, moving from experience to structure, there is an attempt here to disclose how power is concrete in actuality, and operates as constructive social and cultural relations of ruling coded as gender, race and class. This is, in my opinion, an attempt to put together an anti-racist, marxist feminism, and it takes issue with the current practice of conceptualizing in terms of separate or distinct oppressions. Without negating the complexity and specificity of types of oppression, it proposes a more fundamental challenge to imperialist (ex-colonialist) patriarchy. The essays display an ability to "read" and analyze racist-sexist-imperialist constructions of otherness and difference. They can take up the racist typifications or a general object-ification of non-white women produced through what Michel Foucault would have called "the gaze," a lens of/for power. But standing on the analytical-descriptive ground provided by their social location at the intersection of various relations of ruling, they are able to look back at their oppression, that is, return the gaze.

Whether we are non-white or white women, certain dominant aspects of our politics must be taken into consideration, and their homogenization questioned. Feminism in Canada is not a unified (nor unifying) phenomenon. It is riven with its own contradictions and peculiar turns and twists. Living in Canada as I have from 1969 to the present, I have been a part of and an observer of the women's movement. I have watched developments from essentialism to diversity and difference. I have seen a refusal to submit to white feminist essentialism turn to an identity essentialism in a strange twist of theory and politics. What is needed seems to be the working out of a political, analytical/descriptive apparatus which uncovers the specificity of non-white women's oppression while keeping the general context and content of capitalism and class in view. It is this which will make feminism and class analysis responsive to, and integrative of, a critique of racism, colonialism and imperialism.

To think in this way, and to put forward a volume such as this, has become increasingly important over the last ten years or so, as the liberationist/emancipatory thrust of the women's movement becomes weaker. In the name of authenticity, representation, identity and difference, the movement has broken up into self-enclosed segments. This is the ironic reversal of the glossing essentialism that the category "woman" advanced in the earlier phase of the movement. Not that the older "womanizing" essentialism has disappeared completely. There are large strands of it existing among bourgeois, Western feminist thinkers (for example, in Development Studies), who are comfortable with not knowing the "real" difference. But the main trends at this moment are towards various liberal radicalisms which are at bottom marketist and neo-pluralist. There is also an increasing tendency among feminists and feminism towards institutionalization and professionalization — for example, through women's studies or state bureaucracies involving women. And dominant liberal feminism and mainstream feminists have gravitated towards state-facing bureaucracies, with a non-white working token here and there.

With the ostensible view of combating women's oppression, women-run organizations have sprung up in Canada which are a peculiar combination of service centres, feminist politics and self-employing entrepreneurial ventures. Much anger of women has tied itself to funding provided by the Secretary of State and various government ministries to better the lot of women. Small interest groups have emerged which have no basis for collective actions with others, either white or non-white, on the ground of shared politics. Capital, class and imperialism are not seen as being connected to patriarchy, gender organization and racism. It seems to be implicitly believed, though perhaps not explicitly stated, that wrongs of women in these areas can be righted within a modified form of capitalism anywhere in the world. The idea seems to be to exhort capitalism to be responsible and sensitive to "difference" and provide access to "basic needs" for poor women, while, as a whole, structural adjustment is carried out. In addition, a market model for political choice or democracy has become deeply etched into the Canadian women's movement, buttressed by a language of diversity, democracy and freedom.

This anthology is a modest attempt to question all that and aims to go beyond "representing ourselves" in the sense of market liberalism and liberal democracy. Our struggle is for a fundamental change in social relations rather than for a per community quota of representation in the parliament of "races" and "ethnicities." We are engaged in politics, linking theories with practices, examining ideologies through our lives, and our lives through revolutionary ideas. We are not going shopping in the market of cultural differences and relative freedoms.

Himani Bannerji
September, 1992

Beginning
from ourselves

Finding The Way Home Through Issues of Gender, Race and Class

May Yee

Who am I? born in Hong Kong 30 years ago, seventh of eight children, family left Guangdong, China in 1957, immigrated to Toronto, Canada 1964, age two, grew up in East European neighbourhood, lived above family gift and variety store where we all helped out, studied Sociology and International Politics at Carleton University, Ottawa, after 1985 returned to live in Toronto, got involved in Chinese community, anti-racist work, Asian women's writing, teaching ESL to immigrant women workers, Chinese Canadian history and redress, police violence against women issues, community radio 1987-1988, went to China for one year to study Chinese, teach English, travel, and write, returned to family village with parents and brother, returned again to China and travelled to Sri Lanka and India 1990, learned a lot and wrote some more...

Am I ready to write about growing up as a Chinese woman in Canada and returning to China — in an analytical way? A social scientist might say one needs more distance, "objectivity," research, time. But when will I ever have the privilege of that distance, distance from myself, my experience, my pain, my uncertainty? So I write, even as I feel torn about this actual putting to words — because I am not sure I will ever be sure. As a Chinese woman living in Canada, I will never be really "Canadian", whatever that is in this European occupied land — yet I will never know China, of being Chinese, from the inside, even if I were to choose to live and work there. For my place is here, where I grew up, this is what I know. But, this is what I am constantly separate, separated, from — by the forces of racism that always keep me asking questions of identity, belonging, place and voice.

So yes, maybe I am not ready, but then, maybe this is the very state of my position in terms of race, gender, class and age. I have observed enough to see that it is only the privileged who *act* (as opposed to react), without thought to consequences and others. In the same way I will argue that the tentativeness in my writing says as much about us and our position in this society as the very words we so carefully choose, or don't choose. My sentences are often long and full of qualifiers, breaks, brackets, digressions. Or hang unfinished.

But we know the issues that face us because we have lived them, they are our lives. (I/we often switch naturally from the first person singular to the plural — not a royal we but a collective we.) Yet we have too often seen these issues appropriated by white writers and academics, by those who seem to find it easier to write about us (easier for them to write than us, easier for them to write about us than about themselves). Some call it arrogance or complacency, this state of not questioning, not questioning your place to write about other people, the often unthinking appropriation of space that others are still struggling tentatively to claim, reclaim. So it is out of this struggle, this need to reclaim, that I write, however tentatively. I have no honest voice but this one.

The broad issues are simply, for lack of more descriptive words: race, gender, class, economic exploitation, sexism, racism. But these over-stigmatized "isms" include other specific issues — language, culture, history, laws, access, identity, media stereotypes, sexuality, family relations, work relations, the state and all its institutions — to name only a few. This article will touch on almost all of these issues. But, as a Chinese woman who grew up in Canada and has returned twice to China, I want to look in particular at the issues of language, culture, and identity as they relate to displacement —

4

coming from a very old, traditional, agrarian society (which has since seen a revolution to modern socialist society, which is both dealing with feudalism within and international capital without, and is now still rapidly changing) to this modern capitalist society. I also want to examine the effects of changing modern stereotypes of Chinese people and Asian women and whitewashed history as well as the struggles to reclaim our history here and find our identity and voice.

1987 — I'm going to China. I'm leaving everything here, everyone here, all I know. I'm leaving home - to find my unknown home? to find my self, home in my skin. Ma, Baba, "daiga" (whole family), I go to seek your words, the words we never spoke, the words you seek silently, I see silently in your eyes. I have felt your wordlessness has said more to me than a parent's constant speeches and advice ever could have. It has driven me to try and find words for you, for me, for all of us.

Coming here to this strange land where voices cut because of ears that do not listen nor understand, eyes that do not see us. Their voices, loud and complacent like conquerors sure of place, drown out our hesitant and questioning ones.

Ma Baba, I now ask out loud, and loudly, the silence in your eyes. And the answer is the words we all know, but are still unspoken in this hostile vacuum where our words have not resonance. But long resounding in our own ears — we know, we know, we know...

Growing up Chinese in Toronto means first dealing with the issue of language — having to deal with a shift, or split in language. This comes up often from the time language learning begins — by the age of two — if the parents and others (especially grandmothers) speak to the child in both languages, Chinese and English. Sometimes it's not an issue until school age,

age five — which can be even more traumatic if a child has to learn English in the strange new setting of school.

The language I first spoke was Toisanese — a southern Chinese village dialect, related to Cantonese, which is the provincial capital dialect also spoken in Hong Kong. Most Chinese who came to Canada before the late 1960s, the "lo huakew" (old overseas Chinese), spoke a similar village dialect. I was fortunate enough to learn to speak English, but also how to read before I went to school. As in the case of most Chinese Canadian children, the longer I was in school and the more I was exposed to Canadian — or American —culture (TV, books, etc.), the worse my Chinese got. In fact, most Canadian-born Chinese eventually forget how to speak Chinese. I have cousins, all born here, who speak to their mother in English while she answers back in Chinese (they more or less understand each other). This is very sad, one might say, but not uncommon for second generation Canadians from other language groups as well as Chinese.

What research has been done on the effects on the children within our communities of this disjuncture in language? We know the effects could not be wholly negative, despite the strong forces of racism that deny the validity and value of the "foreign" language and culture, the "other" world we often try to hide, and hide in.

I still speak Toisanese - though frozen at the level of a young child without any schooling in the language, and often without even the fluency of a five year old (or of when I was five years old). Actually, my Toisanese has improved since I studied Mandarin (Beijing dialect, "common speech" or putonghua) in China — even though the two dialects have very little in common. I sense it has more to do with getting over the mental block of my teenage years, when I used to proudly answer that I didn't know how to speak Chinese when curious classmates asked me to say something in it.

That I have managed to maintain some Chinese can be in good part attributed to the fact that my immediate family with whom I lived and grew up is almost like four generations — my grandmother who spoke no English

at all, my mother who speaks almost no English, and my father only bro-
kenly, older brothers and sisters who had grown up in China and are still
fluent in Chinese, but almost constitute a separate or buffer generation to us
younger children who grew up mainly in Canada, remembering little or
nothing of China. Yet, it was I, number seven of eight, who was one of the
first to return to China — my year of study there finally prompting my parents, who had not been back to the village in over thirty years, to finally
return there with me and my brother.

> *Hoiping, Guangdong, China — "hengha" / home village: Everyone here
> not only looks like me, but also speaks the same language of my child
> tongue, words of my child heart. This is the language of home, of inside,
> of family, of private - and here it is everywhere, on the street, in the
> stores, in public. So public life merges with private life in a way I have
> never experienced, divided at "home" in Canada by two languages, two
> cultures, two lives. Such a simple thing: that the words you speak to
> your mother you could speak to a stranger (so strangers aren't so strange,
> and Mother is no stranger).*

Let's look at the issue of language in terms of the women of my generation. After 27 years living in Canada, why does my mother, and many women
like her here, not speak English? I have taught English as a Second Language (ESL) to many Chinese women who are garment workers for over 10
or 20 years, who also speak very little English. The interesting thing is you
would probably find very few men who don't have a good working knowledge
of English, unless they came here at a much older age. This has to with past
government language training programs which only gave male newcomers
free ESL classes. But there are also practical issues of economic and cultural
pressures and opportunities, and time. Chinese women of our mothers' generation, born in the 1920s or earlier, grew up in pre-revolutionary China,
where women's place was ideally only inside the home (though rural women,

7

like my mother and grandmother, actually also did a lot of work outside in schooling because her father sent money from Canada insisting she go to school).

But the main reason that many immigrant women never learn English is their double burden of work. My mother had to bring up eight children and cook for and look after additional relatives who stayed in our cramped apartment above the variety store, where she also worked everyday. Under those circumstances, it's a wonder she even lasted the three months of English class she initially attempted when she first got to Toronto.

Her burden, like many Chinese working women, was made more manageable by the help of a live-in grandmother. My father's mother, Ngen, who lived with us until she died of cancer after over 15 years in Canada, never learned a word of English. She, as almost all Chinese women of her generation, never went to school at all. Her husband, my grandfather, had passed away in China. But most older Chinese women who came to Canada in the 1950s and 60s after the repeal of the Chinese Exclusion Act[1] (like my maternal grandmother, Ah-Po, in 1951), came to join usually even older husbands they had not seen for decades because of racist Canadian immigration laws. For these many older Chinese women, the journey from traditional green villages in southern China to cold grey cities in Canada — an unfathomable leap — must have been most difficult of all.

One could say of countless women who came to Canada at an older age and never learned a word of English, that they never really left the village; it was too much for them to adapt to life here, after nearly a whole lifetime in an opposing world. Ngen who first took care of me, then I of her as she became sick with cancer and age, used to forever hark back to life "aw-kei" (home) in "hengha" (home village), as if *that* was her life, and here was only a strange prison made up of the walls of our second-story, off-the-earth, family apartment, with occasional shifts to cramped apartments of her other children here, or occasionally, a Chinese restaurant.

I grew up living in two worlds, where the boundaries of the first world were the same walls that imprisoned my Ngen, and took her off the brown earth and green fields where she spent the first 70 years of her life — her life rooted therein. Her roots, which are my roots, in the end made that world — my family home world, my Chinese self — one without boundaries. Though I was not to find that out until, at the age of 25, I returned to discover China, where in that open greenness of country and deep black/ brown/ red/ yellow soil and countless generations of my people's history, I discovered how horribly bound I had been in Canada — by racism, by displacement, by the painful search for identity as a Chinese woman in white dominated Canada, bound by not knowing, the depth and breadth of my loss.

No place here
in this unreal nation
i am an unrecognized citizen
two worlds
and me   a world apart
from "aw-kei" home
*   "heng-ha" village*

poor village
200 people
one story houses
TVless and timeless
rich countryside
wet rice fields
lush rolling hills
so green
so green it makes my heart
ache
ache with wonder or loss?
*with wonder **and** loss*

9

so I went back to China
in search
of what?
maybe a sense of place
    a sense of history
    a feeling for my people
travelled across vast country
so many worlds within
a billion people and earth
earth my feet had never touched
earth my Grandmother had stood ankle deep in
Ngen, I touch you   *touch earth*
my heart remembered

and all that I found
(where I was not looking)
leaves me constantly amazed
awash in wonder
yet, all that I know I will never know
leaves me forever lost

lost in a sea of broken memories
we crossed an ocean
and lost a world
find ourselves barely
afloat
straddling two worlds
    two seas
drowning in loss
floating in wonder
if the undertow doesn't pull us down

can see all horizons...

And now, 27 years after my arrival on this other shore, and a year after
my return from my second trip to China (and South Asia), I still find myself
constantly pulled under by the contradictions of life as an Asian woman in
this white, male-dominated country, by the violence and horror of what I see
happening everyday to my sisters and brothers around me, here, and around
the world. Still, in 1992, as we in the Americas look back at 500 years of
invasion and resistance, I also find myself lifted abuoy by the strength of my
sisters and brothers all around, by the vision to radically change what has
fundamentally kept us down for hundreds of years.

500 years

in this stolen land
where real estate is expensive
but speech is free,
words are cheap
and I don't know what to say anymore

our words have been falling on deaf ears
for 500 years

they cut the native heart
    cut the native tongue
now say we are free
to say anything[in english]
free
to say anything we want[in any language]
because no one will listen
[except to record your treason for future reference]

the script has already been written

11

written in blood
in the fine print at the bottom
of broken treaties

500 years
we've choked on their language
on the compromise in carefully chosen white words
now choking on our black rage
on words said over and over and over again
genocide, colonialism, imperialism
racism, sexism, capitalism
taken out of our mouths
barely formed
and into fine words
in fine academic journals

turning our pain into jargon
  our rage into jingles
regurgited back to us
in head-ache-inducing fine print
"neo-colonialism," "post-structuralism," "paternalism,"
"multiculturalism," "post-feminism," "deconstructionism"

choking
on their white language
  their twisted words
choking on our own blood

take back our words
take back our lands, our lives

500 years
enough talk

Those of us who are not native but not white live here everyday with
the contradiction that although, through great leaps of history, geography,
language and culture, we make our homes in this country, whether by choice,
necessity or birth, this can never be our home the way it is for white Canadians. We are all (including First Nations people, ironically) familiar with that
seemingly innocent assumption-laden question:*"Where do you come from?"*
(and the answer,"Bloor Street," never quite seems good enough). Or there's
the: *"Do you speak English?"* Well, I *teach* English, I think in English, I love
and live in English — in fact, it is the only language I speak at all fluently
(even if racism and my biculturalism makes English sometimes feel like a
foreign language, like a skin that doesn't quite fit, a skin that doesn't fit my
skin).

At home in one's skin — taken for granted by most people in this society, but not if that skin is not white. I never even knew what that feeling
was, even to put a name to, until I went to China for the first time. And
when I discovered it for the first time blending in with the people in the
streets of Bejing, it was so new, yet so absolutely basic; it really changed the
way I looked at the world, and at myself.

That non-acceptance, that never quite belonging, is, in this
"multicuturally sensitive," "race relations" or let's-sweep-racism-under-the-
rug society, manifested only in small part by schoolyard namecalling of
"chink" or "paki" or "nigger." Much more than that, we have "educated"
racism that knows to not "call a spade a spade," but comes out in those "innocent" questions, their limited choice of small talk (the big favorite, of course,
is Chinese food), the things that don't get said more than what's said, an
awkward silence, a glance or a seeing through you, the tone of voice, or a
patronizing manner that at times can approximate, making you feel like you
have a fatal disease. Then, of course, the basic issues of racism, power and
privelege can take away your job more easily than it is given, can make it
more difficult to get a promotion, find a home, buy your groceries, drive your
car, walk on the street, go to school, fall in love. And, of course your class and

sex also are major factors in that unequal equation of power and privelege.

When we are constantly made to feel like we don't belong here, the issue of "home" becomes central. As I learned more about the actual history here, of the destruction of millions of First Nations people and their ways of life and the theft of the land — the history they never taught us in school — I began to realize that those who have told us to "go home" all these years here are in fact those who have the least right to call this "home" (unless one believes "might is right"). So, who and what is really "Canadian" after all? But this revelation still does not stop profound feelings of "homesickness".

Sometimes I feel so homesick — just listening to Chinese flute music or a folk song. The feeling really pulls me down when I ask myself, where exactly is the home I feel so sick with longing for? I'm not sure. Unless one can be homesick for a whole country that one has never lived in, doesn't have a specific home in, nor fixed address. After all, the Chinese word for country, "guojia," has the word "home" in it, "jia," — country of my home. The lilting of Chinese music reminds me of travelling on the train. And if home, "jia," could be a moving window on the world, then I'd love to take a slow train through the vibrant hills and hollows of the heartbreaking/healing land of China, my home.

Or maybe a slow boat — like the one I took from our home province, Guangdong, to Wuzhou — where I wrote this:

We move upstream in the waters which flow past our mother and father and ancestors' old home. There is no question as to why I have come back — never has been since the moment I saw hauntingly familiar hills and felt my heart turn over (right itself up to come to rest), and open to the sensation of coming home.

*This sense of home is not the home of **hearth**,*
*but the home of **earth**,*
*the home of the deepest and wildest **heart***

14

— as basic as skin, blood, ancestry, the line of life
— for a moment standing still in time, encompassing all of time, no more
is needed. Home as Motherland, returning to the womb of original earth.

I could not live here, but I could stay here frozen in time, would want to
be buried in this earth (my natural home) if I were to be buried in any
earth.

But time has taken me where I have been and am, and so we must live in
the homes of our own making
—the small home of domicile, family, friends. The real day to day sense
of home is a domestic one.

So, Toronto is my real home — living in the circle of family, amidst
friends who know me even if they cannot know me in the most basic sense
of skin and blood and pain. And no, I would not want to live outside the
circle of arms of love, arms and eyes that hold me even if this hostile
white soil and grey concrete never will.

We children, not rooted to white stolen land, must find our rest in small
spaces, our home in small secure places of our own making, in our end-
less struggles - but never forgetting this Motherland, this unending
openness of earth and heart, the roots of our longing, and our loving.

Returning to China was eye-opening and world-expanding for me, but it
was like acquiring new eyes to see and feel something so new yet very old
and familiar. It also gave me the distance to see our lives in Canada in perspective. There's a Chinese proverb about being able to see one's own mountain from a distant mountain — and when that distant mountain is also a
home of sorts then one can see all kinds of things.

Hey, from this distance, these heights, I can see that we never really knew what home was — just knew it couldn't be found nor take root in the pre-fab suburban or urban(e) boxes that most of our families and friends have taken (temporary?) refuge in. If home is where the heart is, then at best we made erratic homes back "home" in Canada.

Broken hearts, broken homes,
we have suffocated in plastic that sanitized our pain,
behind cushioned walls that held in our misery
and held out the horrors of the world,
saran-wrapped our bubbled lives ready to burst
but
some of our bubbles burst long ago
young eyes opened
to our displaced separation within
and the unending horror without

how we have held all those fragments of our lives
and still remain eyes open
I do not know
then
I do not know maybe
what has gone missing a long time ago
what maybe we have lost forever in our hearts
do not know what our eyes cannot see anymore
(after years of being held in pain, privelege, and dust)

but here we are
escaped (not unscathed)
from the modern ruins
and I don't know if we,
so long immersed in the source of the storm

the belly of the beast,
with our precarious privilege and insight on one side
and accompanying self-hate and destructiveness on the other,
we who have learned so well to hate our lives
that we can even begin to call that living and loving,
we,
can we build a society?

or is our vision of socialism
just a vision of smashing the source of our oppressions
only destroying our destroyers (and ourselves)
to sink together into the drowning sea?

our eyes can see
and maybe can even see what needs to be done
but, can our hands move more than a pen?
can they move mountains? move earth? move hearts?

can such broken hearts hold the faith and love
needed to build a new world (instead of just tearing it down)?

see
the world coming down
in huge bloody pieces all around us
it does not need our little hands
to help bring it down
to dip into the sea of blood already too huge to fathom

hands we need
to cradle a newborn baby
build a new world

hold another hand
wipe away tears
write a new book
work the land
grow the food
feed the children
hold back the tide
hold on
to find our way home...

So maybe I am homesick for the home I never had, home I never knew, never knew what I was missing — until I saw the land, the people, felt the history, again — then, in that moment of recognition, I felt a healing wholeness for the first time. These recurring bouts of homesickness are really a missing of a part of myself, that drove me at an early age to write angst-ridden, teenage existentialist poetry.

I'm not sure I'm ready to write about those painful teenage years, now given the name "identity crisis." But when will I ever, then? It's been ten years, a lot of time, tears, work, and questioning. But I've come a long way in learning to see my inner world of woe, well of loneliness, in a much broader perspective — in learning to see the world. It's no longer writing about "I" in relation to an abstract "all." I've come to learn some things about the complexities and contradictions of society, history, culture and economics that press on all our lives. And sometimes the sheer weight of that knowing, and knowing what I do not know, paralyzes me once again in a homesickness and emptiness that I can only begin to express in writing. And maybe what makes it hardest to express is that so much of it is based on what we've lost, on what's missing in the structured chaos of our lives here, in this "postmodern capitalist" hell-heaven (depending on which side of the fence you stand, and whether you're into shopping, consuming, unseeing waste and destruction). Not to mention that in North America, it's all based on land theft and genocide.

I feel this country is nobody's real home, except the First Nations people, who have had so much taken from them I wonder that they must not also feel profoundly homesick. If home is the heart, the land, the people, the history, the interconnectedness and wholeness of all these things, then I think we've all lost our way here, and only the First Nations people can show us the way back home.

Of course, those who feel at home here don't ask these questions of identity and self-doubt and must wonder (sometimes, but not usually out loud), "if you're so bitter about this place, why did you come here?" Or, better yet, "why don't you go home?" But that just puts us back where we started - where's home? Most of us didn't come here by choice (listen, I was only two years old!). If we were not political refugees from imperialist or imperialist-backed wars, then we were economic refugees — or as a friend likes to put it, "we're just following our money..."

I don't think I'm bitter. I'm just trying to understand, beyond our own petty differences and personal concerns, the links, the contradictions, to search for the truth in a world gone mad with destruction and lies. We can't afford to be bitter, for we have survived, when the forces that be have tried to destroy us with racism, sexism, economic exploitation, violence, war — if not destroy us physically in wars back home or the 500 year war on First Nations people here — then destroy our identity. So it is important to work on this nebulous thing called "identity," which can fall into navel-gazing easily, even as the economic situation around us worsens. But a strong, grounded (as opposed to a navel-based) identity — meaning an identity with the people, with home, with history, with land — is what our children need to grow strong enough to fight those forces of destruction. So they don't have to grow up like most of our generation, wanting to be white, not wanting to be Chinese, to be Black, to be Native, to be the Other.

It's interesting to compare this racial self-denial and self-hatred with the impact of gender oppression, because I think most girls here are growing up now no longer wishing they were boys. I don't remember wanting to be a girl, a woman, though there were many times I noticed the privilege of my brothers, both within and outside the home, and I quite resented it — yet I never wanted to be a boy. I think I had an early consciousness of a practical "feminism" that told me things were not at all fair, but gave me the space to fight the already identified stereotypes and inequalities, without ever wanting to be as aggressive, insensitive, selfish and careless as I saw boys being.

But in those years of growing up, when our family of ten or more was very poor, with no extra money to spend on "luxuries" like a house, a car, toys, holidays, fancy clothes, new clothes or a lot of clothes, school camps, dentist visits, of course, then I wished we were rich, or even had as much money as most of the working class families in our neighbourhood to buy all those things kids begged for — brand names we saw on commercials, which became the main source of children's conversations and status. So I always felt doubly excluded at school, on the basis of race and class. The combination of the two compounded the dilemma of the stereotypes forced on me and my inability for the longest time to break out of those racist and classist barriers.

Right through high school and even university I wanted to be white, and I tried to fit in to my almost totally white school and university environment. I pretended I couldn't speak Chinese, I tried to avoid going out with my mother or sitting next to her on the subway, I avoided the handful of Chinese and black kids at school, just as they each seemed to avoid me. I mean, it's not like any of this was conscious, as if I *wanted* to be embarrassed about my mother and ashamed of my culture and people — but it was just common sense, with seemingly a lack of other choices for teenagers here, for whom the world consists of trying to fit in, belong, be "cool" in the midst of a lot of heavy peer pressure, without anyone to really talk to about this, who could warn about the pitfalls. My parents had no idea of this other world, and my sisters and brothers were going through their own silent painful struggles to cope. It is a painful irony that so many of us grow up here thinking we are so alone, and go through hell trying to fit in, when all along there are so many

20

of us going through the same experiences. So we're not alone really after all.

In grade 10, I won awards for getting the highest marks. I had already gotten used to being called "browner," seen as that "smart Chinese girl," accused of studying all the time, being all brains, like a computer — the typical stereotypes about Asian kids in North America. But the awards were like a public confirmation of all those nasty rumours (which were not that true, because I spent very little time studying for school, most of my time devouring all the books, classics and junk, I found in the library). I almost didn't go to the awards ceremony, wondering if there was any way I could refuse it (but keep the $100.00). Of course I went, as did my proud parents. But, from that point on, I studied even less (yet, interestingly enough, my marks actually went *up!*).

So, of course, nobody believed me, or even asked. They just assumed I spent all my time studying, and kept treating me like the quiet, studious, straight 'A' Chinese girl — which was the last thing I wanted to be, especially when everyone else (it seemed) was "going" with someone and spent their time at parties and doing other exciting, cool and meaningful things. So I remember being so scared to speak, thinking I always had to say something "cool" (to counter that constricting preconception of me), choosing words so carefully in my head, that, in the end, if I finally came up with something cool enough to voice, the time would be past to contribute my comment. So, I hardly ever spoke.

I knew I was smart (so much so I could afford not to want to be smart at school), but I had a serious "social" inferiority complex because I could not express what was in my head, was insecure about talking, felt very "uncool" and totally unattractive to boys. I grew up in a school which had a hierarchical social environment revolving almost exclusively around the heterosexual merry-go-round. You were judged to be "in" based on who you were "going around" with and how many relationships you had been in and out of, how many guys you'd "dropped." It was this incredible game, and if you had never had a boyfriend or girlfriend you were completely out of the picture, invisible.

21

I have always hated the term "visible minority," finding it particularly ironic because of how often we find ourselves *invisible*, not even worthy of notice in the heterosexual game of checking everyone out, pursuit and conquest. So I think we learn very early on to not play the game, or else (like a few of the kids I remember in school) go through painful contortions to try to act "white," and to be so artificially outgoing and outlandish that even radically unconscious white kids (into being phoney themselves) know something is phoney and avoid these nonwhite kids who try too hard, or take advantage of them.

Then, of course, there's the kind of attention Asian women get as "mysterious exotic sexual creatures," that makes us feel again invisible. As we get older, we quickly begin to recognize a certain glassy-eyed white male look, that does not see us, but sees some kind of fantasy "suzie wong" or "china doll" image. The pervasive stereotypes of Asian women in Western culture as being submissive, exotic and easily sexually available are tied in with the American military presence in Asia since the defeat of Japan in the 1940s, the Vietnam war, and the presence of huge military bases in the Philippines. This military imperialism led to the American restructuring of, in particular, Thailand and the Philippines into "rest and recreation" areas for their huge population of U.S. soldiers. The economies of these countries have become based on sex tourism to fulfil the fantasies of Western and Japanese men, and the commodification and sale of Asian women — and girls as young as 11 or 12 — as prostitutes and mail-order brides.

From the images manufactured by this economic and sexual exploitation, it is no wonder that Asian women, if they are seen by Western men at all, are often seen as submissive and available alternatives to Western women — who are often seen as having become too demanding and aggressive as a result of feminism. This outrageous image of Asian women (I have yet to meet an Asian woman who is not outraged when confronted by it, whether used unconsciously or not), is also apparent in the way we are treated by other women, even within the women's movement. I don't know how many times I've been confronted by self-declared politically conscious people with the description or expectation of myself or other Asian women as being so "nice," and also the accompanying surprise and incredible defensiveness whenever we get angry, swear, or speak out — "oh, I didn't know you could be like that...", or the quick accusations of being "too aggressive" (from people who are clearly usually *more* "aggressive"!). And I know this to be a common experience among other women here from all over Asia.

The mirrors that mainstream Western society holds up to Asian women are contradictions which distort and refract so many times over that one wonders how we are able to see ourselves and form our sexual identities in this society where sex and women are so grotesquely commodified. It certainly results in deep insecurities that can only affect all intimate and sexual relationships. And, in different ways, it affects all our relationships with people who have internalized these stereotypes, just as we, as Asian women, have ourselves internalized them by accepting, denying, using, or challenging the distorted mirrors held up to us.

But for all the powerful Western stereotypes of Asian women as both passive/submissive "china dolls" and "dragon ladies" who use their "exotic" sexuality to manipulate, along with the effects of our own patriarchal cultures, I am very conscious of the real strength of Asian women of our mothers and grandmothers, the carriers of incredible burdens of family and work, and age-old traditions. We don't have to look just at the new generation of Asian women in North America who are speaking up and organizing against sexism and racism. We all know older Asian women of great strength, wisdom and vitality (not to mention the historical participation of women in revolutions all over Asia itself).

So even as new growing generations of Asian women have been giving voice and political and cultural expression in the struggle to break racist and sexist barriers of silence, we need to put forth first the strength and voices of our mothers and grandmothers, who have never been silent as much as publicly silenced or not listened to. In the first book of its kind to be published about Chinese women in Canada, *Jin Guo: Voices of Chinese Canadian Women*,[2] subtitled in Chinese (Toisanese), "Heung Ngoi Gong...listen to me speak", does just that. This book was a community project seven years in the making, and consists of oral histories chosen from over 100 interviews in English and Chinese. Most of the life stories in the collection are of older Chinese women in Canada, in their 60s to 90s. These women were mostly born here, since racist immigration laws like the $500 Head Tax and then the 1923-47 Chinese Exclusion Act made the immigration of Chinese women to Canada extremely rare until the 1950s and 60s. This collection of the authentic voices of women is a tribute to their strength and contribution to a community that was isolated and damaged by a century of repressive legislative and structural racism.

One Chinese woman born in British Columbia in 1908 speaks about her mother: *"It was always a steady routine of work, work, work for my mother. She'd have a child in her arms or on her back, because there were eight of us. She had to help with the laundry, farmwork, to cook, and maintain us."*

The economic reality for the Chinese in Canada was that, because of racism and restrictive labour laws, the only work usually open to them was for families to start up their own small businesses in restaurants, laundries or farms/hothouses. This meant the few Chinese women who were in Canada worked hard alongside their husbands, shattering the traditional stereotype that Chinese women were housebound and did not work. (There were also a number of women brought over as prostitutes, for the huge "bachelor" community). But Chinese women contributed their strength to more than just working in and outside of the house for the family. They also did much to hold together small communities under siege.

One woman born in the 1920s speaks of the harsh situation in Nanaimo, B.C., which had a "Chinese ghetto" and segregated schools for "Others" (Asian and native children): *"I think, perhaps, we are different, we are stronger. Earlier, the Chinese people have to cling together for support very much. Otherwise, there are enough attacks from outside if we're not strong. The families were very united in their doings. I think, if you've been brought up in Nanaimo, you come out pretty strong — appreciative."*

The same woman also talks about her later political involvement with the Chinese community, including this:*"I was the only woman on the `Committee for the Change of the Chinese Immigration Policies.' Although the Chinese Exclusion Act was repealed in 1947, a fairer law to allow family reunion wasn't established until 1957, after ten years of lobbying. They felt the success of our meeting with Diefenbaker came from having a woman there. It's natural to have your families together — how dare they keep our families separated?!"*

This Chinese Canadian women's oral history collection contains many stories of women surviving isolation, abuse and very harsh conditions. This last excerpt is from a woman named Margaret, who was brought to Canada in 1910 as a "slave girl," first ran away from her abusive "relatives"/employers, then from an abusive husband: *"He wanted to treat me like a dog — I barked at him and ran away. `bow-wow-wow' — can't take things too seriously. You have to laugh a little, cry a little — that's life. You know, life is very complicated. You can't feel sorry for yourself. You should fight for your rights, and away you go! Run, like I did. I'm a liberated woman."*[3]

This first collection of Chinese women's voices is very important, especially for Chinese kids growing up in Canada, not knowing where they belong. I didn't find out about the history of the Chinese in Canada, about the Exclusion Act and Head Tax (even though my grandfather had paid it to come here), about the stories of women like Margaret, until I was well into my 20s, and had started working for this women's oral history project and on the redress issue in the Chinese community in Toronto. We need to bring our children up strong on this knowledge of our painful but proud history here, not on denial. I wish I had learned much of this sooner, instead of feeling confused for so long on issues of identity, place and voice, instead of needing to go back to a country I had never been to — to China in search of some elusive identity, sense of place.

25

There are all sorts of terms, humourous and technical for that "identity crisis" almost all nonwhite children grow up with here. There's "banana" — yellow on the outside, white on the inside (and its equivalents like "oreo," or "apple"). Some say Chinese kids here are like popcorn — "little yellow things that turn white under pressure". These are things that can make you laugh and wince at the same time.

Then there's a Chinese term which can be taken as a serious insult, "juk-sing", which refers to Canadian-born Chinese as being bamboo which empty at both ends, meaning neither Chinese nor Western.

"juk-sing" / hollow bamboo (empty at both ends)

"ai-ya!" but you never knew how
appropriate that insulting term actually was
never knew our loneliness
so different from your loneliness
you who knew
what you were missing
no empty longings, no hollow misgivings
your heart full with the memory
the absolute knowledge of this
beautiful old land

is it worse to be empty
and not know it
not know what you are empty of?
but
finally here
this juk-sing / hollow bamboo
finds myself full
full at both ends

26

knowing where I'm coming from
and even beginning to know
where I am going

strange
how we must come back
to know where to go
to be more
than juk-sing / hollow bamboo
with the wind whistling through us
whatever direction it blows
to find where
bamboo stands in groves
not alone
stands together in circles
erect, strong, but flexible enough
to bend with the wind
yet stay rooted
in this earth

to stay rooted
though the struggle will always go on
I know now
where a tired heart can find rest for awhile
rest awhile
where nothing can hurt you
where Mother earth holds and heals
all the wounds of uprootedness from hostile white soil

welcome home little girl....

This was a poem written in China, on a train heading back toward our
family village in Guangdong. It was written for my Grandfather, Ah-Gong,
almost one year after his death in Toronto. Ah-Gong, who paid the $500 head
tax 75 years ago, one of tens of thousands of Chinese who had to pay this
exorbitant racist tax just to immigrate to Canada, then had to wait almost
half a century before his wife, children and us grandchildren could rejoin him
in Canada, after the repeal of the Chinese Exclusion Act.

Yet this poem is not just speaking to my grandfather, but to all the
grandmothers, mothers and fathers, and even those like my eldest sisters
and brothers who grew up in China. It is a plea for understanding that although I am just beginning to try to understand the world you have come
from and how difficult the transition must have been — it is a plea for understanding those of us, including the very children of your blood, who you see as
too westernized, and either lost or too privileged in our English-speaking
adaptability here to reach. It was not our choice, though we may understand
the economic reality, the famine situation that drove you from the land you
loved so much that you never let us forget our unknowing betrayal of it. But
it was not our choice, how could we have ever wanted and chosen to be so
torn? to have hated ourselves (and sometimes you, who loved us, but not the
way we saw love portrayed on TV) and tried to be white, to deny you and all
you tried to give us. I guess you never really knew what you were competing
against here, or what racism can do to young, growing minds and hearts.
And how were you to know? because what were your choices? And how are
we to know, how much we have lost?

And so, maybe our generation, to find our way, must first retrace the
steps, complete the circle, to attain some kind of closure that would allow us
to go on, healed if never quite whole. Just as our grandfathers, our mothers,
came from their old world in search of new lives, for their children if not
themselves, so then must we, the children now grown, leave all we know here
of this new land to know what our elders left behind. Our people came to
these modern metropolises, and are still coming here, from Asia, Africa and

other nonwestern countries, in search of material security from old civilizations torn by military and economic wars of centuries of colonialism and imperialism.

Many of us have attained here the material comfort the migrating sought (while others have found their old careers as doctors or engineers have somehow led them here to work in restaurants and stand silently in assembly lines). But here we all are in the land of material plenty, where dreams of freedom become the American dream/nightmare of consumption. And many of us who stop to think, between our tedious jobs and cashing our paycheques at the bank and spending it at the shopping centre, find ourselves materially gorged to the point of sickness, and spiritually sucked dry. The irony seems to be that, the more we achieve in the American dream of material consumption, the more lost we find ourselves, and the more we find we have lost our children to a modern high-tech, pop culture of indulgence we have almost no control over, even if we could begin to understand it in this strange new language.

But when I was growing up, my family could never afford Barbie dolls, a car, or anything much beyond absolute necessities. Then it hurt, but now I am relieved by the extent to which I escaped the consumption and superficiality game, and the material addictions. Compared to the early responsibilities of my older sisters and brothers, I was also relatively lucky in the extra privileges, choices and freedom I had as one of the youngest, whose way was paved through the earlier negotiations of my sisters with my parents through a landscape of conflicting values. I was able to choose not to buy into the system, to be stuck in a job or career that gave the necessary economic security to fulfil responsibility to the family. I was able to choose just to study liberal arts out of pure interest (though high school counsellors tried to stream me into maths or nursing), then turn down scholarships, to write and work in the community, to travel, to finally return to China in search of the roots my elders had to forsake for material security and family responsibilities.

29

Maybe I am writing this to pay back. To give back what I have learned and seen in my studies and work here and my trips back to China, to give back to those who went before me and sacrificed certain individual choices, but allowed me to choose to learn, to see the world, to write, to speak, to fight back.

Although I knew my parents and grandparents could never fully understand or even want to try to understand my life, so different from theirs, I do not feel that I have betrayed the traditional values they tried to teach us all. I have learned, but found I had to apply my sense of responsibility to family, to the larger family of community, and world. On seeing the world and all its horrors, yet strength of people, I could do nothing else with what my elders gave me, unless I closed my eyes to it all.

This is an attempt to put what I have learned into words and share it with others who are also trying to make sense of the contradictions which make up our lives.

Giving voice through writing is one way of fighting back, against all the powerful forces which attempt to silence us. For those of us who come from communities which have been silenced through histories of colonization, patriarchy and resistance, the pen is a powerful weapon we must learn to use well. To write as honestly as we can, from the heart, to drive at the heart of a system which is indeed killing us, to expose the truth as we live it, to expose the lie of this capitalist ideology of liberal democracy, which we see before our eyes, during the current economic crisis, is very capable of turning into the fascism which belies it.

The power of the pen is only found in the connection to history, people, and land, the understanding of the material sources of power and resistance. Western liberalism, and its appropriation of the powerful concepts of freedom and democracy, are illusory, empty words. Freedom to exploit (if you own the means of production), freedom to consume (if you have the money), freedom to die (if you don't), individual freedom (depending on the class, race and gender you individually belong to). And democracy is a TV gameshow every four years where the contestants and winners are fixed in advance by the corporate sponsors. We come from old lands and cultures where the basis of society has never been some illusory sense of individual freedom, but the strength of collective responsibility and the connection to land.

On a train to Beijing...

Here is China, I see so many people living lives which they seem to call their own in a way I cannot name mine. I know I am much more privileged in many ways, and I have heard from many dissatisfied university students yearning to go abroad that we in the West are so much freer...

Yes, we are free - free to not know where or what to pin our lives to.

Oh, what can I tell these educated urban youths who speak about "democracy" without thinking about the peasants who make up the vast majority of the people of China? How can I tell them that in the West one is only meant to live for oneself, for material gain, for consumption (consuming each other and ourselves in the process)?

I say that freedom falls into itself, falls into meaninglessness, into nothing more than "liberal" rationalizations for global exploitation, destruction and murder...want such blood-tainted "freedom" no more than want their blood money, their bloody comfort, a luxury cruise on a sea of blood...

I look down deep into that bottomless pit of horror, until I suffer from vertigo. But I don't fall, I hold on — hold on to this, China, the land and people I had lost, now found I hold more dearly...

On a train to Guangzhou...

31

Moving through the heart of a land that goes through my heart, though it is no longer the intensity of first sighting — it must be the intensity of loneliness, my longing, a longing for belonging, belonging to a land more beautiful than dreams, more real than the American dreams we all chase. What is that intense wide emptiness at home in the West that creates this instinctive open fullness of heart here? In this land not stolen — blood too, always blood, but no false treaties that justify genocide. Canada, America — a first nations people without a country, leaves us all nation-less, heart-less.

I look at so much land, so green and brown, that this train moves through. I know I do not know the feel of the earth in my hands, but I can feel it in my heart. Our hands cut off from our hearts — with only these words, this moving pen, as an intermediary between me and this moving land which so moves my heart.

Wake up, wake up, from our modern slumbers,
for this is life, life which comes from the life of the land...

but what life for me? who does not really know what life is like for the peasants, who everyday bend over the fields, hands touching earth (connected to heart), giving life to us all.
Workers of the earth, who look like me, but look at me like I'm something from another world.
And I am. I who know only what I am not. Only what a world cannot be, only of the emptiness and the horror of a world based on taking away worlds, destruction and theft.
My cut-off hands only know the feel of steel, of concrete, of plastic, of mirrors that reflect the same unreality. What do we know of building, building a country from the earth it rests on, with the people rooted in it,

building socialism?

China, land of my people, my past, you have given me hope, an open hope, when I have come from a closed, destructive world that has destroyed people's real hope and replaced it with plastic dreams in technicolour, dreams which in reality are like cotton candy disappearing to nothingness on expectant child tongues. So quickly we learn the many shades of betrayal.

But it is only on going back to China that I finally discover the heartache green of life, the deep brown of earth, this familiar yellow of skin — the real colours of life. This is the heart of the real homes we must build for ourselves to live in — fight for, and die for if we have to — instead of dying in pre-fab, pastel, suburban model homes, cushioned and suffocating — homes of their making, and our destruction.

But to fight, to organize and to build a way of living which is really ours, in these highly controlled, advanced capitalist societies we live in, we must try to understand the sheer complexity and weight of the various structures and histories which press on and into those of us displaced and dispossessed by centuries of bloody colonialism, patriarchy and imperialism. This means looking carefully at the issues of race, gender, colonization and de-colonization, language, culture, identity, sexuality, migration and displacement. These are the pressing issues, relating to the real lives of the growing number of us here who question where we belong in this society. These are the kinds of things I wish I had been able to read about and study when I was in university.

Like many others, I did become politicized when I was at university. I studied Marxism and international politics, and got involved in solidarity groups organizing around Central America and anti-apartheid. But it was only after I returned to live and work in Toronto that I took a hard look at these solidarity groups and the whole international aid and development field — and saw how white-dominated and liberal they were. I began to see that beyond the good intentions and even heartfelt political commitment, there were familiar missionary themes to the whole business. It was like modern missionaries paving and softening the way for modern forms of international capital, just as the old Christian missionaries had done the same for the old traders and exploiters.

And yes, I saw the racism. Then I began to take all the activism and theory I had learned during university, and I brought my politics home. Back in Toronto I became involved in the anti-racist and women's movement. I began to see the apartheid situation right here in Canada. Finally, going to China put it all into more perspective. Living in North America can be like living in a bubble — it seems like "we are the world." Seeing Asia, in all its beauty, poverty and humanity, put that imperialist illusion to rest.

Now, back here in the eye of the storm, I see how much there is a need to understand where we, as Asian women and decolonizing peoples living in the diaspora, presently stand in this current crisis in Western capitalist society, and where we can take our struggles in the shrinking political space and growing racist, anti-feminist and anti-communist reaction. This means challenging the prevailing myths and stereotypes here of Asian women as passive, silent, and either asexual or readily available, exotic sex objects. This means building theory on all the issues that affect our lives, and revealing how these issues interconnect. This means organizing.

There have been recent trends which our communities must begin to deal with in an organized way: growing anti-Hong Kong and anti-Asian immigration sentiments, rising Japan-bashing as the North American economic crisis deepens. The old stereotypes of Asians in North America as living in crowded and poor conditions, and working in family laundries and restaurants, corner stores, and of women bent over sewing machines in sweatshops are quickly being replaced with assumptions that we are all as rich as the newly arrived Hong Kong entrepreneurs, whom the Canadian government has encouraged to buy immigration status with $100,000 or quarter of a million dollars in real estate investments here. But, of course, the state has taken no responsibility for the racist backlash that has grown

34

in places like Vancouver and Toronto as a result of these Canadian immigration policies to attract fleeing Hong Kong capital, which could be seen as a new exorbitant "head tax."

The media is also whipping up fear of the Asian peril taking over in the form of powerful Japanese capital, with the image of Asians as robot-like, too smart, and not quite human. Phillip Rushton, of the University of Western Ontario, recently played up this racist stereotype of the Asian super race who practised inhuman sexual restraint, and were to be feared. The economic roots of racist stereotypes become clear as we see how quickly they can change and become contradictory, depending on what problems we are being scapegoated for or who we are being pitted against.

Unfortunately, there is a tendency in our communities, like others, to react divisively or chauvinistically to such racist attacks. Many people from China have strong tendencies against identifying with Japanese people. Parts of the Chinese community have also tried to set themselves apart from the Vietnamese community in the recent anti-refugee hype over so-called "Asian crime." These and other divisions between Asian peoples come out of real historical enmities based on nations' painful experiences of war and occupations. The older Chinese community has also tried to set themselves apart from the ostentatious wealth of some Hong Kong newcomers — and there *are* class differences. But there are large Asian communities in North America that are here to stay, and when it comes right down to it, we have to put aside our differences and work together against the growing attacks. Because, aside from the politics of unity, it's also clear that, when push comes to shove, we "all look alike" to them, whatever the real differences are. Two white autoworkers in Detroit didn't stop to ask Chinese co-worker Vincent Chin if he was in fact Japanese (and therefore supposedly to blame for lay-offs) before beating him to death.[4]

This is a scary time for all our communities, as Western capital finds itself in crisis and needs to create scapegoats to divide a working class which is facing rising unemployment and economic insecurity. The irony is that

Asian workers (especially non-English speaking) and other nonwhite workers, and women are usually the first to be laid-off, the last to be hired again,
stuck in the lowest paying jobs, and the most economically insecure. These
are the real hard issues our communities must confront — even those of us
who have made it up the hard way to middle-class comfort and good professions. We need to open our eyes and see how precarious our positions really
are, and that there can be no long term individual solutions. For the sake of
our communities and our children, we must organize on as broad a basis as
possible to safeguard our gains and help build a society that is not based on
such divisions and exploitation.

But the basis of that coming together and organizing must be on the
strength of our own communities' abilities to find our own voices and stake
our place here. We have not been silent, just silenced or not listened to. That
is why we must speak for ourselves, and why questions like political and
cultural appropriation are so important. Our various communities need to
organize politically, but we must do this by also first presenting our real
experiences and voices *ourselves* — with all this diversity, contradictions,
pain and uncertainties. There can be no appropriation of these voices, nor of
this theorizing of our position in society, at present or in the future.

Asian women living in the West still have a long way to go in theorizing
the complexities of our lives, as do all nonwhite peoples here. But this is a
task we must begin ourselves. This theory can only truly come out of the
heart of our experiences, the depths of our historical struggles to survive and
resist. It must speak to our hearts and those of our children, and inform our
future struggles. This is the dialectic that moves us into, against and beyond
our various oppressions.

I hope I have helped set down some of the framework for that ongoing
discussion on issues of race, class and gender, which will grow as our numbers and our consciousness grow. I have given not so many answers as I have
asked questions, difficult questions, many of which we *all* need to ask. And,
as an Asian woman, I ask these difficult questions neither quietly nor pas-

sively. Sisters, brothers, the answers must come from *us*. We must look hard into our own hearts, at those things which may hurt the most, the things that may separate us from ourselves and each other, but in the end must bring us together, if we are to focus our energies at attacking our common enemy (instead of destroying ourselves and attacking each other, as we all have witnessed and suffered from too much in our communities, under growing attacks from the forces of reaction).

We have all been colonized and divided. It is now up to us to de-colonize our minds, ourselves, and our communities, and come together to work against the powerful forces of imperialism and patriarchy to which we have been subjected personally all our lives, and collectively, as nations and peoples, for centuries. This means finding our true voice, however tentative, painful or angry that may be, sharing our experiences and analyzing them in the context of the historical, economic and social reality we all live in. We must write of our struggles to overcome the multiple forces of history, society, and culture which press on us, often in the attempt to silence us. Our identity and strength grow out of sharing the struggle to fight that which has tried to dehumanize us, and find the common ground we share as women, as Chinese, as Asian, as de-colonizing peoples, as workers, as humans.

A Jewel in the Frown: Striking Accord Between India/n Feminists[1]

Anita Sheth and Amita Handa

[T]he question "Who should speak?" is less crucial than "Who will listen?"
. . . the moment I have to think of the ways in which I will speak as an
Indian, or as a feminist, the ways in which I will speak as a woman,
what I am doing is trying to generalize myself, make myself a representa-
tive . . . there are many subject positions which one must inhabit; one is
not just one thing. That is when a political consciousness comes in...But
when the card carrying listeners, the hegemonic people, the dominant
people, talk about listening to someone "speaking as" . . . When they want
to hear an Indian speaking as an Indian, a Third World woman speak-
ing as a Third World woman, they cover over the fact of the ignorance
that they are allowed to possess . . .

Gayatri Chakravorty Spivak, 1990, pp.59-60

In writing about our speaking to each other as India/n,[2] middle class, graduate student, feminists located within white, printed academia, we are attempting to shift out of talking about "brownness" as a construction relevant only in relation to racism into talking about India/nness from within the category of India/n itself. The reason we choose this as a starting point is because we have not encountered our experiences of living India/n text books, classroom discussions, lectures, conversations with colleagues, and the like. Our absence has become unbearably conspicuous.

This is not to say, however, that the racist stereotypes of the India/n are missing. We need only to recall the tremendous success of sales enjoyed by the white Canadian business person who sold, and the hundreds of white Canadians who bought, the T-shirts, buttons, stickers and flyers mocking the Sikh RCMP Mountie wearing a turban and sword as testimony to the racism that is present and marketable. Notwithstanding these racist stereotypes, we are nervous about how the silence on India/nness in academia masks over much needed discussion on the ownership of activities of India/ns in the countries of Africa, the everyday oppressive Hindu practices of caste, the cultural-regional, nationalist domination of India over Pakistan, Bangladesh, Burma and Sri Lanka.

Our coming to consciousness about our racial oppression has largely been delivered by Black feminist activists. When we read Audre Lorde, Angela Davis, bell hooks, Michele Wallace, Barbara Smith, June Jordan, Linda Carty, Peggy Bristow, Dionne Brand, Makeda Silvera, Toni Morrison, Alice Walker — truly the list goes on - we come to understand the pain and injustice of, and resistance to, white-supremacist oppression and exploitation, and learn about how this hateful practice of racism, colonialism and imperialism is put together and managed daily. We thus also find in their words an entry point to talk about ourselves, our exclusion, our struggles. We realize that as feminists working towards an anti-racist project, we have not understood our particular experiences as India/ns; we have not drawn on our particular histories of oppression, domination and resistance. Through their works we had access to South Asian feminists, like Gayatri Chakravorty Spivak, Punam Khosla, Himani Bannerji, Nirmala Bannerjee, Partha Chatterjee, Pratibha Parmar, Lata Mani, Chandra Mohanty, Kum Kum Bhavnani, Swasti Mitter. While we have been exposed to the historical subordination of India/n women by India/n men and to the subordination of all

India/ns in general by the white British, we have not found points of entry to discuss the particular prejudices and privileges that we as India/ns in general and India/ns from a particular class have in relation to the spectrum of non-white people.

When we walk down the streets in Toronto, or enter immigration offices in New York, or wait in airports in London, or even listen to our parents and grandparents talk, or when we learned what was available in India/n history books, or hear white friends criticize certain non-white individuals for their political activities, or watch the television reports coming out of South Africa, we notice a curious positioning of ourselves as India/n in relation to Black people. There is always this sense that because of our brownness, white folks find us to be relatively more acceptable, more trustworthy, more dependable. In indulging uncritically in this space, even while actively fighting against white racism, we engage as people of colour in the very practices that divide, rank and exclude us. Given that most of our politicization has come from identification with the work of Black activists, as India/n feminists we feel the need to account and take responsibility for what they have implied and continue to imply about our location. In attending to this, we must ask ourselves difficult questions. For example, how is it that people of colour fight daily against white racism and remain quiet about our taught racism even when no white person is present? Why is it that India/ns have been silent about their economic privilege in the countries of Africa?

The questions we want to raise about our cultural privileging and racial prejudices are sensitive and risky. They are sensitive because we are open-ing up a level of discussion that might not be safe to have at this historical moment. They are risky because we are not sure how white people will appropriate and use this information. But we feel strongly that the time has come for us as India/n feminists to talk to each other about our India/nness. There is a sense of uneasiness that we feel when we choose to be silent for fear of providing material to white groups interested in, for example, further-ing their racist domination. We have learned to be suspicious of even "progressive" white people who choose to interpret the anti-essentialist line as an end in itself, as a way of reproducing the invisibility of differences, thereby offering no radical alternative to the idea of the "generic human" which is characteristic of the the liberal white stand. We have also learned to be suspicious of white folks who put forth the "reverse discrimination" charge as a way of holding on to the centre.

Our uneasiness comes from wanting to resist the white referent point, while knowing full well that the language we use and the systems we live in daily still bind us to it. As we write in this feminist text we know that most of our readers will be people of whiteness. But we want to say to them that in our minds and bodies when we speak to each other we have only the non-white person present. Of course, this is not to say that we want to monitor who will read this piece of work, or that we object to a white reader. The point made, however, draws attention to the fact that when people of colour talk to each other there is a character to the conversation that is typically different in that it images and operates within a context of non-white listeners. The text of conversation here included, then, also has this character and must be understood within this context. We would suggest to the white reader that she needs to constantly position herself *not within* the text but *in relation to* the text. She must recognize her position of whiteness and how it falls outside the experience of the text but not outside the power dynamic of her relation to the history of racial domination relevant to the experiences in the text. To quote a white feminist, Minnie Bruce Pratt, in illustrating exactly this point:

Sometimes we [whites] don't pretend to be the other, but we take something made by the other and use it for our own: as I did for years when I listened to Black folk singing church songs, hymns, gospels, and spirituals, the songs offering, enduring, and triumphant. Always I would cry, baffled as to why I was so moved; I understood myself only after I read a passage in Mary Boykin Chestnut's diary in which she described

41

weeping bitterly at a slave prayer meeting where the Black driver shouted
"like a trumpet": she said, "I would very much have liked to shout too."
Then I understood that I was using Black people to weep for me, to ex-
press my sorrow at my responsibility, and that of my people, for their
oppression: and I was mourning because I felt they had something I
didn't, a closeness, a hope, that I and my folks had lost because we had
tried to shut other people out of our hearts and lives . . .(1984, 41)

There has been much critique of Euro-American (white) feminist theory
and its conceptualization of women as a cohesive category disregarding race,
class, sexuality, nationality, and geographical location. Unlike Minnie Bruce
Pratt, we cannot imagine, even for one moment, making the mistake of
splitting gender from race or vice versa. We are always "coloured" women;
never are we women first and then India/n nor are we India/n first and then
women. However, when working within a white academy, we find that we
encounter various situations when we are unwittingly forced by white feminists to constantly justify our feminist politics when addressing white racism.
They do not realize that the authority they exercise in questioning and evalu-
ating stems not so much from a more advanced feminist analysis that they
think they may possess, but rather from a eurocentric, privileged space of
whiteness which might have little to do with feminist politics. Often white
feminists do not understand that their identity as "woman" is inseparably
tied to their race, so that even the best effort made by them to render an
anti-racist reading reinforces white solipsism when gender is examined at the
expense of race. Clearly within a white body (male or female) the erroneous
and historical splitting of race and gender is so embedded in its way of knowing. White feminists must get to work on unravelling the very relations that
have caused them to historically overdetermine gender at the expense of
race. They must stop expecting feminists of colour who are engaged in anti-
racist politics to constantly prove their feminism. This is similar to the necessity of holding accountable heterosexual women who, instead of critically

examining their sexual privilege, choose to question white feminist lesbians or feminists of colour lesbians on their feminist politics when they decide, at times, to work with white gay men or gay men of colour in struggling against heterosexism.

Although we have not here extended an explicit critical reading of Hindu-Brahmin-hetero-patriarchy and unpacked the specific ways in which this ideology marginalizes and oppresses India/n women on a daily basis, it must be understood at the outset that our project has grown out of, and is located in, feminist consciousness and analysis.

Our readers should know that we have received comments by a white feminist in the pre-publication review process of this paper about our lack of feminist analysis. While we have already provided a reading to the white feminist about proceeding with caution in questioning feminists of colour about our feminism when discussing racism, we still feel that we must justify what we mean. In some ways it is difficult to think how a paper like this is possible without embodying a feminist political project. To see ourselves as India/n women is to be conscious of our historical role and everyday marginalization as women, not just by men in India but throughout the world; this is forever inseparable. When choosing to analyse a particular piece of conversation that we had in talking about ourselves as India/n women, and further choosing out of this those parts that could possibly tell us about what tacitly operated in our coming to be with one another as India/n women, we were interested in and curious about our own construction of India/nness. Of course, our choosing to analytically emphasize India/nness at the expense of woman, if this argument is sustainable, could point to the current limitation in feminist theories and methodologies that have not yet found a way of collapsing the two categories. Perhaps this very limitation is what causes white feminists to examine their oppression as women and not their oppressive practices based on their white privilege; which is also forever inseparable, despite the contradictory positioning. Perhaps feminists of colour have internalized the abusive ideology in the Euro-American academy that sees us as women on the one hand, and as "colour" on the other. Often you will find us building alliances with white women in spite of their racism and with "men of colour" in spite of their sexism; always wandering the in-between, never politically content with either, always resisting the particular brands of feminist and anti-racist politics that split us apart (gender first and race next, or race first and gender next).

From our own domestic experiences, popular Hindu beliefs, mythology, folklore, and through the writings of other India/n feminists, we are deeply aware of the historical subordination of India/n women by India/n men. As early as 1896, Pandita Ramabai, in appealing to those who are easily taken in by the claims of Hinduism, notes,

> *I beg of my . . . sisters not to be satisfied with . . . the . . . beauties of the grand philosophies . . . and the interested discourse of our educated men, but to open the trapdoors . . . of the ancient Hindu intellect, and enter into the . . . cellars where they will see the real working of the philosophies which they admire so much . . . The strongholds of Hinduism and the seats of sacred learning . . . where the sublime philosophies are daily taught and devoutly followed, there are thousands of priests and men who are spiritual rulers of our people. They neglect and oppress widows, send out hundreds of emissaries to look for young widows, and bring them to the sacred cities . . . and rob them of their virtue . . Thousands of yound widows . . . are suffering untold misery . . . but not a philosopher or Mahatma has come out boldly to champion their cause and help . . . There are many hard and bitter facts that we have to accept and feel. All is not poetry with us . . .* (quoted in Uma Chakravarti, 1989, 75-76).

Our decision to focus on India/n as a cultural/racial category, to repeat once again, is driven by our absence in white Canadian feminist academia and by the questions we have regarding the economic activities of India/ns in the countries of Africa. Quite simply, we had never discussed our presence in the countries of Africa with each other prior to this speaking; neither had we come across it in conversation with the few other India/n feminists we know. In fact, what sparked this project was a comment made to Anita, quoted later in this text, by an African Kenyan feminist colleague regarding India/ns in Africa.

In this text, we now make available and analyse parts of our six-hour taped conversation as a way of recovering and making sense of the particular issues, dynamics, conflicts and insights that we have experienced in the process of speaking to each other as India/n women in this Canadian context. It has taken more than 60 hours of discussing, arguing, disagreeing, resisting and negotiating to reach this point of writing. Unfortunately, this part of the reflection was not taped and is therefore absent from our analysis on India/n-ness. Part of the difficulty we experienced in doing this project might have been a result of our choice to present this work as a collaborative piece. Traditionally, printed academia in Canada, as any insider recognizes, largely encourages individual and independent writing. We have discovered that had the singular authorial model of presentation been followed, we would not have recovered the very contradictions, similarities and differences between living India/n in India and Canada.

The excerpts selected out of the the conversational text lack their full significance because of the changed circumstance and audience brought about by this writing. The choice to focus on certain aspects of our oral exchanges and not on others stem largely from, to use Bourdieu's phrasing, "where...[we] expect the maximum resistance:"

> *[Y]ou feel that you owe it to yourself to concentrate . . . on the point[s]*
> *where you expect the maximum resistance . . . to tell each audience, with-*
> *out being provocative but also without making concessions, the aspect of*
> *the truth which it will find most difficult to accept, in other words what*
> *you think its truth to be, making use of the knowledge you think you have*
> *of its expectations so as not to flatter and manipulate it, but to "get*

45

across" . . . what it will find most difficult to accept or swallow — in other words what disturbs its most trusted investments. (1990, ix)

As will become evident in the reading of this paper, we have gone about selecting those parts of our conversation that tell the other what we think the other must hear, even though it is what she might find most difficult to accept.

"Othering" as a process of locating

ANITA - Let's talk about how we came together, how we discovered the India/nness.

AMITA - When I first saw you I thought you were India/n but the India/n that wouldn't talk to other India/ns.

ANITA - What kind of India/n?

AMITA - The kind that rejects your roots, maybe you were white-identified and didn't have many India/n friends, or weren't really conscious of the India/n part of you.

ANITA - When I met you I thought you weren't the India/n that I could identify with because you were probably too conservative, too traditional, following the man, you didn't have your own character or centredness.

AMITA - This is really interesting because when I met you I assumed that you were probably brought up in the West.

ANITA - What indicators were there?

46

AMITA - Maybe the dress, the way you spoke, the way you pronounced my name, the way you carried yourself...I thought you were brought up in the West...but I didn't think you were Anglo-India/n.

ANITA - I am not. My mother is Anglo-Indian. I spent more than fifteen years in India.

AMITA - I know a lot of Indian people who have grown up here who don't want to emphasize the India/n part of them.

ANITA - So, you mean the rejection of India/n culture, India/nness by India/ns?

AMITA - The Anglo-India/n is, in my mind, tied together with being western-ized. When I say you are westernized I think of you as sexually active, loose, and therefore I can see the flip-side of what you are saying about me in terms of subservient female. You are thinking of me as subservient to the male. I am thinking of you as not authentically India/n, but very westernized, mean-ing sexually active, no restrictions...which touches on the class thing. I would think all Anglo-India/ns are upper class.

ANITA - which is ridiculous!

AMITA - which is ridiculous.

ANITA - On the point of sexuality, I didn't think you were conservative, so in this sense I didn't think you were traditional. I knew you were Punjabi right away, you looked Punjabi. I was waiting for you to talk to me first because I was not Canadian and to me you were Canadian. I saw that you were India/n but you were Canadian...the interesting thing is that I thought if you were

47

India/n and Canadian, you might as well be Canadian, what's the point of being India/n. Canada is to me the most racist country I have ever lived in and your accent was Canadian. So there was a distance set up on that level too, as well as on the level of my resistance to this North American culture.

AMITA - What I really meant to say is that I saw you as being allowed to have sex.

ANITA - Which is ironic because I too couldn't do all those things.

The above excerpt illustrates the process by which we each became the "other" in each other's eyes through continuing the language of opposition and exclusion. In attempting to make sense of our experiences, in trying to come to speak of India/nness, we constantly fit each other into whiteness, though acknowledging that we had first encountered the other as India/n. Because we were both operating from a tacit fear of not being India/n enough, we unconsciously moved into a frame of exclusion which meant that we could only validate our own sense of identity by denouncing the other's as false, tainted, less genuine. For Amita, the fear stems from having grown up in predominantly white Canada, though both her parents are Punjabi India/n. For Anita, the fear originates from her mother being Anglo-India/n, even though her father is Gujarathi India/n, and having lived the past 12 years outside India. The language of exclusion and the familiarity of the oppression that comes from being marginalized in Euro-American world mediated between us and our particular backgrounds, silently forcing the notion that "if I can see you as white, I can locate you. And if I can locate you I can then locate myself in opposition to your whiteness." This, despite the fact that we "knew" in the first instant that we were India/n. This process of "whitening" the other manages to shift the focus away from our own identities, away from the pain of insecurity and confusion to a focus on the "other." To accomplish this validation of India/nness, from within the category of

India/n, each of us began by concentrating on what is un-India/n (i.e. what is white and Euro-American). It is here that we began to pull at the contradictions in each other to fabricate and construct the other as un-India/n, not India/n enough, thus solidifying, fixing, and feeling comfortable with our own India/n identity as the more real one. All this in a subtext of rush and competition in a silent beckoning of the question, "Will the real India/n please stand up?"

We choose to examine this particular strategy adopted by us to exclude the "other" for reasons that will become clear as the paper develops. However, in response to feedback by Punam Khosla and Melanie Randall, we must here acknowledge in full agreement with them that exclusion also took place in how we located the other in terms of sexuality. Anita placed Amita in the traditionally India/n orthodox context of heterosexuality as indicated in the utterance "following the man." Amita, on the other hand, placed Anita in the Euro-American, non-conservative heterosexual context; as she puts it, "sexually active, loose...no restrictions," even though she was not clear if an explicit reading of heterosexuality was made (i.e., she merely mentions sexual practice without locating it). Furthermore, we also excluded one another by internalizing patriarchal and misogynist practices: Anita by indicating that Amita did not have her own agency or resistance because she was seen as a "typical India/n female" ("you didn't have your own character and centredness"); Amita by employing the same words used by men to negatively describe a woman who has taken her sexuality into her own hands. Neither of us concentrated on the internalization of sexism and heterosexism that were present and managed in our talk.

The following excerpt of conversation further illustrates our building on the process of othering by fitting the other into whiteness:

AMITA - I remember becoming friends with a Christian India/n and how I saw her as so different. To me, she was India/n but with an important difference because I see the Christian India/n as more westernized somehow.

ANITA - What was the stereotype of the Anglo-India/n that you grew up with, or the Christian India/n as you're naming it?

AMITA - As being westernized and so not really authentically India/n, not growing up with the same Hindu culture as I did, westernized in terms of being formal and cold...

ANITA - Hindu religion to me felt backward, you worship the sun, the moon, the stars, and the idea of reincarnation was the weirdest thing because it said that if people weren't happy it was due to the the fact that they were sinners. But we didn't grow up with a notion of Hinduism because my father rejected it. Intelligence and not religion was more important to him. I remember how Indian people would make jokes about white Britishers, Germans doing silly things, giving importance to petty things. The idea was that they were like their food, bland and cold. So in India while there is an honouring of being British, there was also a rejection, a ridiculing . . . . Part of me wanted to be Indian, part would love to be like my father who is completely Indian, but because I grew up learning different things from my Gujurathi Indian father and my Anglo-India/n mother about India/nness and deviations thereof, there was a lot of confusion and contradictions.

AMITA - How do you now identify with the Anglo-India/n part of you? Do you want to reject this?

ANITA - I've always wanted to reject it, always. If I see an Anglo-India/n I want to go the other way. But with my mother I do not feel this way, on the contrary . . .

AMITA - How did you feel when you were with your father's relatives?

ANITA - Completely not good enough, not authentic. They were cold with my

mother, because she was Ango-India/n. She got the worst part, constantly
othered in that context where whe was the only Anglo-India/n in a household
full of Gujarathis or Hindus. When you see photographs of their visits, she is
always the one standing at the end. My father always used to fight with her
in Bombay about not doing it right, be it wearing a sari, or cooking some
Gujarathi dish, and so on. People who were more accepting of my mother
were mostly Punjabis. They were my mother's best friends; she had only one
or two Guju friends, which is ironic.

AMITA - What of Anglo-India/ns who had more white in them than you, how
did they treat you?

ANITA - More white...I don't think of them as having more white...they are
India/n to me. Anyway, they didn't talk to me either, don't you get it? Muriel
Harding, Grace Jones, they saw us as more India/n so we grew up with this
funny sense with them. We wanted to emphasize the India/n part of us with
my dad and the Anglo part of us with Harding and Jones at school. My mom
was the only one on her side of the family who married a Gujarathi and not
an Anglo-India/n. My father was also doubled by the family: "Why did you
marry an Anglo-India/n?" There was a terrible saying which considered the
Anglo-Indian a bastardized race. . . It's interesting because what you are
naming as Anglo-India/n, I see in white people, in terms of being cold and
formal . . . If you met me in India you wouldn't talk to me because I'm not
India/n enough but I see you as a person who didn't grow up in India, therefore not authentically India/n, so there's something about geography. I feel
now, living in the West, that I have more ties with those who have grown up
in India than to you.

AMITA - But I too feel I have more ties to those people who have grown up in
India than to you because I have more in common with them in terms of
cultural and religious backgrounds, and in terms of values, than I have with

you. You're right that we probably wouldn't talk if we met in India but it wouldn't be because you're not authentically India/n, but because I would see you as formal, westernized, snobby, that you see yourself as above me and it would therefore probably be you that wouldn't talk to me... This conversation makes me realize that the whole term westernized is problematic.

ANITA - Oh yes.

AMITA - Because it means so many different things to different people, depending on their histories, locations and reference points. To me, westernized could be represented by someone like you. To you, being westernized could be me, so what do we even mean by westernized?

ANITA - Hang on a minute, westernized is clearly white . . .

AMITA - But when you speak of westernized values, that definition doesn't really hold any currency. When we speak of "westernized" it's as if we're assuming that there's a cohesive kind of India/n. Who do you consider a westernized person to be in India?

ANITA - Those who go off to study and have families abroad like you, you would be the westernized person in India.

AMITA - Do you have a notion of the westernized person living and based in India?

ANITA - Yes, Punjabis to me were more westernized than I because they could make friends with boys.

AMITA - They did? Not in my family.
. . . . (laughter) . . .

ANITA - Punjabis were the most liberated kind to me...just look at the word I used, "liberated."

AMITA - I think this is a class thing. If we talk of upper class Gujarathis, Punjabis, Bengalis, you'll notice that all of them have adopted westernized values, in terms of the western model of dating, etc.

ANITA - Not all, my family didn't. But what you're not hearing me on is that because you didn't grow up in India, you don't realize that you can't talk about "India/n," you have to talk in terms of Gujarathi, Bengali, etc. There's all this competition around in India about who is the most India/n.

As is evident in this conversation, we continue to participate in a discourse of binary opposition constructed upon the category of India/n/"un"-India/n. As any India/n knows, the western categories of race, class, gender and sexual identification are necessary though insufficient in capturing the construction of India/ness. An India/n can either be a Buddhist, Hindu, Jain, Sikh, Muslim, Christian or Zorastrian, and can come from either a Dravidian, Aryan or mixed race and from varied class backgrounds; and, if belonging to the Hindu majority, is either a Brahmin (priest caste), Kshatriya (warrior caste), Vaishya (business caste) or Shudra (untouchable caste). To this an India/n will add regional, cultural, and lingual differences depending on which state and/or diasporic location one's family originates from. At the time of our conversation, when we each spoke from our own positions of essence and authority, we did not realize that we lacked a language to speak about our commonness, a commonness that exists in spite of this multi-layered way of living India/n. Lacking a language to articulate our similarities cannot fully explain the particular way in which we treated each other with suspicion and mistrust; toiling with each other as we would a white person engaged in anti-racist politics who refuses, denies or forgets at one and the same time to account for her own racial dominance.

In fact, we now can see that we were operating from stereotypes, putting each other on trial, unconsciously compiling evidence to charge the other with cultural impersonation:

> *To persuade you that your past and cultural heritage are doomed to eventual extinction...inauthenticity is condemned as a loss of origins and a whitening (or faking) of non-western values. (Trinh Minh*-ha, 1989, 89)

However, the process of othering that operated between us also took on the appearance of a transference of real power without actually moving out of the power position. In each of us assuming that we were more India/n, we were each making the claim that the other had more privilege without recognizing at the time that this was going on. Although we engaged in and played out the very languaging and reconstructions that come from uncritically honouring whiteness as referent, we also, at the same time, allowed for the implication that to be white or white-identified was to be less authentic, less real; and to be this was to be simply less. But, in this context, less what? It would seem less India/n, meaning having less racial currency because, between us, association with whiteness is identified negatively: the more white you are, the more negative you become. All this might seem paradoxical when viewed exclusively in terms of white privileged centres and non-white margins, but appears less so when experienced, even if only at a glimpse, from the context of refusing the currency attributed to or associated with the white referent.

Losing the connection

> *Being easily offended in your elusive identity and reviving readily old, racial charges, you immediately react when such guilt-instilling accusations are leveled at you and are thus led to stand in need of defending that very ethnic part of yourself that for years has made you and your*

ancestors the objects of execration. (Trinh Minh-ha, 1989, 89)

Our conversation must be seen as taking place in this historical moment within a predominantly white Canadian discursive and lived context, and between two women of the same race, who have class privilege, who do not share the same religious background, country of birth, or history of being India/n. It is noteworthy to track how the notion of westernized, first introduced by Amita, is played against the notion of traditional, as first offered by Anita. When Amita encountered Anita she saw her as westernized, meaning rejecting her India/nness, even though Amita has lived most of her life in white Canada which systematically teaches non-white people to deny their cultural heritage. When Anita met Amita she thought of her as a traditional, orthodox Hindu female that lives her life serving the India/n male, even though Anita knew from her own experience, her mother's, and other India/n Hindu women in India, that this subservience is not always accepted or followed. While Amita saw Anita as a westernized India/n, Anita only used the term to identify white people. Later, she used it to describe Punjabis like Amita who lived outside India. The meaning she gave to it, however, was not the same as Amita's (i.e. being cold or loose) but rather was defined as not being traditionally India/n. From the excerpts of the conversation already included one can see that Amita's Hindu-centric attitude dismisses all India/ns who deviate from this dominant ruling religious frame as "tainted" India/n. Although Anita and her siblings grew up Roman Catholic (according to the stipulation dictated by the church which granted that her Anglo India/n Roman Catholic mother could only marry her Gujarathi, Jain, father under this condition) she constantly witnessed and internalized her mother's pain in being treated by Hindus as outsider, as other, as an object of sexual play, as overly ambitious when compared to all other India/ns. This attitude prevails regardless of the many generations that her mother's parents' parents lived in India and the inter-marriages that took place between them and Hindus.

On the other hand, Anita's nationalistic attitude, which she learned from her Gujarathi father and from living India/n in India, excludes all India/ns born and living predominantly outside India as India/n. This sense of nationalism was fueled for Anita in the mid-1970s when India banned the sale of all foreign-made goods. To be India/n meant buying only India/n made products at cheaper prices at the highest quality - the slogan all over college campuses read "be Indian buy Indian." To be India/n and proud of it also meant being anti-imperialist by belonging to the only country in the world that stopped the sale of Coca-Cola. However, Anita, unlike Amita, does not know enough to speak, read or write Gujarathi or any other India/n language despite living in India for 17 years, did not and does not wear India/n-looking clothes or jewellry, does not now listen to India/n music or read India/n texts, and feels no need to claim her India/nness by these signs when with white Canadians. In other words, Anita positions herself as undeniably India/n without at one and the same time incorporating either in India or in Canada the outward symbols that identify India/nness.

Amita was born in England and came to Canada at the age of one and has lived here all her life. She has visited India nine times, two of which were of one year duration. Because of this location, here, references to India or India/n are constantly challenged and negated by Anita's nationalistic and quasi-imperialistic attitudes. When this is examined in the context of Amita having grown up as a minority in Canada, where being brown means being treated as outsider, as less smart, called "Paki" or "Pun-jab," made invisible, taught to self-hate, to hide, to lie, to feel shame, Anita's India/n nationalistic attitudes and immediate ignorance regarding what it means to grow up constantly made to feel inferior to whites, coupled with the forgetting that India/ns were colonized by white British, further contributes to Amita's exclusion. By disclaiming or challenging any association Amita made to India or India/n culture, Anita touches the deeply embedded feelings of insecurities and inadequacies Amita experienced daily in this country. Of course there is no purposefulness here, Anita quite simply has not lived her childhood to late teenage years having to experience white racism, believing that her colour of skin would impede her growth. In fact, in what follows, Anita continues to insist that being India/n in India is different from being India/n in Canada.

ANITA - I must say right now that I don't hold a notion of authentic India/n in my mind. What I hold in my mind is that to understand the India/n experience one has to live in India as India/n for a substantial amount of time. I think this is crucial to understanding the India/n experience.

AMITA - Your notion of the India/n experience.

ANITA - No, this applies to any active speaker speaking about India/ness. One has to live in India to understad social make up, class divisions, caste, untouchables, temples, politics, churches, the entire urban/rural experience. To understand India in context I believe that one needs to live there.

AMITA - India, right, but I think...

ANITA - India/nness, the India/n mentality.

AMITA - See, this is where I differ from you a little bit because what I realize now is that when you say you see an India/n who lives outside India, there is a certain set of assumptions you have. When I meet someone who comes straight from India there are certain assumptions I have too. What I am trying to get at is that when we spoke about our India/nness I realize how our categories are so false. This made me realize that for you, your sensibility of being India/n is very much tied into having been born and brought up in India. The location and geography is very important for you. But for me, of course, the notion of India/nness does not stem from there because obviously I did not live there. India was represented in my home with my parents because this was a little India to me, because everything is preserved

57

and kept...

ANITA - That is peculiar to me, so in India, nearly every home is little India...

AMITA - We did not assimilate . . .

ANITA - I am having difficulty hearing you on this, as someone who was born and has lived more than a decade in India, because when you speak about India in your home I can also speak about the India in my parents' home in Malta. Their home is a little India, to use your peculiar phrasing, in terms of preserving the India/nness, but for me that's not enough because there is a limitation, an individuality. I just want you to hear me say and acknowledge that India/ns from India and India/ns from outside are different. We must speak of the difference and not collapse it into one. There are commonalities yes, most definitely. I, however, identify in terms of everyday things, from market places to film images . . . I think you can't limit it to what your parents have put in your house in terms of eating or religion, but you need to add architecture, roads it's all different. For me, the question becomes: how can you put an India in Canada, how can you preserve an India in Canada? So when you go into your house and there you will find different kinds of books, different kinds of television shows if you have a set, furniture, the toilets, the everyday things, where you cook your food, your kitchen appliances, all of this is difficult for me to ignore, to hear you say you have trapped India in your own home here in Canada. But how I hear you when you say that you had an India in your house is that you had things that emphasized India (e.g. religious beliefs and the practice, objects) that remind you of India, then there is food and language. This to me does not make India; I can't imagine how it would . . .

AMITA - Even though you are not using this word you are constructing an authentic Indian exeperience in what you are saying which takes place for you in India.

ANITA - Okay, sure (laughs).

AMITA - For me, from where my experience is, authentic India/n does not have to do with geography and of course this had to do with our own different experiences.

ANITA - Do you think Canada or the Canadian experience has anything to do with this...?

Hearing the differences

Through this process of writing, we began to understand the necessity of thinking about the politics of listening, not just theoretically, but also in developing a method of its practice. The question and the struggle, then, centred on our talk, not just in terms of its content, but in terms of analyzing its form. How could we talk without negating each other's experience? We began to realize that we had to create a space for our different identities that were informed, in very concrete terms, by different histories and locations that we redefined and reformulated at specific junctures in our lives. The focus changed from speaking about our different geographical locations in a bid for proving our India/nness to a form that kept intact the India/n in us. We shifted to a way of talking that started from the point of being India/n, accepting that we both indeed were India/n, but had been informed differently, historically, geographically, and institutionally. The following passage illustrates a painful beginning of this process.

ANITA - I notice, when you told me your painful experiences of racism, you disassociated yourself from them. I find this form of disassociation happens a lot with non-white people who are born in Canada and live here. If this sort of thing happened to me, and it does happen to me now here in Canada, I get really mad, I don't disassociate. I get very upset, emotional, I will not let it pass until I have spoken to it or dealt with it in one form or another. I'm wondering if this is what you pick up in yourself too; are you aware that you disassociate?

AMITA - No, I agree with you. I think I disassociated at the time because I was so outnumbered. I was the only person of my kind, the only India/n in the class. I would think, "Yes there is something wrong with me." But I wanted to fight against it, I thought I could resist it. Yet I remember a telling moment when I was in the final year of high school. I was sitting on the step when a friend of mine, who is half India/n and half Dutch but could pass for white, told our classmates that she was going to Europe for her summer vacation. But she came up to me and said, "Amita, I'm telling everyone I'm going to Europe. Please don't blow it but I'm really going to India." A few years later, I too was going to India, and when my classmates asked me where I was going, I was about to construct a little white lie like my friend; it was sort of an automatic thing. But I remember pausing for a moment, looking around at all these white people I had tried so hard to be friends with, and it's as if for the first time I realized their true nature and said, "I am going to India". I came out as an India/n. This is how I felt, which is ironic because it's not as if I could hide the fact that I was non-white. This was a major point of resistance for me, this big burden of constantly trying to hide was suddenly lifted . . . It is so difficult to remember all of this because there are so many scenes like this in my head. In grade 7 or 8 there was a bunch of white people standing around talking, I heard one of them ask the other where they were going for Christmas; I remember her response so clearly. She said, "Well where do you think I'm going, I am going to Florida. It's not like I'm going to India or something," and they all started to laugh, "like who would ever go to India, even for a holiday, it's such a backward and depressing place." I felt so ashamed, I wanted to be invisible.

ANITA - Why did you feel like this; wasn't this more a comment on them than on you?

AMITA - What do you mean? They were laughing at India and they knew I am from there, so I took it as a direct comment on me. There are so many examples like this. I remember another similar situation. A group of white girls were talking at lunch break and one of them said to the other that she had a joke to share. But before she told the joke she turned to me and said, "Amita, I guess you better not listen to this. Can you go stand over there?"

ANITA - Did you actually move?

AMITA - Yes, but I was within hearing distance. I heard the joke. It was a "Paki joke." I remember trying to act cool, like, "you think a small thing like that would bother me, I can take it, I'm tough." I almost tried to pretend that this had nothing to do with me. This was all in my mind and through body language of course, I didn't actually say anything. It was bad enough that she told the joke, but I felt that the spotlight was on me because she asked me to move and everyone looked towards me. I'm sure there is disassociation going on. Yes.

ANITA - That's horrible. The reason I mention disassociation is because I don't feel this way. Maybe this comes from the fact that I did not grow up here in racist Canada. I feel bad telling you this; after all, who am I to say. But I just feel if this sort of thing happened to me I would not let it pass. Gosh, I would be angry. I think I have this take on it because I lived in India for so many years. I would have told all of them to get lost or said something nasty about their culture. I don't really know, maybe all of this is my arrogance of being India/n which touches on middle-class privilege I am sure . . .

While Anita persists in acknowledging herself as an outsider, which is also the way the Canadian immigration policies constitute her status here as a foreign student on visa for the past ten years, Amita moves on to recount stories illustrating how she is regarded as an outsider in Canada, even though she has lived here virtually all her life. Both these forms of othering by Canadian society are racist regardless of whether or not Anita can grasp Amita's reactions. The point of difference between us is not so much related to our specific responses and reactions to Canadian racism, but rather to the experiences of growing up we each had in the countries in which we have lived. Unlike Anita, Amita's growing was inseparably linked to notions of racial shame as created by this dominant white culture. As Frantz Fanon notes in describing his coping while living in white Euro-American culture,

> *[C]ompletely dislocated, unable to be abroad with the other, the white . . . who unmercifully imprisoned me, I took myself far off from my own presence, far indeed, and made myself an object. What else could it be for me but an amputation, an excision, a hemorrhage that spattered my whole body with black blood?...I slip into corners, I remain silent, I strive for anonymity, for invisibility. Look I'll accept the lot, as long as no one notices me!* (1990, 110-112)

The mind/body split pointed to here is intensely present in Amita's recount of the racism she underwent while growing up in Canada. In this context, she experiences a contradictory pull. On the one hand, she becomes acutely aware of her body, her skin colour. On the other hand, she tries to deny this reality through emotional distancing, and camouflages it by adopting white sanctioned codes of dress, hair style and mannerisms in a desperate bid to hide from herself that she is different. She fools herself for a while only to realize, as is clearly evident in the exchange above, that in the end she was the only one she had fooled; no one else had forgotten the skin, the differences. The emotional distancing, the desire to become invisible, the self-silencing all become protective mechanisms of survival for her in an all-white school. Although her coming out as India/n was instrumental in resisting the racism around her, her disassociation still operated as a strategy offering a protective shield to defend against it. Yet, the feelings of inferiority that come with internalizing racist discourse with all its destructive teachings of self-hate and shame is inescapable, especially because its emergence in the psyche at any given moment is unknown and therefore difficult to subvert. For Amita self-hatred, and shame of her India/n culture, were the outcomes of internalizing the dominant white Canadian racist discourse.

What is interesting to us about this piece of conversation is the distance, the gap in understanding between us with respect to this account of racism. For Anita, despite the experience of shame associated with the Anglo-India/n part of her, her mother in particular, and her marginalization from parts of India/n society, this experience did not translate into a whole identity based on shame. Growing up in India meant for her growing up with notions of confidence and pride in being India/n. For Anita, this feeling of strength is accurately captured in the following quote by Hanif Kureshi,

> *I began to wonder why I was so strong - what it was that held me together. I thought it was that I'd inherited from Dad a strong...instinct. Dad had always felt superior to the British: this was the legacy of his Indian childhood - political anger turning into some contempt. For him in India the British were ridiculous, stiff, under-confident, rule-bound. And he'd made me feel that we couldn't allow ourselves the shame of failure in front of these people. You could not let the ex-colonialists see you on your knees, for that was what they expected you to be. They were exhausted now, their Empire was gone; their day was done, it was our turn.* (1990, 250)

Regardless of caste and class barriers, India/n people in post-British India felt an enormous sense of national pride especially in the late 1970s when India was on its way to producing all its own goods and services. Identifying the common foreign oppressors produced a link connecting India/ns together. Of course, there were cruel inequalities; women, working class people, untouchables, non-Hindus were still severely oppressed by the India/n state, by Brahmins, businessmen and educated elites. But as a nation, India was set on building a strong territorial spirit of independence among its citizens. Having participated in this particular period of India/n history, and having grown up in a household where her father, who worked in the ship-building industry in India as general manager, dedicated his life to removing the foreign influence, thereby attempting to make shipping the prime national example of an all India/n endeavour, Anita is unable to understand Amita's seemingly timid responses to racist statements, or why it is that she internalized these statements. Amita is unable to understand why it is that Anita would even question her reaction. She discovered that because Anita did not grow up with the stereotype of the "Paki", she could engage with the racist utterance as as external to her, as a statement reflecting only the ignorance of the person who utters it. Amita cannot shift outside her context, and therefore assumes that the Canadian stereotype of the India/n as "backward, lazy, and dirty" is operative in India and that India/ns living in India know that this is how white people see all India/ns. This is so much the case that Amita believes that the external racist images of India/ns must somehow predetermine the self-image of all India/ns, regardless of geography. Hence Amita, investing so much meaning in the white point of view, fails to comprehend that in India, notwithstanding British colonialism, the white referent, its gaze, its evaluation, is not so consequential and connected to the daily cultural (though not economic) formation of India/n identities and self-image.

Our movement into listening aided in the dislodging of the stereotype, the fix we had on the "other". Amita began to realize that she had to account for her geographical location, that she was not from India even though she had visited it so often and because of this her sense of India/nness was different from that of Anita's. This became a point of discovery for her just as

Anita's learning about how India/ns are treated in Canada as early as child-hood became a point of discovery for Anita. We both realized that the notion of the monolithic India/n was itself exclusionary. Once we ceased to speak from a totalizing discourse that negated each other's differences we were able to participate in a listening which provided space for knowing and learning from each other about each other's constructions of India/nness.

Resisting the silence

"Your silence will not protect you." (Audre Lorde, 1984)

In moving closer towards each other, we were able to discover that what we *also* shared in common is our culture's racial prejudices towards non-India/n people of colour. Since the Euro-American practice of racial categorizaion through colour of skin still acts as one of the prime racial mark-ers through which everyday racism exerts its power of domination, the whiter one is, the more racial privilege one has. Suffice it to say that this type of categorization of race denies the existence of the interlocking nature of op-pression based on differences, of class, gender, sexual identification, colonial legacy and so on. When this categorization of race seeps into the system that reproduces these social relations, the daily production of racism becomes an integral part of all social living. In participating in the system by the mere fact of living in it, non-white people internalize and act upon categorization based on the colour of skin, thereby executing, and consequently reproducing the social relations of racism among themselves that are primarily designed by the dominant whites to exclude all of them. They thus become cultural and political workers supporting the daily reproduction of white racism.

"But when we are silent, we are still afraid." (Audre Lorde, 1984)

Remarks by non-India/n people of colour, mostly African and Chinese women, reflecting their notions of our racial privileging as India/ns forced us to take a hard look at the stereotypes we grew up with of other non-white groups.

"Anita, the Indian you are in Africa, I hate." (African Kenyan feminist colleague, 1991)

In engaging in this process we have come to realize that to stop everyday racism we must also consciously refuse to be the cultural and political workers supporting the daily reproduction of white racism. One of the ways we choose to begin this refusal is by naming our own racial prejudices.

ANITA - The notion of British colonialist racism I grew up with in India was more directed toward Black people...I didn't even know that Black people were slaves...It is only when I left India did I first learn about this. Through my exposure to Christianity in India I internalized Christian beliefs about African people. This means I thought Africans were devil worshippers because I was told voodoo worship was sinful, which I was afraid of being. Without even seeing a single African man, I was frightened of him. Of course I was afraid of the Indian man as well. Surely there is a connection of gendered heterosexual activity here. I hardly remember anyone talking about Africans but they spoke sometimes about "Africa", about ivory, gold, diamonds. I am sure this raises the whole question of India/ns going there to open up businesses. None of my family, to my knowledge, on either my mother's or father's side, emigrated to "Africa", but I know a lot of Gujarathis went. So yes, I most definitely grew up with notions of racism. I was Roman Catholic . . . Although I am talking a lot about Christianity here, I know that Hindus do have some similar stereotypes. I can only extend their prejudices about Muslim people to know this . . . but I do not know what they are exactly. I have not really talked about his before with any India/n so that says a lot about us as well . . .

AMITA - I am sure I have internalized racism towards Black people in growing up here in Canada, even though the memories of Black people I got from
my father, who was politically active, were that of strength and struggle,
and...they didn't accept their oppression, you couldn't mess with them, they
were fighters. Through conversations with my relatives and India/n family
friends I became aware of the extreme racism towards Black and Muslim
people. There was a girl in my class from Pakistan and one day we were
talking about stereotypes and asked each other about our notions of Muslim/
Hindu stereotypes. I said Muslims are considered untrustworthy, not very
clean, not very holy, whereas Hindus are considered holy, clean, virtuous,
wearing white flowing clothes, and my friend said, "No way! That's the exact
same stereotype I have about Hindus: they can't be trusted, they're not holy
or clean," and were both shocked by this discovery.

The issue of racialism[3] caused heated discussions between us. We struggled with the question of how to hold ourselves accountable and responsible
for our own racialism without in the very process of doing so, reproducing
racialist practices. Once again, our histories and locations emerged as a point
of splitting difference. While we both agreed that owning up to the racialism
taught in our families, communities, and schools was important, deciding
how the telling should take place became a point of contention. More specifically, the debate involved whether the telling should name the stereotypes
that were learned.

For Amita, owning up to the learned racialism was important. There
needed to be acknowledgement of the prevalence of India/n racialism toward
Black people. Given her repeated exposure to racism here in Canada, naming
the stereotypes and prejudices that were learned, however, would seem to
reproduce those very oppressive practices. For her, the racial slurs about
herself were all too familiar, so she could not understand the usefulness of
repeating slurs about Black people that she thought to be all too familiar to
them. India/n racist stereotypes about Black people were not any different
than the racist stereotypes she had heard from white people toward Black

people. For Amita, a detailed type of naming seemed no different than an exercise in confessional or guilty telling. The process of detailed naming, she felt, would once more provide space for, and bring life to, the very stereotype. In this sense, repeating the stereotype would serve to reinstate it rather than dislodge it. She did not understand how this kind of public personal account would be beneficial for anyone else except herself. This type of releasing of her own conscience in the name of giving up racialist practices seemed to take place at the expense of others. She felt that acknowledging and being accountable for her learned racialism was the point at which to launch into a responsible discussion on political coalition-building and action.

For Anita, however, her feminist understanding has instilled in her a belief that naming the exercise of privilege in every instance of its execution is as important as, if not more than, simply acknowledging that one has privilege. Amita's question of whether one reproduces the stereotype by naming it at the expense of the other's pain raises serious questions in Anita about her coming to consciousness about racialism on the backs of non-India/n people of colour. If this were so, then, she would still be exercising her relative privilege as an India/n woman. While this remains a political question in Anita's mind, she feels strongly that she would be protecting her access to racial privilege if she settled for merely stating that she has it rather than talking about what that privilege actually looks like. Our two positions are illustrated in the following:

AMITA - I almost feel when you talk with "women of colour" we don't admit these things, that yes "I took part in being oppressive, I had internalized racism at some point in my life."

ANITA - I think we need to tell it like it is, because it's a sense of giving it up which is a process of non-political consciousness coming into political consciousness, which is what this telling is all about...When I read papers it's always those that name and give it up that I find empowering.

For Anita, it is empowering because stripping down all the protective layers by which we hide our privilege involves a tremendous risk that speaks not from fear but rather from a place of giving up the power, no matter how seemingly insignificant it is in the face of the over-riding race ideology.[4] To paraphrase Gayatri Chakravorty Spivak, giving up privilege entails experiencing tragic loss of that privilege. To Anita, then, naming the racial stereotypes is not about releasing personal guilt; instead, it is a process by which we learn to embody the feminist politics of progressive change that we speak about. For example, Anita believes a statement like "Anita, the Indian you are in Africa I hate" necessitates a substantive and politicized, as opposed to a defensive and personalized, accounting of the role played by India/ns in buffering British colonial racism in the countries of Africa. What matters is who is doing the telling. When people of colour tell of the stereotypes we have of each other as a political act, we tell it to untell it, to break it down, to transform it.[5] Anita is of the opinion that to assume that Africans must already know the racialist stereotypes levelled against them by India/ns, on the basis of our common experience of white racism, is itself based on privilege; and does not address the power differential between people of colour according to the lightness of their skin. The subtle grouping of all people of colour implicit in the real fear of naming our India/n racialism inevitably follows white dominant practices of homogenizing all people of colour into one group. This homogenization further fuels racialism by instilling among us a competitiveness that feeds into the enhancement of white power. It is for this reason that Anita holds the position that, to participate in the building of coalition politics among people of colour, India/ns must do their part of critically examining the ways in which they have duplicated marginalizing practices in the non-Euro-American world and with non-India/n people of colour throughout the world. As Sivanandan deliberates, "it is interesting to note how an intermediate colour [e.g., India/n middle class] came to be associated with an intermediate role [in East Africa and now in British society]" (1987, p.97).

While we differed on whether or not describing a racialist stereotype works toward reinscribing or releasing its marginalizing effect, we indisputably agreed that as India/n feminists we must resist the urge to be silent in addressing our taught racialism. We find encouragement in Alice Walker's point that,

> *the truth about any subject only comes when all sides of the story are put together . . . each writer writes the missing parts to the other writer's story. And the whole story is what I'm after.* (1983, 49)

Self-silencing itself becomes instrumental in maintaining the system of prejudice. The very act of speaking, then, though possibly operating from a site of privilege (in our case academic privilege to name but one form), disallows the occasion to pretend ignorance or to be indifferent to racialism. Despite our differences of locations within India/nness we both know that Hindu-centric notions of India/nness feed into practices of superiority which are ultimately exclusionary. For instance, Hindu-centrism rejects, though it tolerates, religious and cultural practices historically traceable to non-Indian contexts. In fact, the very notion of India/n comes to be synonymous with Hindu, a person from another race cannot be regarded as Hindu unless born into this religious group. Clearly, one can see how this purist ideology of Hindu-centric categorizations produces daily racialism. Furthermore, within the dominant Hindu ideological framework itself, there is hierarchization based on caste; people originating from the Brahmin caste are valorized above all others. Brahmins are regarded as holier, where holy connotes the ultimate link to notions of Hindu superiority. It is important to note that this Hindu construction of superiority does not connote, nor can it be likened to, Euro-American notions of supremacy.[6]

However, caste and race in India are inextricably linked to racialist ideologies of nationalism and imperialism. For example, in India, Anita learned that India/ns developed infrastructures in Nigeria, Kenya and Tanzania. The national newspapers, and social studies text books, all of which grew out of right-wing ideology, worked to produce the popular mythology in the India/n mind that these countries of Africa were "backward"; and that India was directly responsible for economic growth in the region. In rethinking that period of learning, Anita can now see how these imperialist notions prepared the India/n psyche for the possibility of India emerging as a major Third World power.

Hindu-centrism and India/n imperialist practices culminating in extreme racialism can be identified in the daily exchanges of India/n people. Privileging based on colour of skin operates in a manner that facilitates the domination of lighter skin Northerners (Aryan) over darker-skinned Southerners (Dravidian). Amita grew up constantly being told to avoid sunlight for the fear of growing darker (read Kali/Black). Those putting ads in the matrimonial section of newspapers make mention to light skin in order to upgrade their chance of finding a suitable match. The cosmetics industries continually pitch skin-lightening products to women; tea was at one time thought to darken skin colour and hence to be avoided. Hetero-patriarchal beauty standards, then, are established on the colour of skin; the lighter the India/n woman is, the more marketable she becomes.

Sherene Razack, an India/n-Caribbean feminist teaching within the academic institution in which we write, pointed out in her comments on this paper that although we address India/n imperialism in the countries of Africa, and have examined racialism based on a colour hierarchy, we have neglected to incorporate a class analysis into this discussion and have made no space for understanding the India/n-Caribbean experience in its particularities. To paraphrase Razack, then,

In the academy, class disappears. We can't let it disappear; race is not pure. You are doing to class exactly what we don't want to do with gender. Talking only about shades of skin promotes a simplistic domino-effect (from white to Black) analysis. But how do you incorporate class

71

into the domino effect? In the Caribbean, Indian/Black relations are very different and specific to the region. In Trinidad, for instance, you're talking about two majority populations where Indians function as a merchant class but have never had political power until very recently. Also, the Trinidadian national identity has very much been constructed as a "Black" identity into which Indians have a very difficult time fitting. So the question of racialism and Indian/Black relations is a lot more complex than a colour analysis brings out and there is a danger in homogenizing or exporting an analysis from and about one part of the world to another. What is interesting, however, is what happens to our identities, what we do to each other here within this context.[7]

Provoked by Razack's comments we asked ourselves for whom do we speak and how? Much of our articulation has come from, and grown out of, our middle-class privileged locations and is justified by our absence as feminists of colour in this white, elitist, male institution. Realizing that women of colour are largely at the bottom of a capitalist arrangement of labour and formalized knowledge means that the very writing of this paper, coupled with its lack of critical analysis of classist oppression, shows how our class privilege works to advance our privilege. Although, like Blauner, we understand that "class and race [and gender] are not antithetical, nor are they reciprocals in a zero-sum relationship where 'more class' must mean 'less race' [and 'less gender']" (1992, 61-62), it is important to point out that without an analysis of, and a politics for, the elimination of classist oppression, we too contribute to the daily marginalization of working-class feminists and women of colour who are exploited not only on the basis of their race and gender but also through their class location. While we must continue to struggle for our place in academia, and speak out against our exclusion from white feminist academic circles and sites of paid work, we must at the same time remember that it is the *same* social relations which also keep us, as women of colour, "on the periphery in academia" (Carty, 1991, 16). We have only begun to understand that we must continually ask of ourselves, as Cherrie Moraga has suggested, "how have I internalized my own oppression? How have I oppressed?"(1992, 23).

In trying to think through Razack's comments regarding the danger of importing an analysis from one part of the world to the other, we began to see how our construction of "India/n" absented India/n-Caribbeans. When critically examined, our hegemonic construction of "India/n" and marked ignorance about India/n-Caribbeans suggests that our exclusion of India/n-Caribbean is based on either nationalistic beliefs or racialist notions. The former rationalized on the grounds that they migrated away from India generations ago and therefore have no ties. And the latter, on grounds that they have taken on cultural and social aspects of African-Caribbean communities and are therefore not India/n. This, regardless of whether or not India/n-Caribbeans seek associative ties with people and cultures from the India/n subcontinent. Our unidimensional analysis of racialism, as Razack correctly points out, fails to provide for an analysis that works out the complexities and particularities of "internalized racism" among and across people of colour. Even our discussion on racialism towards Black people, for example, followed a distant acknowledgement of this practice without direct reference to how it gets generated in the here and now, in Toronto among and across African-Canadians, Chinese-Canadians, Japanese-Canadians, African-Caribbean-Canadians, India/n-Caribbean-Canadians, India/n-Canadians, and other peoples of colour. Our communities must begin to understand the many ways we have been divided and how we continue to participate in divisive practices. In discussing the need for political solidarity between women, bell hooks notes,

> *White women . . . must confront racism . . . Women of colour must confront . . . absorption of white . . . beliefs, "internalized racism" . . . Often women of colour from varied ethnic groups have learned to resent and hate one another...Often Asians, Latinas, or Native American Indian*

groups find they can bond with whites by hating blacks. Black people
respond to this by perpetuating racist stereotypes of these [sic] ethnic
groups. It becomes a vicious cycle. (1991, 36)

While we do not understand the ways in which racialist practices are
exercised between people of colour living in the the countries of the Caribbean, an African-Caribbean-Bajan colleague, now a resident of Toronto,
brought a popular racialist African-Bajan calypso song to our attention which
aired on television's "Banks Pic O' de Crop" program in 1987, in Barbados —
the twenty-first year of its independence. We were unable to obtain a printed
version of its lyrics and have instead transcribed parts of the song from a
videotape recording of the program. The following is a partial transcription
of what we heard from listening to the song, entitled *"Twenty-O-Nine"* (2009),
about India/n-Bajans, written and performed by Mac Finngal, an African-
Bajan male high school teacher

When I was taking a trip through time in the year twenty-O-nine
I became so curious, I wanted to find out about Barbados
so I devoted me time machine [and what I found out]...
was a big shock to me...
Look an Indian here, an Indian there, an Indian everywhere...

Look them in immigration, customs and tourism...
Indian, Indian, Indian
Indian here, Indian there, Indian everywhere
can you believe that...

When I walked by me daily news
man, now me head gets so confused,
only two Indians in parliament...still
I get their control in every cent.

To control your economy
is to control your destiny
that's why I hurried back to let you know
that twenty-O-nine they got to be go...

Indian here, Indian there, Indian everywhere...
Indian, Indian, Indian...
twenty-O-nine they got to be go.[8]

Given the complexities and multi-layered ways of living India/n, it remains extremely difficult for us to self-consciously realize the daily methods by which nationalism, Hindu-centrism, racialism and our middle-class privilege play out these and other marginalizing practices. In some sense, this section on "Resisting the Silence" itself illustrates our inability to confront our racialism against non-India/n people of colour, and lack of knowledge about their racialism towards us. The reality of these practices is much larger than we are able to grasp here. What is beyond dispute, however, is that we need to understand in context the historical and materialist differences between all of us and the ways in which marginalizing practices are played out. Undertaking such a task would necessitate that we begin from a feminist, anti-capitalist, anti-imperialist, anti-colonialist standpoint.

Striking a chord

The claim to a lack of identity or positionality is itself based on privilege,
on a refusal to accept responsibility for one's implication in actual histori-
cal or social relations, on a denial that positionalities exist or that they
matter, the denial of one's own personal history and the claim to a total
separation from it. (Martin and Mohanty, 1986, p.208)

In talking within the category of India/n we have discovered that who

speaks is as crucial as who will listen. Through writing this paper we have
begun to locate both the dominant and marginalized voices within us. Giving
up the internalized master narrative in a move to dislocate the fixity of the
category India/n, while simultaneously politically claiming our India/nness,
gave rise to gripping and often tearing emotions. Our process of writing was
riddled with violent tension, heated debate, sleepless nights, and hours of
painful disagreement. The learning/unlearning that has gone on extends far
beyond the product as presented. To remind our readers once more, we have
only included seven minutes of our six hour long taped conversation. Most of
our discussion then, on patriarchy, gender, sexuality and class within the
category India/n has not been imported into this paper. We are
hyperattentive to the fact that we have not discussed these issues in this
paper, despite our awareness of the interconnectedness of these oppressions,
even as they appear in the conversational dialogue here included. We believe
that one of the ways to dismantle hegemonic discourses is to go about chisel
in hand cracking away at the cement that holds in the interlocking oppressions. In this sense, then, we would like this paper to stand as a point of
entry, another strike that cracked another piece of that wall.

We now break from our own voices to listen to another feminist, Himani
Bannerji, commenting on our attempt to talk about India/nness from within
the category India/n. Himani Bannerji was born in Pakistan, grew up, and
undertook most of her education in India. She came to Toronto in her mid-
twenties for postgraduate study and has lived here as resident ever since.
The following, quoted in her own words, is the response she gave:

I think it's very crucial where childhood is spent. I think so much of the
structures of confidence come from what is mirrored from others around you .
. . I mean no one asks "Who am I?" unless they are feeling totally
disjunctured . . . people don't ask "Who am I?" unless they are feeling circum-
scribed, or denied. . . This sort of existential anguish is not automatically
mental. Basically, it becomes so when a child feels such an outsider always
to one's self. Yet this is the only insight she knows . . . so the inside is the

outside and there is no other space they can go to. The home is also inscribed for them . . . they bring the stories of the school place back home . . .

Why has one of you learned to globalize the term India/n and the other not . . . I think this is where the question lies because one of you has actually lived in the country so it is a historical place, while for the other it has actually been homogenized by being India/n abroad where the category India/n was created whereas, in India it is created by the India/n state. Every province in India is tearing apart because they all want to secede . . . We can't speak of India, I will never teach a course on India . . . I teach a course on Political Economy where I will use examples from that country . . .

I don't understand the contestation over the category India/n, I understand it to be purely ideological . . . It was invented in the course of people living in a racist environment. No matter where they come from, who they were, with completely different histories . . . they all got lumped through their passport. What categorizes it is the passport. Once having been created, however, it actually becomes a pseudonym . . . one of the sub-categories of being categorized as a race . . .

While I agree that this category India/n is very useful to understanding racism . . . the category is also a way of zonalizing people; zonalization is like apartheid . . . I'm not denying the value of the category India/n, but the reason why it's become such a contestation between you two, and such a big issue between the two of you that you even chose to think about it is because you are feeling so out of it here in Canada . . .

[P]eople coming from certain places that have socially, economically, politically, culturally organized in a certain way, and made a finite number of changes, have certain things in common . . . But these commonalities are actually fractured, fragmented and riddled with internal contradictions of this very space. These contradictions are important to specify, and that is what allows us to fracture that category called India/nness; that is what allows us to fracture the essentiality. There are certain general traits we have in common but the specificity of these traits is what breaks it down into actual lived practices . . . What I'm saying here is that the way we use India/n and India/nness in the identity politics scene is essentialist, and I would be very afraid of falling into the trap of that essentialism. I would misrepresent tons of people I know, with whom I grew up, with whom I go to work, I could not do justice to most of the people I knew, if I were to really stereotype them as India/n or having India/nness . . .

The work against racism is actually to be historical . . . If you want to fight racism really, and you want to fight it on the ground of history, then you have to introduce notions of imperialism and colonialism . . . and locate the notion of India/nness within this . . . If there was not a white referent point we wouldn't even be discussing this. In India people are not sitting around and discussing it, they don't give a shit, they live in a society where everyone looks pretty much like themselves, worshipping the same gods. It is a question relevant to non-white people living in Metropolitan countries . . .

If one just goes into cultural categories, I do not see a feminist agenda operating. Cultural categories can only incorporate a feminist agenda by having a zone added to them; this is not incorporation, it is addition.

This is an interesting paper in so far as it is debating the whole category of India/n . . . and you are unsettled in terms of it. Its value is that it might help to get out of the fixity into thinking about history and being able to think about colonialism, capitalism, imperialism in Canada. None of what you say would be relevant, this wouldn't have been your anguish, you wouldn't have been so worried about where you are, and about where you come from, had you not had that big long history of colonialism, capitalism, imperialism whithin which you live right now.

Now it becomes an absolute pipe dream to talk about international solidarity of people and revolution, but I happen to be old fashioned and I do really think from here we could go on to thinking about this in revolutionary terms, where you could point out how it is that you made these types of choices, what is the history . . .

In a lot of the discussions you had, you were empirically able to present to me a lot of the quandaries, the pains, and denials through which you have gone. This is most useful to me because it shows where the entry point of politics is. All the points of denial and absence are points of entrance and politics. What you have said resonates with my experiences, where I work daily. This is useful and it is good to see people doing it, and doing it with such a direct voice. I have not seen it written as clearly as you've written it by anybody living here. I think this is very important.

However, I think you may have partly taken the category of India/n as a given, although not entirely because you have had a lot of debate over it . . . The term "westernized" is used often to trash feminists working in India, which leaves room for patriarchy, classist, casteist, fascist political organizing to happen in the name of being India/n. Students who read this piece of work in Canadian universities may actually think that there is something called India/nness and they may think it all right to equate India/n with tradition; where Western is modernization. They would not see the East as both tradition and modernity as much as they do the West. And so that is a danger. But on the other hand, these students might gain some understanding of the kind of debates that are actually going on in "the community" as to where people want to situate themselves. Your debate is not individualistic, that's obvious, because as I said experientially and empirically it has brought across all kinds of detailing of experiences, and those experiences are not to be negated if one is to become politically active. One has to see what real experience, as ideological categories such as India/nness, can give rise to, and I think part of your paper does make that point. Ideological as it may be, it has actually created real pain. But the trouble is answering back India/nness with India/nness.

Also, one thing you need to state outright is that your paper is about younger people; it is not about us older people. For we are also here. Some of your quandaries are not our quandaries; we don't have identity problems. Whatever other problems your mother might have, her identity is not at stake; her job may be, her everyday life may be . . . she even may be trying to

79

placate . . . but whatever it is, she's not concerned about her Indian/nness. She is not going to stop cooking her food or wearing saris if necessary . . .

I do not want to negate this enterprise in any shape or form but I would like you to be very careful about it. There is a lot of writing being done inside India by extremely right wing people about being India/n and it has become a way of silencing profound questions about sexism, casteism, colonialism, imperialism . . . I would caution against thinking of India as tradition and India/nness as actually an existing entity in the world . . . There is a fear . . . The paper's main intent is to problematize this, but because of the way people have been pre-organized, it inadvertently falls into the trap of fighting a problem with a problem. However, none of us are talking about the huge political crisis going on in Canada right now; we have not said a word about living here in these times . . .

Opening up

What we have learned from the comments offered by Himani Bannerji is that discussions about our "differences within" as women of colour must go on. Although her words caution against and problematize the taken-for-grantedness of the category "India/n" as employed in this paper, discovering that she could enter this text at places and make it her own illustrates our common struggle and the need to enhance and enrich our understanding of one another, perhaps not so much as India/n women but as South Asian feminists.

> *"India" for . . . me . . has been an artificial construct. "India / nness" is not a thing that exists...The name India was given by Alexander the Great by mistake. The name Hindustan was given by Islamic conquerors. The name Bharat, which is on the passport, is in fact a name that hardly anyone uses, which commemorates a mythic king. So it isn't a place we India / ns can think of as anything, unless we are trying to*

*present a reactive front, against another kind of argument. And this has
its own contradictions. For example, when I'm constructing myself as
India/n in reaction to racism, I am very strongly taking a distance from
myself. If an Indian asks me what I am, I'm Bengali, which is very
different.* (Chakravorty Spivak, 1990, 39)

*While it remains difficult to identify every phrase and sentence contributed by
Punam Khosla to the section on "Resisting the silence," we wish to acknowledge that we have benefitted enormously from her comments. We would like to
thank Punam for giving generously of her time, energy and effort. Anita would
like to thank her in particular for the countless hours spent in her home and in
Cuba debating and arguing various points in the paper. Punam's critique
regarding the absence of discussion on, and analysis of sexuality implicit in
the conversational text has caused us to re-think the privileged splitting we
employed in speaking to one another from within the category "India/n".
Thank-you, Punam, your help has been invaluable.*

> *We thank Himani Bannerji for her comments, particularly for taking the
time and finding the energy to speak to us even though she was feeling ill.
Also, we would like to thank her for encouraging us to push this work forward.
We thank the participants of Desh Pradesh; from their words and images we
have drawn tremendous energy. In particular, Amita would like to thank
Vinita Srivastava and Prem Kohly.*

> *Anita wishes to acknowledge the ongoing support and critical comments
she has received from Peggy Bristow, Linda Carty and Himani Bannerji in
collaboratively working for an "anti-racist feminism in academia." She would
also like to thank Tony Xerri for patiently proofreading the many versions,
Rinaldo Walcott for his comments, and Melanie Randall for listening every
time Anita needed her (there were many). Thanks also to Melanie for her final
reading and Phil Masters for her detailed copyediting of this paper. Thank-
you.*

> *Amita is forever grateful to her father, Madan Handa, for never-tiring*

guidance, encouragement and endless discussions on thinking and living through issues of social change.

Storytelling for Social Change

Sherene Razack

Her (story) remains irreducibly foreign to Him. The man can't hear it the way she means it. He sees her as victim, as unfortunate object of hazard. "Her mind is confused," he concludes. She views herself as the teller, the un-making subject...the moving force of the story. (Trinh, 149)

For many of us who would describe ourselves as teaching for social change, storytelling has been at the heart of our pedagogy. In the context of social change storytelling refers to an opposition to established knowledge, to Foucault's suppressed knowledge, to the experience of the world that is not admitted into dominant knowledge paradigms. I have found storytelling to be central to two apparently different strategies for social change: feminism applied to law and critical pedagogy or popular education. In this article, I propose to situate my introductory comments in the context of feminism and the law, leaving the central part of my argument for the discussion of storytelling within the context of critical pedagogy.

For feminists, storytelling has always been particularly seductive; women's stories have not been told. When we depend on storytelling either to reach each other across differences or to refute patriarchal and racist constructs, we must overcome at least one difficulty: the difference in position between the teller and the listener, between telling the tale and hearing it. Storytelling is all about subjectivity: often uncritically "understood as sentimental, personal and individual horizon as opposed to objective, universal, societal, limitless horizon; often attributed to women, the other of man, and natives, the other of the west." (Trinh, "Not You/Like You" in *Making Face*, 373). When, for instance, the Canadian Adviosry Council on the Status of Women, a quasi-governmental organization, collects the stories of immigrant women with a view to their publication, one suspects that it is the sentimental, personal and the individual that is being sought after. To what uses will these stories be put? Will someone else then take and theorize from them? Will they serve to reassure everyone that Canada really is diverse, full of folklore? Who will control how they are used? Will immigrant women tell a particular kind of story in a forum they do not control? Such dilemmas are evident wherever storytelling is used.

Feminists working in law describe for the court's benefit the nature of women's oppression and then make an argument that policies and practices that perpetuate oppression ought to be declared illegal. (In Canada, section 15, the equality rights section of the Charter of Rights and Freedoms, is usually invoked in support.) The Women's Legal Education and Action Fund (LEAF), formed in 1985, is one of the major groups developing and making this argument in Canadian courts (Razack, 1991). The challenge has been to bring into the courtroom details about women's daily lives in a forum constructed to negate or silence such realities. For instance, Western law functions on the basis of liberalism where the individual is thought to be an autonomous, rational self, essentially unconnected to other selves and dedicated to pursuing his or her own interests. To present an individual in her community, and further, to describe that community as LEAF has done as "the disadvantaged, the disempowered, the marginalized" is to pose a fundamental challenge to legal discourse. The individual in her community is less empirically provable, and courts are inordinately fond of empirical proof.

Storytelling in law

Feminists working in law theorize on the nature of the challange they pose to law's "truth." Robin West, for instance, sees the process as one of telling women's stories. Thus, feminism applied to law consists of flooding "the market with our own stories until we get one simple point across: men's narrative story and phenomenology is not women's story and phenomenology" (West, 70). An example of this kind of flooding is the defence mounted by the Federation of Women Teachers of Ontario when they found themselves in court defending their right to exist as a women-only teachers' union. The Federation argued that women were and are an oppressed group and that in this specific context, a mixed-sex union would only perpetuate that oppression. The men teachers' federation who supported the challenge to the Federation's right to exist as an all-female institution maintained that women teachers are equal in every way to men teachers; a mixed sex union would serve all teachers best. Whereas the side arguing for a mixed union only felt obliged to point to the collective agreement as proof of equality between men and women, the Federation enlisted the aid of over twenty women — experts in women's history, women's studies, women's unions, etc. — to flood the court with information about the past and daily lives of women in general and women teachers in particular. For instance, Dale Spender was asked to testify on her research that men dominate in mixed-sex groupings. Joy Parr, a Canadian historian gave evidence that historically, Canadian women have had to fight to protect their rights. Management studies experts testified that "the routines of inequality" blocked women's advancement. Principals, for instance, had to have training in the curriculum studies, which one could only get after school, a time when most women shouldered family responsibilities. At times, the tale became highly subjective, as when Sylvia Gold, then president of the Canadian Advisory Council on the Status of Women, testified that she felt that the Federation had directly infuenced the creation of women leaders. At other times, details about women came into the courtroom in full scientific dress. Margrit Eichler, a sociology professor, quantified inequality for the court's benefit and then measured the Federation by twenty indices of inequality. Her conclusion: the Federation advanced women's interests.

Storytelling as a methodology in the context of law leads very quickly into dichotomies and generalizations. Is the search for facts, Carrie Menkel Meadow, a feminist lawyer, asks, "a feminine search for context and the search for legal principles a masculine search for certainty and abstract rules?" (Menkel Meadow, 49). Gender is the prism through which daily life is viewed and differences among women fit awkwardly into the story. When gender is constructed in its pure form, i.e. uncontaminated by race, class or culture, Norma Alarcon has pointed out, the woman thus imagined names herself; her culture, race or class do not name her. Thus, ironically, she remains the old, autonomous, liberal self, only female (Alarcon, *Making Face Making Soul*, 357).

There are two additional features of storytelling in law that bear mentioning. First, how are the stories going to be received? Can the man hear it the way she means it? This is particularly evident in the courtroom when the story has to do with violence against women, a story that heavily implicates men. A second problem is that one can't be ambiguous or contradictory when playing this kind of game. The stories are being told to make a particular point and they are being heard in a particular way. It will not be possible to squeeze all the realities of daily life into this framework; some realities are distorted to the point of being unrecognizable. Canadian Native women in prisons, for instance, are currently wondering if their stories of oppression are "translatable" for the court's benefit.

Storytelling in critical pedagogy

In the area of critical pedagogy, whether in popular education workshops or the academic classroom, some very similar problems arise. Popular education, writes one practitioner, "stresses dialogue, group learning, and valuing the participants' experience as the foundation for further learning and knowledge. The educator is considered a facilitator of a collective educational process, someone who is able to question critically different perceptions of reality and custom, and to contribute to the formulation of *new knowledge* that addresses the problems of poor communities and the actions those communities want to undertake" (emphasis added; Magendzo, 50). Ricardo Zuniga, in an article called "La Gestion Amphibie," laments the lack of critical reflection on the part of popular educators and attributes it to an us/them mentality. For instance, the funders (the state) are thought to be the bad guys, thus placing emphasis on the unity and internal solidarity of those who receive funding. It then becomes difficult to critically evaluate the project (other than in carefully constructed reports to the funding agency). Zuniga identifies the tendencies that exacerbate dichotomous thinking and make it difficult to deal with contradiction. The popular educator embodies contradiction, he argues: "he [sic] is responsible for training in a context where only self-training is acknowledged; he does not want to control and he is conscious of the distance between him and his 'clients,' 'collaborators' or 'students.' The problems with terminology well illustrate the contradictions" (158). The only palliative, Zuniga argues, that is available for this anguish is the reassurance of being on the right side, the alternative to the status quo.

If you are on the good side, then you define yourself by: reliance on "le savoir populaire," popular knowledge, and not "le savoir bourgeois"; a firm rejection of empiricism, positivism and science and a warm embrace of emotions, stories, narratives, nature, spontaneity (Zuniga, 162). Stories cannot really be critiqued in this framework; they are unproblematically conceived of as suppressed knowledge. There is an assumption that the living voices (and sometimes the written texts) of the oppressed express a truth that will win out. There is little room for questioning that voice or text as the transmitter of authentic "human" experience (Gayle Green and Coppelia Khan, *Making a Difference*, 25). Language is seen as simply representing reality rather than constructing it. (Zuniga, however, is only objecting to the oppositional thinking and not to the view of language and voice as straightforwardly representational of reality. Thus, he ends up arguing for more rationality and less emotion.)

The oppressed, in characterizing themselves as everything the oppressor is not, are seduced into making moral claims rather than organizing to take power (Zuniga, 160). That is, we are on the good side, we are the oppressed, let us have what we need in the name of justice, rather than demand our fair share. Carol Smart argues somewhat differently about feminists working in law: here, women are seduced into making legal claims when in fact they should be making moral ones. In either situation, what remains difficult is the possibility of making ethical claims, that is, claims that take the discussion out of the realm of individual moral choices and into the more political vision of what the good society ought to be and how to get there.

Warning us of the ultimate dangers of dichotomizing, Gloria Anzaldua writes:

> *But it is not enough to stand on the opposite river bank shouting questions, challenging patriarchal white conventions. A counterstance locks one into a duel of oppressor and oppressed; locked in mortal combat, like the cop and the criminal, both reduced to a common denominator of violence. The counterstance refutes the dominant culture's views and beliefs, and for this, it is proudly defiant. All reaction is limited by, and dependent on, what it is reacting against. Because the counterstance stems from a problem with authority — outer as well as inner — it's a step towards liberation from cultural domination. But it is not a way of life. At some point, on our way to new consciousness, we will have to leave the opposite bank, the split between the two mortal combatants somehow healed. (La Frontera, 78)*

To heal the split, we have to think about our way of life. "The massive uprooting of dualistic thinking" (80) which Anzaldua and many other feminists have long called for requires new ways of knowing. Yet, the narratives or stories of which Zuniga complains are frequently advanced as *the* way to challenge patriarchal dichotomies, in spite of the fact that they are primarily described as everything patriarchal knowledge is not. Thus, Bettina Aptheker concludes her book *Tapestries of Life* with this suggestion:

> *The point is that more than one thing is true for us at the same time. A masculinist process, however, at least as it has been institutionalized in Western society, accentuates the combative, the oppositional, the either/or dichotomies, the "right" and "wrong". What I have been about throughout this book is showing that the dailiness of women's lives structures a different way of knowing and a different way of thinking. The process that comes from this way of knowing has to be at the centre of women's politics, and it has to be at the centre of a women's scholarship. This is why I have been drawn to the poetry and to the stories: Because they are layered, because more than one truth is represented, because there is ambiguity and paradox. When we work together in coalitions, or on the job, or in academic settings, or in the community, we have to allow for this ambiguity and paradox, respect each other, our cultures, our integrity, our dignity. (254)*

In the field

There is high demand for stories in the classroom — both the traditional academic classroom and the one in which I teach human rights activists at an annual summer college. There, Aptheker's "respect for each other," acceptance of tolerance and ambiguity etc., frustrates me, however, in the same way that Elizabeth Ellsworth felt frustrated by the fine sounding phrases of critical pedagogy in her influential article "Why doesn't this feel empowering?" Stories intended to serve as an opposition to patriarchal discourse have *not* always felt empowering. This is due, in large part, to two tendencies: our failure to recognize the multiple nature of subjectivity and hence the complex way we construct meaning, and a failure to develop an ethical vision based on our differences.

Ellsworth noted specifically that in a mixed-sex, mixed-race classroom on racism, students enter with "investments of privilege and struggle already made in favour of some ethical and political positions concerning racism and against other positions" (301). The strategies of empowerment, dialogue and voice do not in fact work as neatly as they are supposed to because there is no unity among the oppressed and because our various histories are not left at the door when we enter a classroom to critically reflect. Her students were unable to "hear" each other. The operative mode was rationality and the stories of various groups had to be justified and explicated using the very tools that held these stories to be inadmissible. (Here, the parallel to feminists working in law is obvious. The rules of the legal game structure the tale in such a way that only some parts of it may be told or what is told is unrecognizably transformed by the fancy scientific dress.) Going beyond Aptheker's unproblematic call for a tolerance of ambiguity, Ellsworth suggests that we respect the diversity of voices, of stories, as it were, that we recognize that the voices are "valid -but not without response" (305). In other words, the stories must be *critiqued* and she has a number of concrete suggestions for doing so which I would like to address in order to look for a way out of a return to rationality or to uncritical reliance on stories.

Ellsworth recommends that we work hard at building trust, hence the importance of building opportunities for social interaction (we do this at the summer college by making the program a residential program); that we stress the need to learn about the realities of others without relying on them to inform us; that we name the inequalities *in* the classroom and devise ground rules for communication (for this we used Uma Narayan's article "Working Across Differences"); that we consider strategies such as encouraging affinity groups between those who are most likely to share the same forms of oppression; and that we consciously offer such groups the time to coalesce so that individuals can speak from within groups. All of these recommended pedagogical practices come out of her central piece of advice which is that we critically examine what we share and don't share. We work from the basis that we all have only partial knowledge, that we come from different subject positions. Most important of all, no one is off the hook since we can all claim to stand as oppressor and oppressed in relation to someone else. These suggestions, which I do practise, do not save me from some of the "ethical dilemmas" that arise frequently at the summer college, although perhaps I could have minimized their impact had I paid closer attention to the ground rules above.

Two incidents from the most recent summer college in human rights illustrate some of the difficulties with a critical use of storytelling. The summer college in human rights, held at the University of Ottawa but sponsored by the non-governmental Human Rights Research and Education Centre, brings together sixty human rights activists who work for social change within an organized group. Thus, there are members of disabled women's groups, various anti-racist groups, the Assembly of First Nations, lawyers for human rights in South Africa, etc. Although it frequently happens that individuals from dominant groups work for organizations on behalf of the oppressed, the majority of students can fit, in one way or another, into the "disadvantaged groups." The first incident illustrates the unreasonably high demand for storytelling from those in dominant positions. Here, I take some responsibility. The curriculum is designed to encourage storytelling and the pedagogical practices embraced stress the need to make a space for different voices and, in fact, to forge a politics of alliances based on this sharing of daily experiences. One participant in my group, a white disabled woman, frustrated by the silence of a black woman from South Africa, when South Africa was being discussed, directly confronted her with a firm "Why don't you tell us about your experiences?" Realizing the harshness of what she said, another participant, also disabled but male repeated the request more gently. Instantly, the trust and sharing of the class, built over five days, dissolved in a puff of smoke. The black participant, thus accused, defended herself and then left the room in tears. In the chaos of what then ensued, it became clear that the sentence, so simply expressed by a white woman, innocently inviting a woman of colour to share her experiences of racism, recalled for every person of colour in the room (seven out of twenty) that this was not in fact a safe learning environment. For me, the instructor and a woman of colour, I tried hard to retain my composure. Later, distressed to the point of tears by the "loss of control" in "my" classroom, and not consoled by the learning value of the event, I wondered how it was that I could have been so powerfully affected in spite of many years of experience in just this type of situation. I recall trying clumsily to explain to a colleague the *we* (people of colour) are always being asked to tell our stories for *your* (white people) benefit, which you can't *hear* because of the benefit you derive from hearing them. Suddenly, the world was still white after all and the pedagogy that insisted that the oppressed can come together to critically reflect seemed a sham.

Let me leave this story for a while and tell another that occurred in the same context but among all three classes of the summer college. This story illustrates for me the sheer difficulty of understanding across differences and the need for some ethical guidelines for *listening*. The session in question took place in August, 1990. On the day that the federal government of Canada, at Quebec's request, decided to send in the army to try to end the standoff between Mohawks and the Quebec provincial police (Sureté Quebec), the students of the summer college decided to abandon the curriculum and take action. This, after all, was the basis of the education for social change they had come to get. In the very heated discussions that followed as to the most appropriate actions to be taken, the only two Native participants (not, however, of the Mohawk nation) assumed a leadership role, again in keeping ⟶h the principles of the college that struggles for social change must be led

92

by the groups in question. They both endorsed a march on Parliament Hill to protest armed intervention and made a passionate plea (in the form of stories of their lives as Native women) that we all accept this as the only course of action. As in Elizabeth Ellsworth's class, we, the non-natives in the room then began to process the story we had heard. Some of us then required the two women to defend their position using the master's tools since we felt that the army was in fact an improvement over the Sureté Quebec, a police force well-known for its racist character. In fact, we argued, the Assembly of First Nations who represented Native groups, themselves agreed this was so although they deplored, as we did, armed intervention. The situation soon led to tears (from the Native women), recriminations (from some of the Francophone participants who felt that sympathy for the Mohawks came easily for Anglophones whose daily lives were not touched by the crisis as were the lives of Francophone Quebecers), sheer astonishment at the depth of emotion we had observed, and to our general confusion and failure to find a way out of this ethical dilemma. In a different way, the situation was re-peated when a native woman from an altogether different reserve (Akwasasne) came to speak against the warrior societies of the Mohawks, while a Native leader later spoke in their defence. We had to employ tools of rationality to choose between stories and to determine political action. The brilliant suggestion of Uma Narayan, that we grant epistemic privilege to the oppressed, falls apart when the subject positions are so confused. Unless we want to fall into the trap of demanding that the oppressed speak in a unified voice before we will believe them, we are still left with the difficult task of negotiating our way through our various ways of knowing and towards politi-cal action.

Both these incidents led me to reflect on classroom ethics, indeed on ethics in general, in mixed-sex and mixed-race groupings where there is a commitment to social change. First, I agree with Zuniga and Ellsworth: we do shy away from critical reflection of the practices of those on the "good" side. Ironically, our analytical and pedagogical tools seem to discourage internal critique by calling for respect for different voices with insufficient attention paid to the contexts of both the teller and the listener. Second, the risks taken in the course of critical reflection are never equally shared. This is almost a truism yet we have not been careful to devise a pedagogy that would accomodate it or a political practice that would not sacrifice diversity, again I think because the game of good guy/bad guy discourages it. What would a pedagogy that recognized the inequalities of risk-taking entail? We know more about what it would not entail, for instance, Ellsworth's comments that acting as though the classroom is a safe place does not make it safe.

From feminists and practitioners of critical pedagogy alike has come the suggestion that caring is as important as critical pedagogy. For instance, Methchild Hart warned of an overemphasis on cognitive processes (135). We can't absolutely know what is required in any instance. Is the best we can do to remain open and to care? There are, however, boundaries to our caring which have to be worked out when deciding how far we will commit ourselves to action. Furthermore, these boundaries are hard to discern across cultures and caring sometimes gets in the way. Lynet Uttal, writing of her experience of the differences between Anglo feminist groups and those of women of colour, notes that in Anglo feminist groups, the emphasis on providing care and support leads to passive listening of diverse voices. There is seldom any heated discussion or disagreement; those who fail to fit in simply leave the group. She describes the "blank looks of supportive listening" and the absence of critical engagement with the ideas proposed (Uttal in *Making Face*, 318).

Richard Brosio reminds us that our professions notwithstanding, education is not the leading route to social change (75). Perhaps we ought not to have the expectation that a pedagogy can be devised that will help us to transcend the dichotomies and the bind of partial knowledge. Iris Young wisely notes that "too often people in groups working for social change take mutual friendship to be a goal of the group" (235). I interpret this to mean that we often forget that community has to be struggled for, which I think Ellsworth very forcefully demonstrates by her critical analysis of her course on racism. What might assist us to promote that struggle?

If there is no automatic friendship, goodwill or community, where do we begin? The answer is, of course, an axiom among us: we begin with critical thinking and critical pedagogy. But where critical pedagogy has traditionally begun is not far enough below the surface. We have to begin with how we know, giving this more attention than we have traditionally done. Epistemology, perhaps without using the word, has to enter into our pedagogy and our political categories. It is not an auspicious beginning to build on the feminist insight that women appear to know differently than men because the universalizing tendency of the category "woman" has been every bit as destructive as the universal category "oppressed" has been in critical pedagogy.

Carolyn Steedman well illustrates the point that how we know what we know is central to our political practice because it helps us to locate the inconsistencies, the cracks we might then use to empower ourselves. Commenting on the fact that all women learn about patriarchy in the family, whether by the father's absence or presence, she remarks:

What is a distinction though, and one that offers some hope, is the difference between learning of this system from a father's display of its social basis, and learning of it from a relatively unimportant and powerless man [as in the case of her working class father], who cannot present the case for patriarchy embodied in his own person. (Steedman, 79)

Our different subject positions, borne out in how we know, tell, and hear stories, are ignored at our peril. Maria Lugones describes the dilemmas that confront her as a Chicana woman in an intellectual context that is predominantly white, when invited to tell her stories. White/Anglo women, she writes, "can see themselves as simply human or simply women. I can bring

95

you to your senses *con el tono de mi voz*, with the sound of my - to you - alien voice" (49). This, at any rate, is the assumption behind storytelling. For the woman of colour, however, the situation is altogether more difficult:

> *So the central and painful questions for me in this encounter become questions of speech:* En qué voz *with which voice,* anclada en qué lugar *anchored in which place,* para qué y porqué *why and to what purpose, do I trust myself to you* . . . o acaso juego un juego de *cat and mouse for your entertainment* . . . o por el mio? *I ask these questions out loud because they need to be asked.*

If we are sensitive to this difference which Lugones brilliantly demonstrates, and we heed Ellsworth's practical advice on this score, that is that we problematize what the limits of our knowing are, based on our different subject positions, I think we end up realizing that storytelling serves various groups differently and that it should never be employed uncritically in mixed groups.

Trinh Minh-ha's work is a courageous attempt to delineate modes of storytelling, to explore the complex interplay between the subject positions of the tellers and the listeners. "There is more than one way to relate the story of specialness," she observes, and stories can perpetuate domination. For instance, specialness can serve the dominant group as entertainment, as "that voice of difference is likely to bring us *what we can't have* and to divert us from the monotony of sameness" (88):

> *Eager not to disappoint, I try my best to offer my benefactors and benefactresses what they most anxiously yearn for: the possibility of a difference, yet a difference or otherness that will not go so far as to question the foundations of their beings and makings.* (88)

As a listener, one can be drawn into such a process very easily. I have seen students literally feeding off the tears of stories from the Third World, basking in a sense of having visited another country so easily and feeling no compulsion to explore their own complicity in the oppression of others.

The problems of voice and identity are packed with internal dilemmas not only for the listeners but also the tellers of the tale. Often women of colour are asked to tell their stories while others will do the theorizing and the writing-up. Yet the chance to speak, to enter your reality on the record, as it were, is as irresistable as it is problematic. What kind of tale will I choose to tell, and in what voice? Trinh Minh-ha asks, "how do you inscribe difference without bursting into a series of euphoric narcissistic accounts of yourself and your own kind? Without indulging in a marketable romanticism or in a naive whining about your condition?" (*Woman Native* Other, 28). There are penalties for choosing the wrong voice at the wrong time, for telling an inappropriate tale. Far better, one might conclude, as the black woman from South Africa did, to keep silent. I found myself exploring, at the summer college, this right to silence and offer in this regard another of Trinh's observations: "Silence as a will not to say or a will to unsay and as a language of its own has barely been explored" (Trinh, "Not you/Like You, 373). As a popular educator, however, I find the idea of silence extremely unsettling, reminding me of my own compelling interest in encouraging the telling of stories.

In storytelling, then, while asking ourselves what we can know and not know is important, particularly in terms of listening to others, and then deciding how to act in a particular situation, I think there is a more basic task at hand. This is the task of calling into question knowledge and of being both the teller and the listener, struggling for ways to take this out of the realm of abstraction and into political action. "What we do toward the texts of the oppressed is very much dependent upon where we are," writes Gayatri Spivak (57), echoing a Quebecois proverb that "on pense où on a les pieds." Again, I turn to Trinh Minh-ha who has illuminated for me most clearly why neither rationality nor emotional sharing will suffice. Trinh suggests we

consider breaking the dichotomy mind/body, reason/emotion as is done in
Asian martial arts for instance, by adding a third category, instinct, by which
I think is meant subject position or point of departure. Instinct does not
stand opposed and it requires us to relate to the world with immediacy, from
the basis of where we stand. Instinct requires us to reactivate the "radical
calling into question in every undertaking, of everything that one takes for
granted" (40). Give up, in other words, the quest for knowledge, that is to
definitely know, either through the heart or the mind. Instead, question
one's point of departure at every turn so that reversal strategies (such as
replacing rationality with emotions) do not become end points in themselves
(43).

Trinh Minh-ha is optimistic about her proposal to engage in the ground
clearing activity of radically calling into question:

> *The questions that arise continue to provoke answers, but none will domi-
> nate as long as the ground-clearing activity is at work. Can knowledge
> circulate without a position of mastery? Can it be conveyed without the
> exercise of power? No, because there is no end to understanding power
> relations which are rooted deep in the social nexus — not merely added to
> society nor easily locatable so that we can just radically do away with
> them. Yes, however, because in-between grounds always exist, and cracks
> and interstices are like gaps of fresh air that keep on being suppressed
> because they tend to render more visible the failures operating in every
> system. Perhaps mastery need not coincide with power. (41)*

The mestiza consciousness described by Gloria Anzaldua in her book
Borderlands/La Frontera requires ground-clearing activity. The future be-
longs to the mestizas, Anzaldua writes, "because the future depends on the
breaking down of paradigms, it depends on the straddling of two or more
cultures. By creating a new mythos - that is a change in the way we perceive
reality, the way we see ourselves, and the ways we behave - la mestiza cre-

ates a new consciousness" (80). Anzaldua makes concrete the tolerance for ambiguity called for by Bettine Aptheker when she situates it in the radical calling into question of all our subject positions. The first step of the mestiza is to take inventory: to ask critically, "Just what did she inherit from her ancestors?" (82).

Pedagogically, then, ground clearing activity is my suggestion for re-shaping education for social change. In one way this isn't any different from the axiom to continually critically reflect. What it refers to, however, is reflecting critically on how we hear, how we speak, to the choices we make about which voice to use, when and most important of all, developing peda-gogical practices that enable us to pose these questions and use the various answers to guide those concrete ethical choices we are constantly being called upon to make.

Concretely, I envision a more complex mapping of our differences than we have ever tried before. In the case of the summer college, for instance, it will mean that more space is cleared in the curriculum for the meaning of privilege from our various subject positions. Colonization from within and without will become a major theme and not just in terms of what colonization means for Third World peoples but also how it constitutes the colonizers themselves. The project at hand is Spivak's "unlearning privilege" (30) so that "not only does one become able to listen to that other constituency" (42). In the past, it had seemed such an enormous task to enter into the classroom some of the realities of various oppressed groups that it did not seem possible to concentrate on how we are "processing" this information differently based on our respective subject positions. In effect, were I to redesign my pedagogi-cal approach in the summer college, I would want to pay more attention to how we know rather than primarily to what we know. It seems simple enough but the complex ways of telling stories act as a reminder that the task is anything but simple.

To conclude, I endorse Trinh's passionate plea for a movement away from defining and boxing ourselves into one subject identity:

You and I are close, we intertwine; you may stand on the other side of the hill once in a while, but you may also be me, while remaining what you are and what I am not. The differences made between entities comprehended as absolute presences — hence the notion of pure origin and true self — are an outgrowth of a dualistic system of thought peculiar to the Occident. (90)

Without absolutes, no true self, no pure origin, it becomes all the more imperative to pay attention to how our multiple identities are constructed and played out at any one time in any one context. The white disabled student might then have not asked for the stories of the black South African; she might have focused on critically examining her own need to hear those stories (to what end?). Similarly, we would not have been paralyzed by guilt upon hearing Native women call for a particular form of action which did not meet our rational criteria. We might instead have asked what was affecting our comprehension of events (as indeed they might have asked themselves). More secure in our respective commitments to probing beneath the surface of what we know, to how we know, an alliance might have been possible. In the classroom, ours "is a responsibility to trace the other in self" (Spivak, 47), a task that must become central to our practice.

I would like to thank the many colleagues and friends who sustained this critical reflection including Judith Whitehead and Homa Hoodfar for reading the draft, and Dominique Boisvert for the many conversations which prompted this article in the first place.

A revised version of this article appears in Gender & Education *5, 1 (1993): 55-70*

Mirrored
in the world

Re-imaging Racism:
South Asian Canadian Women Writers

Aruna Srivastava

Foreword, afterword, afterwards

Revising this paper for consumption by readers of a conference proceed-ings (Imag(in)ing Women, University of Alberta, March 1990) has proven to be a difficult task: the revisions requested and suggested were by no means major and would undoubtedly "improve" the paper, but Imag(in)ing Racism is so much a product and a process derived from its oral, conference context that I felt I had to come up with other ways of de- and re-forming that context so that it was still recognizable, recognizably different. What follows, then, is the paper as written/spoken with authoritative intrusions — afterwords, afterwards — afterthoughts, both mine and others, responses to the paper, post-paper elaborations, even re-visions, recreations. As I sug-gested earlier, below, the academic convention of foot — or end-note post-scripts violates my intention(s): fallacious as they might be, I choose to inter-rupt your reading with these afterwords, my hope being to re-create through re-writing, re-visioning, re-imagining (racism) (women), a conference that has been the most important for me, both personally and politically, that I have had the opportunity to attend.

Scene (appropriately enough):

An Ethiopian restaurant in Vancouver. Time: Late evening. Topic: Being stuck halfway through the paper I'm to deliver in two days. We ruminate on the presence and absence of racism, repression, displacement, academia, conferences, frames, contexts, language, and the imagination. I return to my computer the next morning am able to finish the paper which I fully intend to be made up of women's voices only, among them my own. The male voices to intrude are my own creation: those mythical white male colleagues of the story I have written and which you are here to hear. But I cannot quite sustain that fiction, or relegate my intellectual and personal debt, academically, to the feet and ends of my narrative. One doesn't read out the footnotes, after all. And, as we post-colonials know, the margins define, redefine, and undefine the centre... All writing is autobiography, someone said. Someone else said all writing is plagiarism. And yet another someone said this tale grew in the telling. The tale I have written, and have headed with this footnote before I tell it, would have been an entirely different one if it were not underwritten and inhabited by the voice of my friend and colleague Richard Cavell.

[Afterwards: The tale, re-taled, clamours with other voices, conference voices, voices from the past, afterword voices: four women, Linda Hutcheon, Jamelie Hassan, Asha Varadharajan, Anila Strivastava, who ground this story; two men, Thomas Hastings and Ashok Mathur, shifting the grounds. A question put to me after reading this paper on male mentorship and feminist theorizing still haunts me, directed not only to considering other feminists and the men in their theoretical lives, but to myself as a feminist as well. The problem of men-in-feminism is not a subject of this paper but certainly (in forms) the subject(s) in this paper. My answer? Male mentorship and influence, patriarchal theorizing, can be subverted, created anew, hybridized by the feminist for her own strong theories. Does this weak answer necessarily elide the indisputable contributions of my male mentors to this work, this process?]

The tale

Once upon a time there was a girl of seventeen, away from home for the first time to start university in Sudbury, Ontario. Entranced and enchanted by the perils of residence life and the cold, lunar landscape of her surroundings (a far cry from the steamy sunniness of southwestern Ontario), this girl came face to face for the first time with the word PAKI. To her puzzlement, it referred to her, and was meant, she later discovered, all in good fun and the spirit of friendship. *What an odd word,* she remembers thinking, *I am / we are not from Pakistan.* This girl had a lot to learn about words (she was just staring a translator's degree after all), about the power of words, the subtlety of metaphor, about racism, both her and others. *I am not from Pakistan.* Perhaps it comes as a surprise that this literal-minded girl ended up doing her doctorate in English Literature.

Years later (I am under no constitutional obligation to specify how many, on the grounds that it may discriminate me), or twice upon a time, this woman is writing her PhD dissertation. (She is a woman now by virtue of years and her immersion, meanwhile, in feminism.) She has been asked-because she is a woman and a rapidly-becoming ethnic-to speak about Women in Indo-Caribbean Literature. She can't locate any, and is pondering, between thesis chapters on the British Raj, how she will write this absence, to be presented a week from now (our heroine's work habits are by now entrenched). It is a beautiful summer day in downtown Sudbury, Ontario and, as she ambles homeward mulling over this difficulty, she encounters two men and a bulldog. Don't get too close, enjoins the dog owner, to the PAKI broad. She forgets the incident immediately, later to ruminate about her first encounter with that Freudian fiction, repression. What a perfect ending to the paper, though. So she relates the incident to conclude her ironic discourse about academic feminism, identity formation. First World arrogance, and postcolonality. To her minimal surprise, the published version of her paper has been substantially condensed, ironic musings, and most importantly, the story of the encounter with dog and man editorially excised. What place for imagining racism in conference proceedings?

Thrice upon a time, roughly a year later. Interview time at the University of British Columbia (the ending of which chapter you can all guess). The same paper, re-ironized, over-theorized, focusing more resolutely on how we academics come up with our narratives. The racist incident unrelated, lesson learned, is displaced instead with the following poem of Madeline Coopsammy's by way of conclusion. But before that reading, a comment on the responses of her colleagues-to-be to said poem: not, thought two of the, inappropriate ending to a fragmentary and unfocused paper; why in/con/clude with such polemical, and at that, poor poetry? Not to worry, they themselves answered their rhetorical question: *this is only the view of a woman* (said one), *and an immigrant* (added the other).

Thus, the second migration:

Whoever were those mocking gods
who thought it fit to lead us
from the green wastes of the Indo-Gangetic
to the sweet swards of the Caroni
then in a new migration
to Manitoba's alien corn
never thought to state
the price to be exacted
or how or where it would be paid.
Images of a just society dangled
harlot-like before our eyes
we thought that here at last and now at last
the spectres of colour
would never haunt
our work, our children's lives, our play

that in the many-faceted mosaic
we, angled and trimmed to fit
would find ourselves our corner of the earth.
How could we not know
that time, which heals
just as frequently destroys
and like the sixties flower darlings
we too, would soon become anachronisms
be reminders of a time
of joy and grooning
We are mistakes of a liberal time
you did not really court us, it is true
rather, purging us with sugar-coated pills of
medicals and points and two official languages
your tolerant humanity
festered woundings of "brain drain"
While our leaders pleaded, impotent in agony
"Do not take our best!"
"We want your best,
No Notting Hills for us, you warned.
And so again we crossed an ocean
Convinced that little Notting Hills we'd never be.
Now lounging in our bite-sized backyards
and pretending that we do not see
the curling vapours of our neighbour's burger feast
(the third this week)
wafting across the picket fence
we know that careless of our birthright
we have sold it for
a mess of pottage. (72-73)

[Afterwords: An assault on my / self, this whitewashing reduction: only an immigrant's, only a woman perspective-hers, Madeline's, and mine: partial, incomplete, unjustified...images of a just society. So many migrations in the immigrant women's life, from place to place, self to self, from whiteness to brownness, back and forth. This job interview is the start of a new migration for me. South Asian Canadian women, *into gainful academic employment. This paper, imagining racism, my second migration, a year later, not to Manitoba's, but to Alberta's alien corn, so that I can find myself a displaced voice-among imagining women-with / in the academy, that bastion of liberal values, my values? We are the mistakes of a liberal time....]*

If, as Gayatri Spivak would have it, the lesson of "heroic liberal women" is "to return to the third person with its grounds mined under" (89), the lesson of our less-than-heroic question is now to return to the first person with its grounds similarly giving away under my feet. Besides, I can't get further than thrice upon a time, as convention will have it. And so to my latest encounter with the imagination of racism. March 1990. Term is ending and trees are blossoming at the University of British Columbia. The Engineering Undergraduate Society publishes their infamous newsletter with its usual dose of sexism, homophobia, and racism, a longstanding tradition. What particulary catches and horrifies the imagination of the university community this time, however, is a (Native) "Indian Job Application Form" covering almost an entire page and containing almost every hateful stereotype directed against native people imaginable. *[Afterwords: Resisting the temptation, here, to reproduce, and thus reinscribe, examples from this not-so-blank page, marginalized on two sides by jokes directed against women and against gays. A tale within: that this funny "job application form" is proudly tacked up in a bank in the interior of our fair province. Another story, true: a proliferation of chapters in our fair province of the Ku Klux Klan, one of the largest and most active being in a town with the highest population concentration of Indo-Canadians.]* The university administration acts quickly and punitively, to many people's surprise...*There is a place for racism and sexism, you know; boys will be boys* intones a liberal (white) (male) colleague, angered at the furor, especially the threatened suspensions for the students involved. Native as always, I am entirely taken back. *[Afterwords: Freedom of speech, academic freedom constantly brought forth as justification, explanation. These freedom, as opposed to others? thought to be absolute, inviolable, true.]*

But my most pressing anxiety *is how am I to deal with this in class?* I am so enraged, so personally offended and involved, that my first instinct is not to mention it at all. But how, in good conscience, can I, who have attempted consistently to foreground the issues of racism, sexism, homophobia and their direct relation to literature, avoid them now in my classes on Canadian and Commonwealth literature? I cannot be silent this time. Nevertheless, the issue raises for me an irresolvable pedagogical conflict-how to maintain decorum, distance, a level of analysis which I myself cannot muster? In the first, a second-year Canadian literature course, I drop all pretence at dialogue and discussion, silence my students, preach at them, and still barely able to keep myself professionally intact, make a grand exit after the sermon. *Racism*, I intone, *is a failure of the imagination.* I've had an effect, but not, I am certain, on those who chuckled appreciatively over the offending page with their First Nations classmate present and speechless. *[Afterword: "First Nations" is becoming among many a term preferred over "native" and certainly over "Indian." In the Canadian context, I suggest that the term is an ironic reinscription of the historical and cultural priority of the First Nations people and more than an innocent political gesture pointing to the role of nationalism in the oppression of indigenous peoples.]* I read with cynicism the predictable response in the student newspaper of an upset Engineer: *I am not Native and don't know how it feels.*

In my fourth-year Commonwealth class, I introduce the issue in the last twenty minutes of class, fully intending to pack up my briefcase and flee immediately. My cowardice doesn't protect me this time. Decorum abandoned, both I and my somewhat startled class voice our emotion and frustration and anger, our academically sanctioned inaction, our worried complicities and silences, our belated recognition that the university, especially in the eyes of its pupils, is not a sanctuary of higher education, but like the "real world," a place of fear and hate as well. Gay students (in) articulate their oppression, women talk about Montreal murders, we wonder what we can learn in this institution of higher learning. We ask whether these graduates can take anything from the class. As a cynical observation later noted, we are testifying. Many of us are in tears. I don't preach or profess this time and never as a (fledgling) professor have I felt more professionally threatened, undecorous, out of control, and full of doubt. Himani Bannerji's "A Savage Aesthetic" seems a timely reminder, and a comfort:

> *"Remember, poetry too is architecture all else is redundant except the form, the style-what you call-the texture."*

> *...and so the poetry class unending.*
> *Always the same. Sharp, academic*
> *an exhibition of smug narcissism. Full of apt*
> *and self-conscious quotations, allusions and message*
> *in a voice that plays with a joke or two, calculation, avoiding*
> *emotional excess.*
> *So stands this hour of aesthetics, an exact reflection, of the confidence of*
> *the glass and concrete phallus*
> *that arises on an erased slum or broken shanty town.* (46-47)

Imagining racism. The title for this paper is suggested not only by the conference's title, but by encounters with students reading Bharati Mukherjee's "An Invisible Woman". To a person, it seems, these students accuse Mukherjee of imagining things, of interpreting incorrectly, of not being fair, not looking at all sides of the question. None of them close readers, they refuse the once upon a time-ness of Mukerjee's story of Canada, her claim that it is indeed a story of "politics, paranoia and bitter disappointment" (36,38). After reading her short story "Tamurlane," student opinion is confirmed: Mukerjee is *extremist; these things don't happen. There is always another side to racism.* The racists' side, I assume. *[Afterwords: Racism exist elsewhere, in the United States: how dare she find sanctuary, there? Become American?]* And I begin to wonder, quite seriously, about what racism is: I've heard it modified in so many ways: *benign racism, benevolent racism, unconscious racism, institutional racism, yes, even harmless, justified racism.* I am, for instance, tempted to say that I myself rarely encounter racism, but hastily qualify that to overt racism. Again, Himani Bannerji:

> *And a grenade explodes*
> *in the sunless afternoon*
> *and words run down*
> *like a frothy white spit*
> *down her bent head*
> *down the serene parting of her dark hair*
> *as she stands too visible*
> *from home to bus stop to home*
> *raucous, heyena laughter*
> *"Paki, Go home!"* ("Paki Go Home," 15)

What, then, am I to make of those who make so much of my patron? Who accuse me of being a "professional ethnic"? Who, benignly, assume my automatic knowledge of and identification with a particular community? Which one, I want to ask? South Asia? Do any of us/them identify with that geographical fiction? India? Pakistan? Trinidad? Sri Lanka? The Phillipines? What really unites us/them, makes us cohere? Not any fictional nation. For we are all here now, for now, *Canadian South Asian* women, deterritorialized, unhoused in a country that has severe doubts about its own territory, its homeness-the myths of multiculturalism, even of biculturalism and bilingualism, unravelling as I speak. Our otherness, inessential,

111

ephermeral, defined by-what???-perceived gradations of colour, by accent, by name, is defined against our Canadianness, so that we "not-not quite Canadians," to use Bharati Mukherjee's apt phrase, are always, already continuously, continually, dispossessed, and displaced. [Afterwords: And I cannot do better, afterwards, than to cite the readerly marginalia of Ashok Mathur here: "and ..... invisible often, to use Mukherjee's terms. The consciously `othered' communities are so often gendered. ("All the Women are White, All the Blacks are Men, but Some of Us Are Brave)."] Suniti Namjoshi tells us

"How to be a Foreigner"

First,
You take off your clothes,
Your titles and name
And put on a robe,
Sterile and clean,
With neat black letters
Marking THE STRANGER
Then,
You walk down the street,
Alone in fancy dress. (14)

Sometimes, a stranger to myself, I imagine the matriline, the Scot in me asserting it/myself, parading the fancy dress of kilt, not sari. But then I wouldn't be "The Stranger", wouldn't be one of those immigrant once-children who is "precluded by their skin colour from merging inobtrusively into the society at large" (A. Mukherjee 59); I have both chosen and been forced to assume and profess my ethnic identity. Am I therefore fuelling an imagination of racism? Surely not; surely I am conscious of the pitfalls and the pleasures of the "politics of identity formation," situating myself as a *South Asian Canadian Women* in a rigorously "strategic use of positivist essentialism in a

scrupulously visible political interest" (Spivak 205). I often turn, as I have
just done, to Gayatri in times of need and theoretical self-doubt. And I cling
to that notion of strategy for it is empowering, just as strategically asserting
my identity as a woman is. But... it was strategy that sent me racism-hunt-
ing in Canadian South Asian women's writing and a *scrupulously visible
political interest* that found me wondering what to do with the amount of
writing that is not *about racism*. Cultural displacement, yes, especially in
children: many of these women write stories for children, encouraging them
to celebrate their multiple identities, often in the face of ridicule: or-as in this
poem by Parameswaran-they explore the poet's pain as she watches her
children go through this process:

> *Ma, you think you could change my name*
> *to Jim or David or something?*
> *...When the snow comes, ma,*
> *I'll get less brown, won't I?*
> *It would be nice to be white,*
> *more like everyone else*
> *you know?* (15)

or questions, like Lakshmi Gill, her own place in a new home:

> *blue ice*
> *(O My Canada)*
> *can I call*
> *you mine*
> *foreign sad*
> *brown that I*
> *am* ("Song" 6)

I cannot argue, as I have myself, that these writers repress racism, fail

to imagine it. Their act of dis-placing racism, in their own political and
personal interests, warns me of the signal failure in the imagination of a
critic, especially a *Canadian South Asian woman*, who reduces writing to
theme, to its about-ness. I read with renewed interest, then, Surjeet Kalsey's
poem of "Farm Worker Women" in Vancouver:

Women come and work in the broccoli fields
smiling energetic they come
tired with aching feet and
hands sore they go home
Women women women
working working working

Women from the Punjab
come and work in the Canadian farms
brides wearing silk and gold
with soft henna coloured palms
women with pre-schoolers
women with grandparents
women with large families
women work for them
Women work in the blueberry
and raspberry fields
Women pick mushrooms, cut
broccoli and sprouts
Women work on the marshy land
Their hands get blisters
their feet get swollen
their eyes and noses become
watery they breathe in fumes
and their arms, necks, faces

get infected with killer pesticides
women work round the clock
late at night after coming home
women cook food for their children
for their men, for their large families.
women wash every body's dirty clothes
women wash every body's dirty dishes
women take care of the crying hungry
or sick children in the house
women look after every body's needs.
They go to bed very late and get up very
early to go to the fields again.

In the fall when the season ends
and they get their stamps to live
through the winter, farm worker women
usually join English classes in their
neighbourhood to learn how to talk
to the strange world around who do not
understand their tongue
Farm worker women are brave: ZINDABAD!

[Afterwords: The un(literary)-critical contexualizing of my subject posi-
tions vis-a-vis these poems to break down here: we have more poem than "text".
I recall a question about the literary quality of "ethnic" poetry: what do we do
with the fact that we perceive some poems to be, simply, "better" than others? I
answer, predictably, by pointing out that notions of literary quality are inevi-
tably situated, and that, additionally, my reading of the above poems fails (in
a way that Surjeet's own readings don't) to capture the repetition, monotony,
drudgery of the work these women are subject-ed to and to capture the celebra-

tion-through repetition of their woman / women-ness. For the moment, I leave the poem whole. To "speak" for itself?]

As I read (and type) this poem, however, I become increasingly conscious of how difficult it is going to be to (re) cite a poem like Nila Gupta's "So She Could Walk," visually dependent as it is on conventions of typography: *[afterwords: but reading it aloud is a searing experience, conveying to me (the performer) the pain, the fragmentation of self that accompanies the imagination of racism.]*

> *and a man is pushed onto the subway tracks*
> *the train go home paki is coming the*
> *young men shout and laugh the t.v. screens*
> *a young family on the elevator up holds open*
> *the doors on the 10th floor to let some*
> *adolescents in who brandish broken beer bottles*
> *in return the parents must fall on their*
> *children to protect them felled spray of*
> *glass jagged blades and everywhere stabling*
> *child developmentalists say everything*
> *is as it should be everything is unfolding*
> *according to plan.* (163)

As if in answer to Bharati Mukherjee who, some years ago, wrote, "My Indianness, is fragile...my use of English as a first language has cut me off from my desh (homeland)" (Calcutta), (170) and that "to be a third world woman writer in North America is to confine oneself to a narrow, airless, tightly roofed arena" (285), some of these Canadian South Asian Women writers use English literary forms and the language "as she is writ" against itself, trans-formatively. Gupta's "poem" is, yes, about racism but is not reducible to it.

Jamila Ismail's "poetry" *From the Diction Air* continues in the feminist project of rewriting and rethinking the words we use, of deconstructing that Great Book, the dictionary. An example: "patriarchally 'am I going to be a father,' she wondered, patriarchly." Or Jamila's re-and de-definition of the word serendipity:

> *about serendipity, oxford and britannica have it that sarandib, a former name of ceylon (now sri lanka), is an arabic 'corruption' of the sanskrit simhaladvipa...& that an englishman hitched-ity into serendip to make serendipity. well, that's one way to do it. english a word by romanizing an arabesque of sanskrit & grafting on a latin tail. it's a tail that wags the dog, for latin sends on its imperializing ways. but a colonizing ono-matopoeia (ceylon became a crown colony in 1802) needn't be an onomatopooper. one could learn by it to resuffix paris-ian with an-ite, or decline 'british' to 'brutish', me, i like e.s.l. trips, such as 'united states'.*

> *when serendipity was coined in the 1750s it meant the 'faculty of making happy & unexpected discoveries by accident.' a brutish example, from the 1750s might be, the takeover of bengal; which financed the english 'indus-trial revolution,' & so england went to Empaaah. no of course i hadn't it figured this way when the word first buzzed me, testily, in the 1960s in hong kong.*

I want to continue this excursus on these writers' resolute attention to the surfaces of language and form, the (to some) radical notion that all language is metaphor, and that therein lies its power....

At the same time, I want to make connections, to point out part of what underlies my narrative, to use Bharati's words again: "Indianness...is not a fragile identity to be preserved...but a set of fluid identities to be celebrated...Indianness is now a metaphor...for partially comprehending the world" ("Introduction," 3). I want to do this because, comfortingly, it takes me back to Gayatri, to strategies, to that simultaneous assertion of and

117

undercutting of my identity, my identities. It leads me forward to that optimistic ending of many of the stories, poems, and plays I've read, to that space opened up by reading elsewhere that "the postcolonial inheritance is that of hybridization" (Trinh, 13). Strategic identities: I imagine wearing a kilt one day, a sari the next, jeans the next. Hybridity: a costume of kiltsarijeans, parts thereof, with holes, in tatters, unrecognizable.

[Afterwords of South Asian American *"immigrant"* poet Meena Alexander:

Appearance then was a problem not just how to appear-saris, kurtas, jeans, the choice of garment, women's issues in the weak sense of the word-but the very fact of appearing, of existing for the eye. To what extent, I might ask myself if I were to take a theoretical distance from all this, was my sense of self-identity invaded by the gaze, by the look of a world to which I was Other. But there was no way in which I could stand apart from this question. It was what I was and in many ways am, this perpetual reconstruction of identity.]

Unimaginable.

At the same time...at the same time, something buzzes me, testily, for there are those men (and women) who take up their positions, too, strategically situate themselves in scrupulously (?) visible political interest, some of which I, too-shifting-share. And they say there is a place for *racism and sexism, they say she's just a woman-and an immigrant, they say where's your sense of humour?* they say *i am free to speak: you are free to object they say they're just words they say PAKI go home.*

[Afterwords: A salutary warning in those of us (un) comfortable with our strategic identifications:

I confess that I have been increasingly suspicious of the recurrent

118

appeal to "political strategy" or "tactical necessity" in recent critical
disputes....for no mater how reactionary or dangerous a notion may be, it
can always be salvaged and kept in circulation by an appeal to "political
strategy"....Perhaps the question we must always keep before us is: "politi-
cally strategic for whom?"]

Imagining racism. I said. I preached, you will remember, to my silent
students that racism is a failure of the imagination. And in certain way, I
still believe that. I am a fan of literature, after all. But my imagination, too,
failed. Failed to recognize that there is no such thing as racism. Racism is as
inessential as race. It is a metaphor: not just a word, but a word none the
less. Racism, in all of its forms, is an act of the imagination.

[Afterwords: my words, racism is a failure of the imagination, caught the
imaginations of several people who heard or read the paper. But to stop there
is an imaginative failure. Some resisted what they perceived to be the political
implications of what I see as a crucial idea, worth repeating: that racism is
also an act of the imagination, depends on ways of imagining the world.
Perhaps the conflict here lies in how we imagine the imagination: as indi-
vidual, transcendent, and transcending, unfettered, essentially free, independ-
ent, creative in all the best ways? A romantic view of the imagination which
still has great power; indeed, can be empowering. But those who create images
of harm-racism, for example-however passively, do not lack imagination: they
fail only to conform to a particularly limited and liberal image of the imagina-
tion. We must recognize the power of all manners of imagining.] Racism, as
imagination, has a grammar and a syntax, a pervasive and almost imperme-
able narrative power, a power that makes a poet like Himani want to stop
writing, stop using words, remain silent. This is her poem "doing time,"
which opens her collection of the same name:

This is not a poem, nor the introduction to my poems, because I

119

cannot write poetry anymore...

as I was saying I cannot write poems anymore because I don't know what
language, what words, what metaphors or myths I could use to describe
the world around me or express what I feel or think about it. And I am
not sure that there should be any more of these metaphors around, or
myths, or signs and symbols, or whatever they call them. In fact never
more than now have I felt, things have been ever more themselves. They
are what they are. They are fully un-covered. All the bricks, barbed
wires, concrete, chrome, glass, gasses, bombs, helicopters, dogs and
Wallstreet Journals are there for us to see. (9)

Of course, her story, her poetry does not end there: she does not fall
silent: who among us can forget the image of those racist "words run [ing]
down/like frothy white spit"?

There is a series of discussion at my university called "Hate Hurts". The
slogan seems almost trite, cliched, and of course, this cliche underwrites my
rhetoric, my story here. As long as hatred exists in the form of racism, that
imaginary and imagined concept, I can and will, if uncomfortably, inhabit the
interstices and contradictions of my own-and others-imaginative theories.

For me, there is a value-always to be questioned-in my trying to find
homes in imagined communities and in participating in the fight against the
power that racism holds over our imaginations.

I have felt the effects of racism's power and will continue to hunt for it,
track it down, and wish to eradicate it. Contradictorily and finally, then, I
claim the authority and the community experience. *[Afterwords: "How are we*
to negotiate the gap between the conservative fiction of experience as the
ground of all truth-knowledge and the immense power of this fiction to enable
and encourage (us)"...] Theoretically, politically correct? Of course not; but I
myself must be the first to criticize, question, shift my positions, both personal and political. It is this self-examination that I have attempted in this
paper and I have been informed by the context, the frame that this confer-

120

ence has provided. I will therefore not complete that other frame and end my story [even afterwords] with a "happily ever after". Instead, I begin again, imag(in)ing racism and imag(in)ing women with the help of Himani Bannerji:

If we who are not white, and also women, have not yet seen that here we live in a prison, that we are doing time, then we are fools, playing unenjoyable games with ourselves. I won't go so far, however, as to say that we deserve what we get.

Racism, Sexism and Partiarchy

Lee Maracle

This paper is concerned with the historical development of racism and sexism and their relationship to patriarchy. It is not concerned with the pre-history of racism or sexism, that is, it is not concerned with either of the two subjects prior to their conjoining after the development of colonialism. There is some speculation that the colonial process is a continuation of patriarchy on a world scale but I will not deal with this here. Further, some authors argue that racism has its roots in the development of Mediterranean civilizations, but again, I remain somewhat aloof from this issue. The reason for this is simple: the colonial system of Europe which seeded the industrial revolution was the only social order to birth a system, global in extent, that joined both racism and sexism ideologically and guaranteed patriarchy a much longer life than it deserved. Here, I categorically negate any pleas to pay attention to the fact that certain Asians conquered the "known world of their time." At no time were any parts of the world completely unknown to human beings.

Neither am I willing to concede that certain feudal systems were both patriarchal and chauvinistic. Feudalism lacked two things to bind racism and sexism together in an unholy marriage against women. As possessed vestiges of matriarchy, in which the lady of the fief's house shared power with the males as young women and as grandmothers assumed power and control over the household. The feudal lord was unable to entrench this philosophy so deeply that it actually reflected class differences between serfs of different race or sex. A serf was a serf regardless of race or sex.

The previous paragraph is almost irrelevant and is written for the pedants of history, because of course, feudalism never did achieve global proportions. My last reason is rather pragmatic. The study of the history of development of patriarchy, racism and sexism is a fascinating subject, however, it is their modern context that currently prevents the defeat of any. Therefore, I am very much concerned with their modern context because I suffer from all these three mountains.

Very few Native women writers, or colored women writers in general are terribly concerned with the history of European women in the Americas. The reason for this is also quite simple. White women have with terrific consistency negated our sexuality. For instance, "the suffragettes were the impetus behind the women getting the vote." Now, A-holt and Audre Lorde both know that the suffragettes did not get them the vote. There I begin. How did some 15 million women in North America become non-women?

You see I remember well the eloquent statements of the likes of our grandmothers made to the hypocrites in Canada, who decried the racism of Americans, when discussing the civil rights movements of the 1950s and 1960s. It was a battle waged by Blacks that won us our votes. It was not because anyone seriously considered us people entitled to full citizenship that changed things but the threat of a mass movement of Natives. We are not known historically for our non-violence when upset.

The Canadian Voice of Women, bless their hearts, pointed to Pauline Johnson and the threat of violence in their quest for our right to citizenship. Few women today know that Natives were confined to the department of immigration until 25 years ago. But I remember the day of sorrow that our family suffered when my sister married a Native man from the U.S. Standing in the immigration hall before a citizenship judge was my sister, swearing allegiance to queen and country and "immigrating" to the country of her birth and the birth of all her ancestors! In exchange for dis-enfranchising herself, she became Canadian, white in the eyes of the law and thenceforth, entitled to vote and drink with other white folks. She lost her status as "child in the eyes of the law." She became an adult.

The gains for Canada in this sort of institutionalized race and national oppression were enormous. Canada gained the second largest country in the world, a country rich in natural resources. The decimated population of Natives was easily conquered, erased and consigned to small reserves. Racism never travels alone, however. Sexism is always close behind. Native women alone were forced to relinquish their right to be Native and live off the reserve if they married "non-Natives." White women gained status, Native women lost. Racism/sexism eclipse. Because white women gained by these circumstances and Native women lost — no unity around "womanhood" was in danger of springing up. The racial distinction between white and Native eclipsed the issue of sexism. Unfortunately, since the colonial process began, the issue of race has eclipsed sexism; where the conflict involves women of colour the cause is usually racism. In general, the major economically profitable division in the world is along racial lines. The dark nations of the world are the producers of wealth; the light nations of the world are the privileged consumers of this wealth. Racism is the social division of people along racial lines. It is rooted in the actual conditions of the people of the world. The ideological justification used to be racial superiority. Few people will argue racial superiority in today's world. Yet racism persists. It is a condition, not just an ideology.

It is my contention that racism is the culture that arises out of the division between people along racial lines: "you are rich because you are white, you are white because you are rich." The consciousness that arises out of our different social reality is much more difficult to deal with then the more obvious myths of racial superiority. It is an automatic response for Canadians to ignore Natives. In the classrooms of the nation they sit — apart from the rest of the students. The children pretend that the Native kid isn't

124

really there - after all, she will not finish grade school or she will move away because "these people are drifters."

When the school my children attended realized that I had lived in the same spot for two years and had no intention of "drifting," they stopped ignoring me. They were visibly afraid of me. They listened very carefully to every word I had to say. They were overly careful about choosing their own words. This is not seen as racism, but it is. A division between people that is based on race is racism.

The division is quite simple: Canadians stole our country and have done nothing to redress that theft. Until they do, there will be a racial division between us. I have often heard white people accuse Natives of being racist. There is a real difference between not respecting white people who do nothing about the racial division between us and them and being the perpetrator of racial divisions. The Native who has no love and respect for white folks is responding naturally to an unnatural condition. White people who perpetrate this division are protecting their racial interests.

It is not in the interests of white Canadians to be anti-racist. The basic redress of the racist history of their country is going to be personally costly to all Canadians. No Canadian person will admit that he ought to be burdened with the cost. Get it from the government, get it from the corporations but leave us alone. That is protection of your racial interests at the expense of another race of people. That is racism.

What is little known to white women is that it was the birth and growth in strength of racism that gave rise to sexism. Legalized sexual discrimination of sorts did exist before the 1500s in Europe. But the total subordination of women to men is a recent phenomenon which was hothoused by the birth of capitalism and the consummate industrial revolution. What preceded the glorious revolution that transformed language, culture and consciousness for Europe was: the enslavement and commercialization of an entire race of people in Africa and the enslavement of the more populous Natives of Central America; the transformation of European women and children into beasts of

125

burden, cheap labour; and, the plunder of the colonies as both sources of raw material and markets for the dumping of excess goods and people. This major re-organization of the world's hitherto separate economies into a single global system gave rise to the ideologies of racism and sexism among the oppressed classes. The cultural renaissance of England that preceded capitalism's ascendancy included equality between men and women and the weakening of patriarchy. The industrial revolution, the supremacy of science over nature, production over humanity and the negation of love and morality in the interest of profit invigorated patriarchy.

All sorts of debates about the "humanity" of people of colour arose: in Spain, the debate within the church about whether or not "Indians" were people of culture; in England, between the naturalists and civil society philosophers; and in France, Rousseau and finally Chauvin. Chauvin won the day. Nationalism and racism infused life into patriarchy and bent the direction of feminism before it was ever fully conceived.

The women's movement in Europe, and most particularly North America, was exclusively white and centered on achieving white male status for themselves. Yet, the granddaughters of the suffragettes were mightily surprised at the strength of patriarchy 80 years later. Imperialism can always re-arrange the world in the interest of keeping a minority silent. It cannot re-arrange the world to appease the demands of the majority.

Imperialism has shown that it will always concede to the demands of the white minority if they exclude people of color. The trade union movements owes its peaceful existence in North America and its satiate concessions to its white exclusivity, historically. Had the union been made up of Natives, Blacks and Asians (who by the way, formed the majority of workers in this province until 1909), massacres, jailings, etc., would have been their reward.

Every concession made to white people in their exclusivity strengthens their own enemy against themselves. It is very much like picking up a stone to drop it on one's foot. Women organize, demand certain things from government - white women are conceded too - and the next thing you know it is more difficult, more complicated to secure the concession and you are spending all your time securing the concession and not fighting patriarchy. The government is now extending privileges to certain Native groups. We started off determined to dismantle the colonial empire once and for all and rid ourselves of this beast — racism. Funds are handed out to the organized. Within a decade, the goal is all but forgotten and much time is spent in organizational self-perpetuation. We can't see the forest for the trees. Patriarchy wins again.

The reason for that is simple: self-interest. It is hard to put the struggle of people on a world scale ahead of your own national interests, particularly, when your nation has so little. White women are raw with the lash of male superiority. Natives hunger for land. We are on an escalator of our own making marching backward against our long term interests. Patriarchy is secure for a while yet.

The women's movement embraces 2-1/2 billion women in the world. The enemy of women (and men) is imperialism. This system of financial enslavement that organizes and re-organizes the world is beset with financial chaos, recession, and political rebellion. None escape the web of this voracious spider. Apartheid in South Africa, war in the Middle East, rebellion in Africa, Asia and Latin America characterize its strength and its weaknesses. The women's movement is ill-concerned with the imminent monetary crisis that threatens whatever gains have been made by North Americans. Yet, we are all threatened with the collapse of an aging empire.

Imperialism is a maddened patriarchy gone wild. It requires white male kings of finance and their (ex-colonial) cousins to hold it together. It requires a definite lack of unity between North Americans and third world people. Racism is the fulcrum of this dis-unity. It is rooted in the conditions of whiteskinned privilege that is barely 100 years old.

In 1949, a peasant in Asia stood up on a balcony and announced to the multitudes below that "China has stood up." The shock of it, the magnitude of this statement has never been understood. Despite the ups and downs, the twists and turns of the Chinese revolution, a profound point was made by people of color in 1949: we are capable of standing up. Never again would the pragmatism of success or not success deter us. Under the most severe police state, black youth of Soweto rose up and took on South Africa. Children inspired the armed struggle of the Blacks, coloreds and even white supporters of Black majority rule in South Africa.

Mothers rose to the defense of children. Mothers, armed with only a sense of justice, organized themselves and launched the only resistance to military rule in Chile, in Argentina, Guatemala and a host of other countries. Women are on the move. It does not surprise us that "Cory Aquino" effected the only "peaceful revolt" in modern history.

It is time to take a breath and look at what has happened. Everytime a person of color stands up in the world its significance emboldens women of color here. It confuses white folks. White women are baffled when they open the doors of their organizations to ungrateful women who assume that they are entitled to share power, not just presence.

What a mess. Here we all are, trying to re-order our minds and hearts and we have no standard, no starting point from which to take example. The culture of Patriarchy precludes exhibiting the kind of honesty between us that could lead to our untangling the mess. Based on cutthroat competition and profit-making as this system is, the culture of patriarchy is steeped in mutual deception, power-mongering and the manipulation of hidden agendas. Gossip, hearsay, and the hoarding of certain types of knowledge, specifically the methods of organization and the contact lists, etc., are common practice.

White people still invite people of color to participate in social actions as subordinate to the organization as a whole. The bureaucratic machinery to ensure continuity is withheld from the people of color. The real planning takes place on a level separate from people of color. We remain a peripheral validation of the lack of racism in white organizations.

The hidden agenda of white folks involved in their organizations is the security of power that they think goes hand in hand with resistance to the power of the established order. Old habits die hard. A good many of these people are not even conscious of their own hidden agendas. They are simply repeating the style of work of the patriarch, their defences ring out much the same as the defense of patriarchy in excluding women. "No wonder us guys still rule the world, women aren't capable." There is an assumption that in order for the thing to work, power must be hoarded by the few who think they know what they are doing, and that is the basic style of work of patriarchy. For women of color it translates into racism from white women directed at women of color.

Most of the conflicts between women of color and white women are a result of the patriarchal style of work inherited by white women that have them deadlocked against us.

To alter conduct and attitudes requires a fundamental change in character. It requires that white women consciously test their motives at all times: question their actions and test their attitudes in the crucible of relations between themselves and women of color. It also requires that women of color differentiate between what is stock patriarchal style of work and what is truly racism. It requires painful honesty.

All dis-empowered people seek *empowerment*. Patriarchy defines empowerment as the equivalent of power — over someone. This is the unifying philosophy that binds racism and sexism together. Power over the natural world, power over people, power over the seas, the air, time itself. Empowerment is the personal quest for oneness with nature, oneness with people, the seas, the skies, and time. The quest for power dis-empowers the very people who need to be empowered in order to alter the course of our story.

Our very survival on this earth is at stake, yet we find time to waste in bickering over who has power. The answer is simple, patriarchy has power firmly in his hands with every quarrel between us that goes unresolved. Arrogance is the opposite of empowerment. To submit oneself to nature, people and time requires great modesty. Yet so humiliated are women of color by racism and so humiliated by sexism are white women that modesty between ourselves is the very thing we lack. We are mutually influenced by patriarchal styles of work. Our mutual survival requires that we cut the strings that tie us to patriarchy and find a new thread to bind us together.

We are going to have to give up the quest for power and seek self-empowerment. Our language will have to change. When there is a quarrel between us, each will have to look in the mirror at our own self to try and figure out "what could I have done to prevent this discord and promote unity." Instead, we point at the other person and say "she did this and that." What happens when you point the finger at someone else as the cause and perpetrator of discord? You dis-empower yourself. No one *makes* you behave in a certain way. Force is not useful to the enemies of empowered people. "The spirit of people is greater than technology." A person in command of their spirit, at one with humanity, will labor over discord between allies until a solution is arrived at. She will take responsibility for the conflict, in order to resolve it. An empowered person always has the initiative in her own hands. She is in command of herself at all times. An empowered woman will never bow to pressure or abuse, nor will she promote discord between natural allies.

(Our Lives, Vol.2, No. 5-6, Summer/Fall 1988)

Right Out of "Herstory": Racism in Charlotte Perkins Gilman's *Herland* and Feminist Literary Theory

Arun P. Mukherjee

"The problem of the twentieth century is the problem of color line."
W.E.B. DuBois

This paper has emerged out of my frustration with the consensual readings of Charlotte Perkins Gilman's utopian novel *Herland* by feminist literary theorists. Serialized in 1915 in *Forerunner*, a monthly journal written, edited, and published single-handedly by Gilman, *Herland*, was first published in book form in 1979 and holds an extremely important place in the feminist literary canon. Prestigious feminist journals like *Signs* and *Women's Studies* have published several articles on *Herland* and new feminist publications continue to accord Gilman an inordinately large amount of textual attention. A new edition of Gilman's autobiography and a collection of her non-fiction, both prefaced with scholarly introductions, were published in 1991. A rather voluminous biography came out in 1990. And editions of her letters and diaries are currently in preparation. Both *Herland* and "The Yellow Wallpaper" figure prominently on Women's Studies courses (in fact, that is how I became acquainted with this "recovered" text). Obviously, Gilman is, in the terminology of feminist discourse, an important foremother.

These consensual readings, as the blurbs on the back cover of the novel by four very well-known American feminists immediately indicate, find in *Herland* an articulation of feminist desire. The separatist utopian community established by Herlanders, a community apparently based on principles of equality, dignity of labour and communal sharing of resources, has been applauded enthusiastically by a wide range of feminist readers. In fact, to Susan M. Gilbert and Sandra Gubar, two very important priestesses of the feminist inner temple as editors of feminist journals and shapers of the feminist literary canon, the word "Herland" is "a literary landscape populated by women writers."[1] In fact, they have further expanded the metaphorical reach of the word Herland. In the Winter 1988 issue of *Critical Inquiry* they tell us that the title of their most recent book -*No Man's Land: The Place of the Woman Writer in the Twentieth Century* - has "simultaneous meanings of a deadly terrain for men and a potentially life-giving `Herland' for women."[2]

It would appear that to Gilbert and Gubar, *Herland* is not just a celebratory text of triumphant feminist creativity; it is also an important trope. In its metaphorical sense, "Herland" is the female literary tradition which for them stretches across the boundaries of race, class, time, and cultural and geographic differences of languages and nationalities. In Gilbert and Gubar's "Herland," as in Judy Chicago's "Dinner Party," Virginia Woolf and Sojourner Truth, the Indian goddess Kali and Emily Dickinson sit at the same table and thus affirm women's universal sisterhood.

I suggest that the metaphor is imperialistic in its Eurocentrism and that Gilman's *Herland*, instead of being "potentially life giving for women," is, in fact, life denying for some. In this paper, I shall examine the racist and imperialist designs of *Herland* that seem to have eluded the feminist literary critics thus far, a rather surprising omission on their part, given the fact that they have demonstrated a microscopic sight for detecting misogyny. I shall also speculate on the theoretical underpinnings of feminist theory that brackets the issues of racism and imperialism.

Although much reader response criticism is ahistorical and formalistic in its approach, it did open up the possibility that subjectivity of the readers may have something to do with their gender, race, or ethnicity. However, feminist theorists such as Laura Mulvey, Annette Kuhn, and Judith Fetterley[3] have speculated only on the gendered reader or viewer, and their speculations have not gone beyond the gender differential. While I respect the work of these theorists, I would like to suggest that their implied viewer or reader is a white bourgeois female, and however acute her sight vis-a-vis the inequities of patriarchal textualities, she too often fails to see misanthropy and condescension expressed as racial and cultural superiority of the Western way of life.

The following words of Kenneth Burke are useful here for me to explain what I encounter as a racially and culturally different reader in my perusal of many canonical texts of Western literature:

> As...[an] instance of how the correctness of form depends upon the ideology, we may consider a piece of juvenile fiction for Catholic boys. The hero will be consistently a hero: he will show bravery, honesty, kindness to the oppressed, strength in sports, gentleness to women — in every way, by the tenets of repetitive form, he will repeat the fact that he is a hero. And among these repetitions will be his converting of Indians to Catholicism. To a Catholic boy, this will be one more repetition of his identity as an ideal hero; but to the Protestant boy, approaching the work from a slightly different ideology, repetitive form will be endangered at this point.[4]

Burke is talking here about the connection between ideology and aesthetic form. What pleases us, he says, does so only because it is consistent with our ideology, our sense of rightness of things. For the Catholic boy, nothing could be more proper than converting the Indians to Catholicism. However, the Protestant boy reading this fiction will be jarred at this point in the fictional discourse.

Burke does not speculate about what an Indian boy or girl might think

133

reading this fiction about his or her conversion from darkness to light. But we can be sure that for them the "repetitive form" will be equally "endangered," if not utterly destroyed. That, certainly, is what happened to me in my encounter with Charlotte Perkins Gilman, in *Herland* and elsewhere. I discovered that not only was she not writing for me, but that she had constructed me and my kind as the dreaded Other.

Feminist literary theory and feminist historiography claim that Gilman has written the "first truly feminist work in the American utopian tradition."[5] And they claim that for doing so, she deserves to be revered as "our" foremother. These theorists claim that Gilman's "re-visioning" "empowers" all women. I am compelled to say that, like Cinderella's step mother, Gilman loves only her own kind, and not only does she not speak for me, or to me, in fact, she wishes oblivion for me and my kind.

Let me try to reconstruct here the moment this unpleasant realization dawned on me. At the end of Chapter Four, some of the Herlanders find out through their questioning of the naive and chauvinistic male American visitors to Herland about the cruel ways of our patriarchal world. Specifically, they find out that in our society, we have no respect for the right of the calf for its mother's milk. Vandyck Jennings, the male narrator tells us: "It took some time to make clear to those three sweet-faced women the process which robs the cow of her calf, and the calf of its true food; and the talk led us into a further discussion of the meat business. They heard it out, looking very white, and presently begged to be excused."[6]

That phrase, "looking very white," caught me off guard. For, given the geography of the text, I had decided that the utopia was located some where in the Andean mountains and had gone on to paint the Herlanders in my imagination in somewhat dusky colours. My first response was, "Ah, she paints them in her own image. For her, to be `sweet-faced' is to be white." Jolting as this discovery was, this much of Eurocentrism I was willing to overlook. However, it made me wonder about what Gilman might have thought about the non-white minorities in the U.S. That is to say, I began to worry about this "absence," this "lack" in the text. For if Utopia is to be a country of our desire, it must have justice, and this unresolved problem, this absence of the colours other than white in this utopia of feminist revolution broke the spell of the text for me and made me, in Judith Fetterley's words, a "resisting reader."

Subsequent readings made me realize that the "absence" of non-white people in *Herland* was not due to an oversight but the result of that same "Providence" that Benjamin Franklin and Cotton Mather had invoked in the cause of the destruction of native Indians. That same "Providence" that told the colonists that it was the Manifest Destiny of the Anglo-Saxon to replace the "degenerate" races of Asia, Africa, and the Americas, that same "Providence" that impelled the promoters of colonization plans for the ex-slaves to go back to Africa so that America's whiteness would not be stained or darkened is also active in Gilman's text.

Abdul JanMohamed and Gayatri Chakravorty Spivak suggest that texts dealing with the project of colonization usually resort to "the construction of a self-immolating colonial subject for the glorification of the social mission of the colonizer."[7] That is, the native characters in these texts are eliminated without the active agency of the colonizer. Franklin assures us in his *Autobiography* that rum is the instrument of Divine will and will eliminate the howling beasts without the civilized man's having to spill blood. In Gilman's text, something equally providential happens so that by the time the three white American males reach Herland in the early years of the twentieth century, the women they find are of "Aryan stock,...`white,' but somewhat darker than our northern races because of their constant exposure to sun and air" (54).

Gilman places the process of extermination safely in the distance, 2,000 years before the textual time. We are told that Herlanders were originally "a slave-holding people, like all of their time" (54). However, in one of their wars, the men were all buried by "a volcanic outburst." "Very few men were left alive, save the slaves; and these now seized their opportunity, rose in

135

revolt, killed their remaining masters even to the youngest boy, killed the old women too, and the mothers, intending to take possession of the country with the remaining young women and girls" (54-5). Faced by such brutality, the young women "rose in sheer desperation and slew their brutal conquerors" (55).

While this passage interests me greatly in the way it reenacts the nightmare visions of slave rebellions that plagued the mind of Antebellum America, what I wish to focus on here is the way Gilman goes on to eliminate the offending racially Other so that when we enter the utopia in the textual present, only the Aryan stock is left. Another repressed desire, a desire not only Gilman's but one repeated in may guises in American history, literature and other forms of representation, comes to the fore here. It is a desire encountered quite frequently in the texts dealing with the project of colonization: to have the subjugated assent to the justice of their subjugation and extermination.[8]

The passage is riddled with various ambiguities. How is it that "There was no one left on this beautiful high garden land but a bunch of hysterical girls and some older slave women?" (55). Does it mean that the male slaves killed "the mothers" and young children of their own race as well? The answers to these cruxes of the text are hidden in Gilman's profound racism which accords the terms "boy," "mothers," "young women and girls" only to white people. In order to reach her goal of the all-white utopia, Gilman forgets the need to convince the readers that the slave mothers and the young slave women were eliminated by the men of their own race, that is to say by their own brothers, fathers, lovers, and husbands. And if we remain unconvinced of that, we will have to come to the conclusion that slave mothers and young slave women were "exterminated" (144) by the author herself so she could create her all-white utopia.

Then there is the question of the agency of the slave women. Did they, for example, side with their men or with "the young women" when they "rose" and "slew their brutal counterparts"? And prior to that, did they participate in the uprising in any way? The text is silent about any details having to do with the agency of the slave women during the slave uprising or the treatment of the slaves by their masters prior to the rebellion. However, it does tell us, in the only sentence accorded to the female slaves that "Some of the remaining slave women rendered invaluable service, teaching such trades as they knew" (55). The slave women, dispensed with in only one sentence, are like the black mammies of southern U.S. mythology: in bell hooks' words, "a mother figure who gave all without expectation of return, who not only acknowledged her inferiority to whites but who loved them."[9]

And yet, despite such sisterly co-operation on their part, the creator of the text grants progeny only to the white women. After rendering "invaluable service," the female slaves die off of old age whereas the white Herlanders begin to reproduce through the miraculous process of parthenogenesis. Providence of a Darwinian nature obviously favours the white Herlanders, for only they are selected to multiply through parthenogenetic birth. And thus does Herland become an all white utopia.

As I have suggested earlier, in her construction and destruction of the Other, Gilman's text resembles several other American and European texts written at the high tide of imperialism. Her imaginary, guilt-free, providential genocide sublimates the actual genocide that imperialism had been visiting on the non-white populations since the sixteenth century. And like the other imperialist texts, *Herland* justifies and finally obliterates the memory of this traumatic encounter with the Other so that the colonizer is ultimately left with only "the empty land" of Turner's frontier s/he can justifiably possess and build on it the "city on a hill."

The analogy of Winthrop's "city on a hill" is quite appropriate for *Herland*. For this racially pure utopia remains surrounded by "savages" "down below" (144) who have extinguished the light of *Herland's* civilization except for its impenetrable geography. In the closing scenes of the novel, the three American men discern the possibility of "penetrating those vast forests and civilizing - or exterminating - the dangerous savages" (144). However, they talk about it in private because the Herland women "had a definite aversion to killing things" (144). Lest this be considered as an example of Gilman's disapproval of male proneness to violence, in the sequel to *Herland* and *Women and Economics* she states in no uncertain terms her approbationary attitude towards colonization and the violence it entails. "Women," she says, "can well afford their period of subjection for the sake of a conquered world, a civilized man."[10] She applauds "the superior fighting power developed in the male, and its effects in race-conquest, military and commercial."[11]

The impression given in these other texts is that the violence of the past has been a necessary step towards civilization. And women have no right to consider themselves superior because they did not participate in it. In the sequel to *Herland*, Ellador, a Herlander who has married the male narrator, has the following exchange with him on the subject:

> *"We have made a nice little safe clean garden place and lived happily in it, but we have done nothing whatever for the rest of the world . . . The savages down below are just as savage, for all our civilization. Now you, even if you were, as you say, driven by greed and sheer love of adventure and fighting - you have gone all over the world and civilized it."*
> *"Not all dear," I hastily put in. "Not nearly all. There are ever so many savages left."*[12]

The sequel to *Herland*, which brings Ellador and her husband to the United States, is full of the most bigoted statements about Africans, Chinese, Jews, East Europeans and the Mediterraneans. However, the various "herstories" constructed by bourgeois feminist historians and literary critics do not tell their readers about Gilman's racist, anti-semitic, imperialist, and xenophobic pronouncements. Since these "herstories" quote quite extensively from Gilman's books, one presumes that the writers must have read them. I wonder how they have gone about sanitizing Gilman's racism that is presented quite directly in her non-fiction and in the sequel to *Herland*. For example, Eleanor Flexner's *Century of Struggle: The Women's Rights Movement in the United States* describes Gilman's *Women and Economics* as "the outstanding text for twentieth-century feminism."[13] It does not tell us that the book is also the expression of the Anglo-Saxon supremacist ideas popular at the time:

> *The Anglo-Saxon blood, that English mixture of which Tennyson sings, - "Saxon and Norman and Dane though we be," - is the most powerful expression of the latest current of fresh racial life from the north, - from those sturdy races where the women were more like men, and the men no less manly because of it.*[14]

Of course, it is quite easy to pick out passages from these texts where Gilman speaks of "the subjection of women."[15] However, within the body of the text, "women" refers only to "Anglo-Saxon women," and "the race," only to "Anglo-Saxons." Non-white women in her discourse are part of the groups that are described again and again as "savage" and "degenerate," "races" that, according to Gilman, are on the road to extinction due to the process of natural selection.

Unfortunately, the whole of what Showalter characterizes as "the intensely feminist period from 1880 to 1910,"[16] is shot through and through with racist pronouncements about the superiority of the Anglo-Saxon race and the savagery of the natives. Indeed, as Angela Davis points out in her *Women, Race and Class*, the legacy of racism in feminist thought and organization goes back to the nineteenth century suffrage movement.[17] However, feminist "herstories" give us no inkling of the racist and imperialist views held by these foremothers. We have to turn to histories written by black women like Angela Davis and bell hooks to find out that these early feminists believed in white supremacy, approved of the denial of suffrage to black American men and women and barred black women from women's rights organizations. In the "herstory" versions, these early feminists appear as brave fighters, battling for "women's rights." The premise in these histories is that women in nineteenth century America shared a bond that stretched across race and class lines. As Nancy Hewitt suggests, this underlying premise has led to a mythicization of history. In this version

> Women on wagon trains heading west, worshippers in evangelical revivals and in Quaker meeting houses, prostitutes on the Comstock Lode, mill workers in Lowell boarding houses, and immigrants on the streets of Lawrence and the stoops of Providence loved and nurtured one another, exchanged recipes, gossip, and herbal remedies, swapped food and clothing, shared childrearing and domestic chores, covered for each other at work, protected one another from abusive fathers, husbands, lovers and bosses and supported each other in birth and death.[18]

I agree with Nancy Hewitt that it is this version of history that is "widely quoted, reprinted frequently, summarized in textbooks and popular histories, reproduced in curriculum packets, and elaborted upon in an array of scholarly studies."[19] There is never a hint in this hegemonic version that the bourgeois elite women may have participated in oppressing black women and working class women or that they may have enthusiastically approved of and participated in the racist and imperialist projects of their men folk.

In her *Ain't I A Woman: Black Women and Feminism*, bell hooks demonstrates how white feminists have consistently used the unmarked word "women" when they were really speaking about white women. In this usage, contemporary white feminists are following the example of turn of the century feminists like Gilman who used "women" to stand for "Anglo-Saxon women." However, the contemporary feminists should have been aware of the oppressive nature of the word "man" when it is made to stand for humanity. It needed black feminists like bell hooks to point out the oppressive and exclusionary nature of feminist analysis where "the white American woman's experience is made synonymous with *the* American woman's experience. She goes on to say that the practice of universalizing the middle class white women's experience has led to "women's studies programs being established with all-white faculty teaching literature almost exclusively by white women about white women and frequently from racist perspectives."[20] It has led to the publication of books such as Gilbert and Gubar's *Madwoman in the Attic* and *No Man's Land* which on the one hand exclude non-white women's writing and, on the other, enthrone white supremacists like Gilman in the feminist canon.[21]

To understand the conscious and unconscious racism inherent in such practices, we will have to examine the paradigms of feminist theory in general and feminist literary theory in particular. The problem with feminist literary theory is that while it wishes to distinguish itself from androcentric literary theory and practices, the only thing different here is its enthronement of white women writers in the canon. In all other ways, it is really the same old New Criticism in new packaging. For example, in the *Critical Inquiry* article I have mentioned earlier, Gilbert and Gubar declare that "though as feminists we deplore the misogyny expressed by some of the men of letters engaged in the battle we discuss, as literary critics we have long believed that it is necessary to disentangle political ideology from aesthetic evaluation" (389).

However, the problem that I have wished to bring out here is that these canonized women writers are not free from racist and imperialist ideologies of their time and hence discerning readers may justifiably find themselves disagreeing with judgements about their universal appeal. It makes little sense to me that while feminist literary critics are so indignant in denouncing misogyny in male writers, they remain blind to the equally reprehensible moral failures of female writers. From my perspective as a woman of colour, the following remarks by Ann J. Lane in the "Introduction" to *Herland* encapsulate white feminists' insensitivity to the centuries of racial oppression many non-white people have undergone and the terrible price that it continues to extract from them: "Gilman's views of immigrants, blacks and Jews, however typical of her time and place, are sometimes unsettling and sometimes offensive, though characteristically clever" (xvii). As a woman of colour, I must protest that they are always "unsettling" and always "offensive," and never, ever, "clever." And I must keep my distance from those who think so.

In a recent review of *The Living of Charlotte Perkins Gilman: An Autobiography*, and *Charlotte Perkins Gilman: A Non-Fiction Reader*, Elaine Showalter lets out not a word about the endemic racism of Gilman's writing. While she writes about the "profound contradictions in her work around the ideas of female sexuality and maternity,"[22] there is absolute silence about her xenophobia and racism and about her enthusiastic approval of the project of colonialism. Such insensitivity on the part of such prominent theorists makes non-white women like myself highly cynical about their brand of feminism.

As things stand today, much of bourgeois feminist theory has focused exclusively on gender oppression, as experienced by middle class white women. They have been presented as prisoners of domesticity, as evidenced in such canonical texts as *Jane Eyre*, *The Awakening* and Gilman's "The Yellow Newspaper." The prison of domesticity is, indeed, the predominant metaphor of feminist literary theory. The writers who can be fitted into this paradigm are valorized while the rest are either ignored completely or their works are grossly misread to fit into the paradigm.

Historians of minority and working class women have suggested that this paradigm of the prison of domesticity has led to the exclusion of minority and working class women's experiences from feminist discourse and "has cost the field the ability to provide a broad and truly complex analysis of women's lives and of social organization. It has rendered feminist theory incomplete and incorrect."[23] To introduce a few "token" Black, Asian or African women writers in women's literature courses and books on feminist theory will not help unless the paradigm itself is exploded. For the paradigm regulates how these texts by non-white women will be read and talked about. I am afraid that white feminist theory is teaching and writing about these texts only in terms of gender oppression. For example, Gilbert and Gubar imply that Black women's texts are similar to white women's texts because they too are about women fighting men. This, of course, is a complete distortion, for, first, Black women's texts are about racism in American society, and secondly, they treat male-female relations from a perspective that does not fit the model of white feminist theory that refuses to acknowledge that some men may be both victims as well as victimizers.

I am suggesting, then, that feminist literary theory has become a totalizing, universalizing discourse, very much like the androcentric theory it had revolted against. While it may have unsettled reigning patriarchal monarchs from the house of literature, those of us on the margin feel that in its instalment of equally oppressive replacements in the seats of power, feminist literary theory has staged nothing more liberatory than a palace coup. In its mythologizing and romanticizing of women's history, in its turning a blind eye to the rabid racism of writers like Gilman, in its exclusion of non-white women's and men's experience and its ahistorical context, and in its exclusive focus on the "private sphere" texts of middle class prisoners of domesticity, feminist literary theory appears to be only one more addition to the forces that keep today's racist and imperialist world order in place.

Popular Images of South Asian Women

Himani Bannerji

Even though South Asian women are members of the so-called 'visible' minority groups — and visibility should have something to do with visual images — research shows that there is a remarkable paucity of their images in the Canadian media (a situation not unlike that of Native Canadian women). The few images of South Asian women that do exist are primarily non-sexual, passive, docile, and feminine. There is a small sub-category of sexualized imagery, but this sub-category of pagan, exotic, over-sexedness, judging by Pratibha Parmar's article in *The Empire Strikes Back,* seems to be more prevalent in ex-colonial Britain than in Canada. However, this absence of visual images of South Asian women does not connote the absence of our images from the social space as a whole. In fact, this absence is compensated for at other levels of society, and is intimately connected with the few types of images that do exist.

My point that the scarcity of visual images is compensated by other types of images on other levels needs elaboration. In order to do this, the situation of South Asian women has to be contrasted to that of middle-class white women. We have to acknowledge that we do not suffer from the obsessive preoccupation the advertisement agencies or the sex industries show towards the bodies and faces of white middle-class women. South Asian women are not seen as aids to trade and, as such, are not used to sell a wide

variety of objects — ranging from sexual fetishes or objectified sex to gadg-
ets — which uphold the happy, white bourgeois home. That an Indian
woman likes a certain kind of toothpaste is obviously no recommendation for
the product, and certainly the sexual appeal of a garment is not enhanced by
a Sri Lankan model. Needless to say, the clothes that we bring with us - our
saris, shalwars or churidars - are not seen as an aid to beauty. The small
sub-category of images which straddle the sexual and the exotic are insignificant in number and dissemination. They are to be found in the occasional tourist poster or film, such as *Siddhartha*. But the usual "orientalia,"
such as *Passage to India* or *The Jewel in the Crown*, are more concerned
with the imperial saga of the Raj in India than in objectifying Indian
women. If anything, these projects are engaged in such over-all reification
that they do not waste time with piece-meal attempts at individual
objectification. In any case, the women who clean Heathrow airport, or work
in their usual jobs in the factories of Canada are hardly associated in the
Canadian mind with the world portrayed in these (or any other) films. They
are considered a pair of working hands.

From all that I've written above, one may jump to the mistaken conclusion that I am competitively and aggressively seeking to get ourselves a
shelf in the marketplace of images. That definitely is not my project. I am
simply saying that there is no reason to believe, from the general absence of
our images, that we have escaped the fate of others in being objectified and
packaged as commodities. Our situation is even worse in that we can be
treated as objects directly, without the necessity of creating a separate plane
of representation for our de-humanization. The status of social subjects
who, at the least, need a secondary level of visual images in order to be
made the creatures of a capitalist patriarchy, is denied to us. So, while we
do not have to worry about our representation in the media, we do have to
worry about the fact that, negatively or positively, we live in a vacuum, in a
state of constant facelessness.

If one were not aware of statistics there would be very little to suggest that in the province of Ontario tens of thousands of South Asians are trying to make their homes. It is as if we were not here, even though Mackenzie Porter of the *Toronto Sun*, in his infinite kindness, has pronounced the verdict that it is indeed okay for Sikh members of the police and armed forces to wear turbans. How have we arrived at such a state of exploitation and non-entity?

In answering this question, a little history and a little knowledge of Canadian political economy goes a long way. Our social location of here and now was developed through the long history of colonialism and imperialism in which white settler colonies like Canada played subordinate but favoured roles. The economy still continues along the same imperialist path, and its long worked-up justificatory ideology of racism still continues to be the important ideological force. This, combined with the neo-colonial nature of the South Asian countries, ensures South Asian women our place on the lowest level in the scale of exploitation in Canada. One should not forget that Canada's economic involvement with South Asia has been very profitable (for instance, investments in major hydro-electric projects or manufacturing industries in our so-called free-trade zones such as Sri Lanka). Neither should one forget that bringing in and keeping in place a vulnerable labour force is profitable, and therefore, to the profit-makers, reasonable. This becomes twice as easy when using a population about whom there has existed a substantial body of racism for English and American sources. How we are seen or not seen can only be accurately determined from the *terms of our entry* into this country. We were not allowed in to create the middle-class or even the skilled labour class. In fact, whatever skill we did possess became de-legitimized upon our entrance to Canada. Farm work, factory work — these are our labour mandates. Since we have already been allocated a space in the lowest level basement of Canadian society, it is entirely appropriate that we are visually and socially invisible. This invisibility is physical as well as geographical. Many researchers have shown, for example, that South Asian women are generally found in factories which are farthest away from dense population centres, working in areas with almost no transportation, in the lowest or the inner-most part of the factories. Even as white-collar workers, they tend to be put in jobs that do not demand much public contact. This is the analogue, in practice, to our visual absence for the social space.

The visual absence, as I have mentioned above, does not mean an absence of images; but the images that exist are best understood as images of mind, which in the current language of social analysis are called "stereotypes." They form the common-sense of Canadian society and work as a device for social regulation of South Asian women. The social environment is suffused with them, and expectations and images are spun out of them. Passivity, docility, silence, illiteracy, uncleanliness, smell of curry, and fertility are some of the common-sense things that the dominant culture "knows" about us. They provide the content of our racist experiences — that well-aimed spit or cry of "Fucking Paki bitch!" These assumptions function as expectations and injunctions at the same time, and they operate not only at the level of direct exploitation, but also indirectly in other areas of education and administration. They are images of sorts, but of a particular kind best summed up as images of ascription and prescription. They are created in the process of ruling and help to maintain that rule by signalling to keep us in an assigned place. They make us objects of the ruling social organization.

However, since in spite of this continual objectification we go on being the subjects or authors of our actions, our political struggle at this level consists of the production of images and accounts which we might call images of resistance. They consist of descriptions of our lives as they are actually lived, they refer back to the historical and present relations of exploitation. They give a sense of how we really live and, as images of resistance, they also embody how we want to live. This not only helps at the level of culture, but also at what we call the social, that is, our lived reality, to politicize the environment.

But before we go on to talk more about what could be called a war of images (which we must wage in all areas of social production, attacking the

147

images of mind as well as visual images) we have to spend some time thinking through the relationship between our being ascribed a status of visibility
and the overall invisibility of South Asian women in the superstructural
areas of this society. This category of visible minorities is perplexing. On the
surface it seems to be a simple euphemism; it seems to work as a way of
classifying or categorizing, without appearing to be in any way racist. It
seems to be an attempt at nicety. But its first impact is one of absurdity to
anyone who bothers to reflect on it. All forms of material existence, except
air, have visibility. All people, black or white, South Asian or Scandinavian
are visible. So in what way are we more visible than others? Thinking along
this line of greater visibility brings home to us the fact that this category,
upon closer examination, actually reveals more than it hides. Some people, it
implies, are more visible than others; if this were not the case then its trivial-
ity would make it useless as a descriptive category. There must be something "peculiar" about some people which draws attention to them. This
something is the point to which the Canadian state wished to draw our attention. Such a project by the state needs a point of departure which has to
function as a norm, as the social average of appearance. This well-blended,
average, "normal" way of looking becomes the base line, or "us" (which is the
vantage point of the state), to which those others marked as "different" must
be referred, and in relation to which "peculiarity" is constructed. The "invisibility" of these men and women depends on the state's view of them as normal, and therefore, their institution as dominant types. They are true Canadians, and others, no matter what citizenship they hold, are to be considered
as deviations from the way Canadians should look. The category visible
minority, then, is actually based on notions such as "different," "not normal,"
"not like us," "does not belong." One might say it encodes rather than bla-
tantly states any of these things using the physical attributes of people, to
put them into groups, and assign the slot of "us" or the "other." This "us and
them" distinction is based on criteria of normalcy which are very similar to
those used by the Nazis, or those which are used to organize apartheid in

148

South Africa. They put everyone, no matter where they come from, if they
don't have white skin, into one category - the "visible minorities." Needless to
say, this practice totally overlooks the difference in the histories and the
cultures of the people themselves. They have no identity or entity other than
the one conferred upon them by the Canadian state and the racist attitudes
and practices of a people that used to pillage, plunder, commit genocide and
carry out colonial and imperialist exploitation. "Visibility" in such a case
means that people are "selected-out" as not only being different, but also as
inferior or inadequate. Thus, their own bodies are used to construct for them
some sort of social zone or prison, since they cannot crawl out of their skins,
and this signals what life has to offer them in Canada. This special type of
visibility is a social construction as well as a political statement. There is no
intrinsic truth to it.

This category of "visibility," and the construction of one's self as a "minority" (a suffered member of society, even though a citizen and socially
productive), are ways of rendering people powerless and vulnerable. They
work as operative categories not because they possess any truth, but because
they enforce the racist and imperialist relations which are already in place.
They are injunctions, or codes of command, which bid us to be silent, to
remove ourselves from areas or places where we may be seen. To be labelled
"visible" is to be told to become invisible, to get lost. It matches the stares -
not just of curiosity but of contempt - that we get in public places. This
category is the abstraction of that "look" which cuts one out from that necessary anonymity without which no ordinary life can be carried on. The incredible cost in terms of emotional energy in fighting against that singling out
and the reducing cold look is compounded by other actions which reinforce
this, actions such as having no one sit beside you on the bus. This "look",
interestingly enough, is both a look and a judgement. It is also the look of
the mentally blind which does not see what is actually in front of it, but only
sees inward into a mental image of those terrible stereotypes which are
pasted onto us with invisible glue every time someone looks at us. Through-

out this process we are standing in a third degree light that streams out of the stares, the administrative procedures, the assembly lines, against the white wall that has been erected around us.

Often, intensely desiring relief, we wish we were other-wise. Skin whiteners, hair-straightening, and dressing with obsessive care, are all part of the same response. We forget that those who make the rules can change them and that while we can make small gestures of self-mutilation, we can not really flay ourselves out of our skins and features. And even if we could, this wouldn't help. In situations where visibility was ostensibly lacking in physical terms, as in Nazi Germany, it has been constructed by the forced pinning-on of symbols which marked people out, and cut them apart from the rest of society. The yellow star of David, the red star for communists, the pink triangle for homosexuals, were all ways of producing visibility. There were also images of grotesque kinds, but the people being imaged had no right to produce their own images. Their "visibility" was a token of absence of power.

Living in the interstices of an imperialist society and state, what can we do to counter-act these images of mind and eye? Each time we open a news-paper or turn on a television we see ourselves as images of despair and hunger, extending our begging bowls to the West, to America, to those who in the first place produced our misery and continue to aid it. How can we combat the menace of charitable organizations who find a reason for their existence in fabricating our helplessness, and give alms to our hunger but not help to our struggles? How can we convey to the world that many more women in South Asia are involved in political struggles, including armed struggles, than have ever been in the history of the West? And how can we bring across the struggle of our women, of ourselves, a struggle in which these so-called passive women show the resourcefulness and endurance of guerilla fighters? How can we convey in images as clear as crystal, that from the Pizza Crust factory of Toronto to Grunwick in England, South Asian women have said "no" to racism and the hydra-headed oppression of their bodies and their minds? How can we vindicate our intellectual, political, cultural life in the face of the imagistic assault of the passive, obedient woman, not the least of which is the myth of inverted motherhood? I call this inverted in view of the fact that the myth of the Holy Family is not operative for us; to the Imperialist eye, there is nothing beautiful in the motherhood of South Asian origin. That beatific vision is replaced by an animal-like fecundity, which complements her mindlessness with her unending breeding capacity. These are images of ascription and prescription even through the magic of the so-called 'disarticulation'[1] process. But the question that faces us is what are we to do about these images? What should our strategies and tactics be in this war of images?

This war cannot be waged unless we remember that we continue to be substantive entities even though we are not in a position to control all aspects of our lives; that we are not and never were wholly subsumed; that even though we do not control the means of cultural production and reproduction, we continue to generate images which validate us within our own communities. With languages, lores, social interactions, festivals, and all other aspects of an everyday life, we continue to generate strength which forms resistance. But this is not enough. We must be able to produce, be in a position to disseminate and validate militant, resisting images of ourselves. In order to do this we must not only turn to the histories of our countries in anti-colonial struggles, but to the history of the South Asians in Canada. The memory of Komagatamaru,[2] the fight of the farmworkers in British Columbia, the strikes of South Asian women in different sectors of industries must all be revived, resurrected, and put forward in whatever cultural work we engage in. We also must revive the memories of women fighting in other parts of the third world, and take strength from the anti-apartheid struggle in South Africa, or the resistance put up by the women of Vietnam. These images, which are rightfully ours, must provide the third dimension of our struggle to fight against the images of mind which both express and create the conditions of our domination. In short, we must fully politicize ourselves, in the smallest details of our everyday lives. As a part of this process we must also resit the attempt by the 'anthropologists' of the ruling class to 'discover' and incorporate us.

In conclusion, I have to point out that it is not at the level of images, of commercial newspaper photographs, or pornographic magazines that our real subsumption or objectification happens. This happens to us actually, physically, in our daily life. When a people can be commanded to be silent, *to become the images,* then it is obvious that it is the practice of social, political and economic domination that has overdetermined the image. Therefore the thing to remember is that although images do have an effect on us both in terms of our own and others' perception of us, it is not the image but the relations of domination — the practice — that kills. We cannot even begin to fathom the presence, the absence, the nature of the images, unless we stop thinking of them solely as a set, or system of cross-referencing signs, of reality as discourse. We can only begin to read this code when we approach it from what it is that they en-code. Visual images in that sense are congealed social relations, formalizing in themselves either relations of domination or those of resistance. The politics of images is the same as any other politics; it is about being the subjects, not the objects, of the world we live in.

This article is based on a talk given by Himani Bannerji on "The Heat is On: Women on Art on Sex" a three-day conference held in Vancouver in November 1985.

Thinking through Angela Y. Davis's
Women, Race & Class

Cecilia Green

It is becoming increasingly apparent that white upper and middle class North American women can fight for and partially win their "liberation" from patriarchal oppressiveness, leaving the "innermost secret" of capitalism -- relations of production/exploitation based on race/nationality and class -- untouched.

This does not mean that women's liberation is not "relevant" to non-white and working class women, nor does it mean that middle class women do not suffer sexist oppression, even in fundamental ways. In fact, it should be clear that a focal undertaking of revolutionary politics has always been to establish the terms and conditions of a *necessary* alliance, whose bottom line is the defence and advance of *working class interests*, between the working class and middle class groups and individuals, some of whom serve the revolutionary movement, as we well know, in critical leadership capacities. It is also clear that mass campaigns around specific "women-related" concerns such as suffrage, birth control, abortion, equal rights amendments, rape laws and daycare have brought and could bring together women of all classes and races, in however limited a way. Furthermore, individual middle class women have, especially during the long period marking the formation of the welfare state in Britain and North America, played crucial pioneering roles in the struggles of their constituencies as precisely working class women, families and communities, and often played their roles with courage and proselytizing zeal.

Our opening statement does, however, mean that mass campaigns around issues of critical concern to all oppressed women have all too often come to be interpreted, socially constructed and indeed appropriated by exclusivist white middle class interests within those versions which claim media, government and academic attention, and which can be accommodated within related hegemonic structures. As Angela Davis has definitively demonstrated in *Women, Race and Class*, issues like abortion can hold different meanings for women of different classes and can occupy different locations within the total repertoire of class experiences and interests of these different women.

It also means, of course, that reformist middle class leadership of working class women's struggles can give way to a tendency to distort the direction and objectives of such struggles, as history has shown. Thirdly, it means that through the medium of an "autonomous women's movement," an increasingly sophisticated and aggressive theory and praxis of feminism can come to predominate which refuse to treat class and race as issues central to its paradigm and which mark the widening of the gap (objective and subjective) between white middle class women and working class women of all colours. This ongoing fine tuning of feminist existentialism and its concomitant praxis have reached a point where those who attempt to re-introduce the centrality of race/nationality and class (to the question of capitalist patriarchy) are dismissed with convenient cliches and not-so-cliches: they are seen as nationalists, imbued with false consciousnesses, guilty of simplistic analysis, male-dominated left "politics" etc. Nonetheless, those of us who are painfully cognizant of the skeletons of working class defeats strewn over the battlefields of history do not need to be convinced that upper and middle class women's struggles against intra-class sexism do not necessarily attack, except tangentially in some cases, the roots of racist and classist patriarchy,

154

whose most exploited and oppressed victims in North America are working class women of colour.

There is a further ironic twist to this, the implications of which Angela Davis explores for Afro-American men: non-white working class men are often particularly maligned for their alleged brutishness and sexism. Thus these men who are surely bound to be organizationally and socially beyond the pale of the white middle class feminist encounter (especially if their own organizations do not unequivocally take up the struggle against women's oppression) stand doubly damned: they are seen as the rapists and as ignorant oppressors. Some white middle class men in whose interest it is to adopt as quickly as possible the accoutrements of non-sexist language and styles are getting all the badges forthcoming, to denote their individual triumph over the disease of sexism and the rapid disappearance of all its traces from their constitutions. Once again, the victims are seen as the perpetrators of society's problems. The crime of rape, after all, is hardly readily associated with "respectable" white upper and middle class men. Sexism among working class men, which is undoubtedly a huge problem, and semi-official, institutionalized male supremacy both get obfuscated.

Toronto's relatively new non-white immigrant communities are having to deal with increasingly horrible social, psychological and economic pressures at the same time as they are having to get these problems politically recognized and articulated while also distinguishing between authentic and in-authentic extra-community allies. Although there are definitely some genuine alliances, the problems Third World immigrant women in particular encounter with white feminist groups come in three forms: (Davis,1) a push to popularize "women's struggles" which do not incorporate an address to the special class oppression of immigrant and working class women; (Davis,2) a strategy pursued by some groups of cynically demonstrating that they are fulfilling the requisites of a multi-ethnic feminism by forming spurious and token alliances with "ethnic" women who bear no politically significant relationship to "their" ethnic communities; (Davis,3) the attempt by some "feminists" (who rather amazingly manage to maintain their credibility with their less aggressive counterparts) to make a career out of "taking over" immigrant women's struggles, ostensibly with the noble aim of injecting them with the "correct" feminist theory.

Recent struggles within organizations serving immigrant women in Toronto cogently bore out these concerns. These struggles also taught the following lesson: that the immigrant/working class women's movement (broadly conceived) in Toronto urgently needs to articulate a theory — of its constituencies, their oppression and its struggle. It needs the "weapon of theory," both as a ready critique of ethnocentric and petty bourgeois feminism and, most importantly, as a means of clearly and decisively advancing its own interests and shaping the struggle for women's liberation. This theory is, of course, partially embedded in the areas and experiences of, for example, the Toronto activists who recently rose to defend the control of organizations for immigrant women by representative immigrant women and their allies. However, it needs to be pulled together, deepened and articulated.

Enter Angela Davis.

In a way, the United States provides a particularly legible and useful context for the exploration of the issues just raised. It has a relatively long tradition of movements of middle class white women who have had to deal every step of the way with the intractable presence of a huge American born-and-bred subordinated non-white population. This history is a source of widely applicable insights and lessons.

Davis powerfully establishes the two conclusions reached through the unfolding of that history: white women's organizations which fail to incorporate in their analyses and praxes a frontal attack on the racist and class base of U.S. society inevitably become racist and elitist themselves, less and less by default and more and more by intention. Secondly, an examination of the historical and structural location of Afro-American women within U.S. society holds the key to the inner chambers of its racist male supremacy. As a corollary of this, Davis documents the militant resistance with which Black women have met their oppression all along the way, a story that has often been deliberately down-played or hidden, even by feminist historians. Indeed, to date, in spite of the recent proliferation of writings on the history of the women's rights movement in the U.S., one of the most honest and inclusive accounts remains Eleanor Flexner's *Century of Struggle*,[1] first published in *1959*. Davis pays homage to that work as she does to all the fearless white women who risked incurring the terrible wrath of their society by their refusal to compromise on the discomfiting questions of race and class. Two of the pioneers among white women to combine a struggle against racism, sexism and class exploitation, whom Davis singles out for special attention, are the Grimke sisters, Sarah and Angelina, the famous anti-slavery agitators.

Davis begins her account with slavery. She takes "the starting point for any exploration of Black women's lives under slavery" to be "an appraisal of their role as workers" (Davis,5). Thus, in the nineteenth century, while many white women were labouring under the burden of a new "ideology of femininity" which legitimated the transfer of the productive centre from the home to the factory by inflating and glorifying the attenuated domestic and sex-roles of (house-) wife and mother, Black women were fulfilling the unequivocal functions of worker (mostly in the field), breeder (of slave infant property) and sex object (of their white masters).

The forced incompatibility between the slave woman's role of worker and "breeder" on the one hand and mother on the other was starkly symbolized by the painfully swollen breasts of newly confined mothers working in the field and the grief-stricken cries of mothers whose children were being sold away from them. It was also symbolized by the rebellious response of some slave women who chose abortion over giving life to children destined for slavery, or infanticide over letting them endure it. Such defiant acts, and the disguised form of rape that Black women had to constantly endure at the hands of their masters, were perversely inverted against their already beleaguered selves through such myths as their strange and inhuman lack of "maternal instinct" and their "natural" immorality.

Thus, "Black women enjoyed few of the dubious benefits of the ideology of womanhood" (Davis,5), and if they were "hardly 'women' in the accepted sense, the slave system also discouraged male supremacy in Black men" (Davis,7).

According to Davis (and most writers on the subject), the slave relation of production practically obliterated gender and made for a minimal sexual division of labour, since slave men and women performed essentially the same tasks in the field. (In addition, she de-mythologizes the "Black Mammy" figure of the house-servant). But while the system of slavery imposed a "terrible burden of equality in oppression" (Davis,19) on Black women, Davis sees this "negative equality" being transformed on another level into a positive force: both in terms of the pride Black women were able to attain in their work, hence a source of confidence and identity for them, and in terms of the "egalitarianism characterizing their social-relations" (Davis,18) in the domestic sphere (i.e., with their men).

Davis's thesis, that through their work roles and by escaping "the dubious benefits of the ideology of womanhood" slave women were ironically able to achieve relatively healthy self-identities and relations with men, has been supported by writers of many different stripes and contains an extremely important truth. However, there are some problems with her argument. By arguing along a single path, Davis effectively steers clear of the more nuanced controversies and contradictions by remaining embedded in the more easily resolved ones. Obviously, her analysis provides a clear refutation of the "Black Matriarchy" Moynihan theses: firstly, Black women are among the most exploited victims of a racist patriarchy; and secondly, a degree of sexual equality within the Black community has been both a historical necessity and evidence of health and strength rather than social pathology. Davis also implicitly provides a challenge to grossly overrated theories about "Black Macho" such as those spread by Michele Wallace in her viciously distorted little book *Black Macho and the Myth of the Superwoman*,[2] much loved by some white feminists, even if its author indiscriminately maligns Black women and white women along with Black men. (For white men she seems to reserve either an ambiguous admiration or silence. Wallace herself is Black.)

But many questions remain. Why does Davis neglect to throw light on the shaping of the structure of sexism among Black working class men? If we agree that every clearly demarcated social formation under capitalism is imbued with its own "pathological" potential (emanating partially from the structure of its exploitation), what is the "pathology" of male-female relations in the Afro-American sub-culture? Is Black male sexism a post-emancipation phenomenon then? And if this so-called pathology is merely a received reflection of prevailing and dominant mores in the wider society (as some argue), what, anyhow, is the Black community's version of male supremacy? If Davis wants to talk to Black women she cannot simply make these questions out to be tangential ones.

There is also a question about the uses Davis makes of writers like Eugene Genovese and Herbert Gutman. These writers, having undertaken the somewhat dubiously conceived task of restoring the beleaguered "dignity" of Afro-Americans by means of a re-writing of their history, seem at pains to point out either that Blacks made fantastic and heroic slaves[3] or that against all odds their yearnings and behaviour patterns were indistinguishable from those of whites.[4] While Davis is cognizant of these problems, she does not sufficiently question Gutman's thesis that the slaves and freed men magnificently achieved, wherever they could and within the limits imposed upon them, "stable" two parent families complete with the "appropriate" sex roles.

By this argument and the one that the female-headed Black family is to be more precisely understood as a modern phenomenon, Gutman, supposedly well-intentionedly hopes to quelch the "disorganization" theses. But many Blacks are suspicious of what they see as a glorified trend among white chroniclers of the Afro-American experience, even the well-meaning ones. Nathan Hare has a point when he warns us to beware those who would deny the terrible ravages that Black family relations have suffered through a romantic and even celebrationist rendering of their reality.[5] While it is not clear whether Hare is lamenting the "loss" of patriarchy as some Black male scholars do (I did not get the feeling that he was), we cannot easily ignore this aspect of things and its attendant problems. Finally, of course, as Davis herself notes, both Gutman and Genovese assume the superiority and desirability of white cultural norms (sex roles) and impute to Black people behavioral patterns premised on these. At least one other writer has gone further than Davis and questioned Gutman's quite explicit refusal to consider the slaves' adherence to their own reconstituted African norms and his tendency to "read off" European patterns from the behaviour of the slaves.[6] Also, quite apart from the question of cultural origins, one remains curious about the sexual- and class-political implications of "stable" slave families. All in all, it is clear that while Davis has managed a stunning breakthrough, she has not adequately brought together the questions of culture, "deviance" and the intransigent effects of exploitation in relation to Black women's triumphs and tears.

Most of the first half of the book is actually taken up with a discussion of the roots and development of the women's rights movement in the U.S.; however, I consider the opening chapter which takes up the above issues to be of crucial importance.

According to Davis, "(t)he inestimable importance of the Seneca Falls Declaration was its role as the articulated consciousness of women's rights at midcentury" (Davis, 53). Nonetheless, it "proposed an analysis of the female condition which disregarded the circumstances of women outside the social class of the document's framers" (Davis, 54). Davis examines the politicized transposition of white women's energies, in their own interests, from the abolition movement to the women's rights movement in nineteenth-century America. Male supremacy within the anti-slavery movement (especially grating in view of the hard work done by the female participants, together with the transfer of production out of the home, leaving it a glorified prison for the new well-to-do "housewife" often educated and with a lot of time on her hands), contrived to bring home sharply to these women the contradictions of their existence. The Seneca Falls Declaration, a pioneering attempt to systematically articulate their grievances and demands, was therefore a "rigorous consummation of the consciousness of white middle-class women's dilemma" (Davis, 53). It did not address the situation of slave and free Black women, or of white working class women, especially the "mill girls" of the Northeast.

The eventual concession of the women's rights movement to explicitly racist arguments and principles has been documented by writers other than Davis. Angelina Grimke, from very early on, had criticized the racism of the women's anti-slavery societies and herself embodied a radical rejection of that racism. The circumstances of Sojourner Truth's famous 1851 "Ain't I a Woman" speech is now well known. Davis reminds us that the women who formed the early suffrage movement had graduated from an Abolition Movement which was not in the least opposed to Northern capitalism nor in favour of workers' rights. In relation to the slaves, the movement did not see, and was not interested in looking beyond, the single act of emancipation, considering it, and that explicitly, to be all that was needed to correct the wrongs of slavery. Frederick Douglass and William Lloyd Garrison had fought over this position.

Davis skilfully urges us to look at the famous and unfortunate debate of votes for the Negro (men) versus votes for (white) women in that light as well as in the context of the reign of terror which had been unleashed on Black people in the South by their former masters. Of course the debate should never have taken place: its terms were imposed by the exigencies of the situation and the restrictive parameters of the capitalist legislative process. However, the issue of the investiture of "the Negro" (unfortunately through the male, according to patriarchal capitalist law) with common citizenship in American society, at a time when men and women were at the daily mercy of the lynch mob and the subject of constant schemes (government and otherwise) for mass deportation to foreign lands, stood by itself as an absolute

161

priority. Although Davis points to the limitations of the vote per se and criticizes Douglass for his exaggerated and naive belief in its range of possibilities, I still think its importance should not be underestimated, especially when looked at in conjunction with other demands that the "Black Liberation Movement" was making at the time.

The fact that the debate was shaped into a bitter contest was also directly attributable to the white supremacist foundations of the arguments used by the women's suffrage movement to advance their own cause. From arguing no votes for the Negro without the vote for women, especially since they had held their (middle class) suffrage demands in abeyance during the Civil War, they regressed to votes for intelligent and civilized white women instead of votes for ignorant and brutish Black and immigrant men. Votes for white women would save the race; and with that they struck up an alliance with those Southern white interests who were intent on brutalizing Black people back into a second form of slavery. At the 1903 convention of National American Woman Suffrage Association (NAWSA), Belle Kearney from Mississippi could say with impunity: "The enfranchisement of women would insure immediate and durable white supremacy, honestly attained . . . (Davis,125). And this, as Davis notes, from the organized white women's movement at a time when capitalism was evolving its most advanced and most terroristic ideological and economic apparatus of racism.

Davis documents much the same story for other movements, notably, later on in the book, the early birth control movement led by Margaret Sanger, who moved from Socialist party membership in 1912 to an alliance years later with those who openly advocated the racist strategy of population control in order to save the "superior" race from the "inferior." In addition, she notes the organized white women's years of silence and stalling on the question of lynching at a time when Black women were leading the fight against it, their racism towards Black members and Black sister groups of the Club Movement, and their lack of protest when Black women were forcibly prevented from exercising their newly won right to vote.

On the positive side, she documents Black women's own efforts at organization - against slavery, for suffrage, against lynching. The latter struggle occupied the militant energies of two outstanding Black female leaders, Mary Church Terrell and Ida B. Wells, and scored impressive successes. Davis briefly explores the needs and struggles of white working women as well and their relationship to the causes of abolition and suffrage, which did not occupy centre stage in their lives until a powerful argument could be made linking the need for suffrage to the struggle against class exploitation. Finally, on the positive side, Davis celebrates the unprecedented and unsurpassed solidarity achieved between fighting Black and white women during the Reconstruction campaigns to educate the freed men.

The rest of the book, from chapter ten onwards, does not follow the highlighted historical progression traced up to then, but constitutes a series of related essays, on "communist Women," "Rape, Racism and the Myth of the Black Rapist," "Racism, Birth Control and Reproductive Rights" and "The Approaching Obsolescence of Housework: A Working-Class Perspective." Of these, by far the most powerful and most important is the one on rape and racism.

The chapter on Communist women constitutes a clearly inadequate substitute for an analysis that Davis seems not to have bothered to undertake. Why Communism? This question does not raise an objection to Communism but to the fact that the question never gets asked. If Davis' book is meant to be a grassroots account for a grassroots audience then it is seriously presumptuous in its leap from a careful presentation of the documented historical factors to the miraculously conjured up communist requisite. Communism is conveniently asserted as non-problematic, both on the woman question and on the Black question presumably. If Communism as a *concrete* movement with a *concrete* history in the U.S. is the answer, then surely Davis owes it to her fully intelligent and anxious grassroots readership to provide *concrete* (and theoretical of course) proof beyond mere sketches of individual and undoubtedly heroic Communist women? Davis has left us at the stage where Black women are mostly domestic and service workers. How did the not-exactly-harmonious relationship between Northern white industrial labour and Southern Black non-industrial labour become resolved? What happened when Black labour went North? What was the role of Communist organizations in all these processes? How does the Communist party of which Davis is a member pull together the questions of class, race and gender? What is its relationship to Blacks? To women? To Black women?

The questions are not hostile ones. Black women in particular will want to know for sure, and are willing to learn. It is a pity Davis has chosen not to explain.

Davis's final chapter is also a bit weak. One is disappointed that she has not chosen to tackle the all important question of Black women and welfare frontally and to provide us with her characteristically militant and incisive insights. Again, Davis seems not to be connecting quite as directly as in the first two thirds of her book to the demanding reality of Black women's lives and the need for a working class Black woman's perspective. She focuses almost entirely on a critique of white feminist theories and practices. But her critique of the "Wages for Housework" group is not particularly powerful (which is unfortunate for Toronto readers), and her call for the socialization of housework is somewhat abstract and question-begging. This criticism is not as true of her solid contextualization of the abortion debate and her prioritization of a call for an end to sterilization abuse.

The chapter on rape, though brilliant, is problematic in ways with which one has grown familiar by this stage of her book. Davis neatly reverses Shulamith Firestone's absurd thesis that racism is an extension of sexism by arguing that rape, the most brutal weapon of sexism, is an extension of racism. Davis views rape from the point of view of an act of violence essentially governed by racist class relations between white men and Black women. She also attacks the crude assumptions by some white feminists on rape that Black men are particularly prone to the latter (through no fault of their own of course...) as a racist concession to the hundreds of hysterical, false charges of rape that became a weapon of legitimation in the hands of the Southern lynch mob. She raises the all important issues of the discrepancy between reported and unreported rape, the association of "police blotter" rapists with rapists in general and the classist and racist bias of rape prosecution.

It is true that rape by white men of Black women, especially when called by another name and justified by the alleged "looseness" of Black women, has been historically a fundamental building block and index of capitalist America's racist patriarchy. It has borne the distinction of being officially or semi-officially sanctioned by the racist order. Furthermore, Black men, too, are victims of that racist patriarchy, as manifested by the false rape charges of the lynching era and the negative discrimination against them (i.e., in relation to white rapists) in the system of arrest and prosecution for rape. In fact, Davis shows that, in sharp contrast to the prosecution of Black rapists, only three white men were tried, convicted and executed for lynching between 1865 and 1895, during which period more than 10,000 Black people were murdered in cold blood (Davis, 184).

Davis's analysis is an absolutely crucial intervention into the still blurry debate on rape. It is in the immediate interest of Black people in particular to find out the truth about rape, and Davis certainly clears away a lot of the cobwebs. However, she does not sufficiently highlight the distinction between rape as an expression of class exploitation and rape as an intra-class and intra-ethnic (not to speak of domestic) phenomenon. Rape, after all, has a relatively autonomous sexist existence, and as such Black women bear a double burden — racist rape and intra-ethnic "sexist" rape. When a Black woman is being raped by a Black man it is small comfort to her that rape by white men has been an historic weapon in the construction of a racist patriarchy or that Black men have been historic victims of malicious false rape charges. Davis offers little insight into that problem.

On the whole, Davis's book stands as a principled if uncompromising account of the meeting place of women, race and class. Ironically, while one or two self-styled Black feminists have denounced the racism of the American white women's movement in particularly cynical (a-historical and theoretical) ways, Davis, who probably would not call herself a Black feminist without some qualification, does so in a far more principled and concrete manner. She does not allow spurious fads to lead her to compromise her scientific assessment of such historical figures as Frederick Douglass, a Black man, or Angelina Grimke, a white woman, both of whom she establishes as firm allies of the Black and working class women's struggle for liberation. If the unorganized Black working class women's voice sometimes appears to be muted or lack spontaneity in her book, Davis has nonetheless given us an indispensable lesson in how to listen to that voice and what to listen for when it speaks its oppression and attempts to resist it. For sure, for those of us who know the bottom line, we shall be able to detect when that voice is missing entirely, even amidst the most strident mouthing stories for "liberation."

Talking
about structures

"Visible Minority" Women
A Creation of the Canadian State

Linda Carty and Dionne Brand

The Canadian state does not relate to all people(s) equally, and as far as it relates to women at all, it tends to treat Native, South Asian, Black, Chinese and other non-white groups of women as quantitatively aberrant and qualitatively homogeneous. In this scenario, the reality is often as implicit hierarchical structuring of women; the placing of all these groups of women together, on the pretext of attempting to deal with their shared experiences of oppression, does nothing to negate the importance of that fact. Our goal here is not to deconstruct the term "visible minority," but suffice it to say that the term is void of any race or class recognition and, more imporantly, of class struggle or struggle against racism. It is therefore ahistorical and serves to reduce to meaninglessness the specific parts it purports to elevate.

Indeed, attempting to unify the oppression of women of different racial backgrounds is not only absurd but impossible, precisely because their racial histories cannot be unified. To be different, therefore, if it is merely a matter of difference, is not to be assumed as similar, but ought to be recognized as unique. It is against this background that we attempt, within the necessarily restricted scope of this article, to address the inefficacy of state-formed or state-sanctioned organizations such as the National Organization of Immigrant and Visible Minority Women (NOIVMW).

In 1981, the federal government was instrumental in organizing the National Conference of Immigrant Women purportedly to look at some of the primary problems facing immigrant woman in Canadian society. Out of this came a National Immigrant Women's Network and an Ontario Immigrant Women's Network. Two years later, the Race Relations Divisions of the Ontario Human Rights commission and the Ontario Women's Directorate put together a conference to deal with the issues of sexism, racism, and work as they relate specifically to women of different racial minority backgrounds. Out of this conference a resolution was passed to form the Coalition of Visible Minority Women to deal with the special needs of immigrant and visible minority women. In 1986 the National conference on Immigrant and Visible Minority Women was held and out of this NOIVMW was formed. The latter group claims to represent over 500 immigrant and visible minority women's groups in Canada.

Perhaps the most striking thing about these conferences and organizations is that they were all state-initiated. Because the state in capitalist society, by virtue of its goals and interests, does not operate within the interest of the working class — to which most immigrant and visible minority women belong — the limitations of any state-formed organization with a mandate to do so must be recognized and questioned. More important, whether such organizations perceive their limitations, and if so how they do, ought to be examined.

With a few exceptions, most of the women who organize, or rather advise on the organizing of, immigrant and "visible minority" women's conferences (for the state originates the idea, assigns staff and consultants, and then forms a community advisory board) and who form the executive bodies of such organizations are, whether by intentional state recruitment or otherwise, largely women of middle class background. While this in itself does not preclude their ability to work with working class women, for the state to assume that both classes have shared goals is perhaps naive, providing of course we see the state as totally benign.

The role of the state in capitalist society

In advanced capitalist societies the state operates in the interest of the economically dominant class or the bourgeoisie. While this is not a relationship of collusion, that there is a close relationship based on shared interests is inevitable because of the institutions which constitute the state. These are:

> *the government, the administration, the military and the police, the judicial branch, sub-central government and parliamentary assemblies — [altogether and their] interrelationship shapes the form of the state system. It is in these institutions in which "state power" lies, and it is through them that this power is wielded in its different manifestations by the people who occupy the leading positions in each of these institutions — ...the state elite.*[1]

Because the state represents the interests of the most privileged class, it cannot at the same time work for the benefit of the working class because there are substantive differences in the interests of both classes and the two are always in conflict. This indeed is the fundamental contradiction of capitalism. The relations of production which are the propelling force in capitalism are a primary determinant of class relations. Since the ruling class is the only class which is in a position within advanced capitalist society to exercise state power, the class character of that power cannot be mistaken. "When we say that a class holds state power, we mean that what is done through the state positively acts upon the (re-)production of the mode of production of which the class in question is the dominant bearer."[2]

It must be pointed out that the state in advanced capitalist society expends a considerable amount of time and effort legitimizing the dominant class position. This results in the seemingly neutral position of the state, and

gives its representatives an appearance of political diversity in its institutions. For example, though it appears that all classes which make up the
electorate have a choice between political parties with profoundly opposing
views, and that through the voting process they can actually decide the fate
of their country, in fact, this is hardly the case. Because the members of all
the main parties are often of similar class backgrounds, they more often than
not have similar class interests. What may be suggested to the electorate to
be fundamental differences in political perspectives of government representatives, upon closer scrutiny are seen as minor. And "profoundly opposing
views" can be seen to be not so profound and not so opposing at all. "What is
really striking about . . . political leaders and political office holders, in relation to each other, is not their many differences, but the extent of their agreement on truly fundamental issues.[3]

The above argument is not to deny the fact that the state does enjoy
some independence of the bourgeoisie and this allows it a certain amount of
"relative autonomy"; neither is it meant to negate the importance of other
classes in advanced capitalist society, most notably, the petit bourgeoisie.
This is the class which falls between the bourgeoisie and the proletariat, and
is commonly called the middle class in capitalist society. It is this class we
refer to here when we address the issue of the organizers of different immigrant women's groups attempting to work with working class immigrant
women on the assumption of having shared goals. It is easy for the state to
work with the petit bourgeoisie as there is hardly ever conflict between the
ruling class and the middle class. Again we cannot assume that there is
collusion between the petit bourgeoisie and the state but any conflict which
exists is mediated or negotiated through the ideological liberal-democratic
processes which legitimate advanced capitalism. Consensus-making is therefore key to the maintenance of this kind of state. Indeed, the two classes find
it to their mutual benefit to have a relationship of compatibility.

Moreover, the petit bourgeoisie is not itself a unified class. In the Canadian context of Anglophone and Francophone groups and interests which

172

predominate, the immigrant and racial groups among the petit bourgeoisie
can be said to be class factions precisely because they are new entrants into
that class.[4] Though their interests are similar, discrimination and racism
contribute to their subordination in the middle class.

The phenomenon of "ethnic" politicians is a manifestation of these class
fractions. Although women have not yet emerged among the elected "ethnic"
politicians, reflecting the similar sluggish movement of white women through
the white Anglophone and Francophone bourgeoisie and petit bourgeoisie,
the appointment of Ann Cools to the Canadian Senate and the nomination
battles of women like Maria Mina signify their presence within these classes
and within these class fractions.

"Visible minority" and "immigrant women's" groups prior to state intervention

It is worth mentioning that prior to the conferences we referred to and
to organizations such as NOIVNW and OCVMW, which because of their
origins now enjoy quite a high profile, there were already women's organizations in the different immigrant and racial groups. These included the various Black Women's Congresses, the South Asian Women's Groups, the Immigrant Women's Centres and support groups, and women's committees and
projects which started "grassroots" organizations with direct interaction with
the women's communities they serviced before state involvement turned
them into social agencies, so that now they have become quite bureaucratic.
Much of the staff's time is now spent fulfilling the requirements set by the
bureaucracies. These are requirements which do not take concerns of class,
the *raison d'etre* of these organizations, into consideration. This
bureaucratization adds to the staff's already heavy work load meeting the
dire needs of the groups' clientele.[5]

Besides the different immigrant and racial minority communities' success in setting up their own self-directed organizations, many of them had

already devised strategies and models for working across communities and
for working with each other to share their experiences and their goals. This
effort resulted in organizations such as Women Working with Immigrant
Women and the Cross-Cultural Communication Centre. It was not the state,
therefore, that saw a need for women in immigrant and racial minority
communities to be organized and stepped in to do so. These communities
were already doing their own organizing and focusing on issues of racism and
sexism, as well as examining how some state-initiated or supported policies
facilitated these practices. The crucial aspect of their work was challenging
the state in different contexts such as equal education, equal employment
and fair immigration policy, and at the core of their analysis was the class
conflict.

"Visible minority" and "immigrant" women: a constituency to be recognized

It was neither by coincidence nor accident that the state became involved in immigrant issues and specifically immigrant women's issues. Rapidly increasing immigration in the 1970s, the revolutionary movements
sweeping the international scene, and the popularity given women's issues by
the women's movement, combined to make Native, Black, South East Asian
and South Asian women a constituency to be recognized. The state could no
longer ignore a constituency which was in the midst of its own politicization
and represented two important poles, its immigrant and racial connections
and its women's organizational contacts, both of which had potential to make
the state uncomfortable. The state was therefore forced to add issues affecting these women to its agenda. Interestingly, the chosen response of the
state to these women's concerns is reflective of how it deflects the genuine
concerns with interests which conflict with its own into forms which it finds
manageable and adaptable to its own agenda. Therefore, the state, at the
Ontario government level, decided to organize all the different women's

groups which were not white into the 1983 conference mentioned above. There had already been an "Immigrant Women's" conference two years earlier.

The state's efforts were meant to create a containing women's network, while simultaneously diffusing the tensions against itself which were building up in each individual women's group, but because of its inability to deal with the different issues such as racism, sexism, better wages and better jobs, its organizing created new divisions. A primary division was the state's decision to exclude white Latin American women from the conference because of its ill-conceived notion and its creation of what constitutes "visible minority." There was debate on whether these women should be included in the conference, and the implication was that they ought not to be since neither their accent nor their documented experiences of discrimination in Canadian society made them "visible minority," because they are white.[6]

Native, Black, South Asian, and South East Asian Women's issues redefined

A large portion of the organizing time for the conference was spent on deciding what constitutes "visible minority." Furthermore, all the different groups' struggles — for example, Black women fighting around issues of employment or education, or South Asian women fighting for better wages in the garment industry — were all subordinated to the "visible minority" question. More important, in working out the logistics of the conference, the state created certain conflicts which did not exist before or which were on the way to being resolved, such as trying to tell women how to work with each other. All specific issues were subsumed and women were actually consumed with state-generated conflicts, the major one being as mentioned before the question of who are "visible minority"; or whether the question of accent was important enough to determine minority status. The question of telling women how to work together, and why they should do so, threw the onus of

responsibility for the success of the conference onto the shoulders of the
women. The implication was that the problem was not the state but the
women and their "disorganization." The conference, therefore, was not a
conference to question state practices which produce inequality. Instead, it
became a conference to question the various constituencies' "shortcomings" in
making their demands heard by the state. The state set up an Advisory
Committee to plan the Ontario conference on "visible minority" women and
the committee was made up of individuals chosen by the state who were not
representatives of different women's groups although they may have had
some kind of association with them. However, the status of "advisory" meant
that these women were assigned the task of carrying forward specific state-
designed ideas to the different women's groups. Because of the Canadian
state's historical lack of concern for the represented communities, the question arises as to why the affected communities should trust these "advisors"
who are reporting to, and working with, the state.

The larger notion, however, was the effect of the state-designed conference. The idea of the state putting together a conference on "visible minority" women seemed rather impressive and genuine, and as a result, repressed
many people's analytical capabilities. It also overwhelmed the material
capabilities of the affected women's groups and organizations, since the state
had massive resources to throw behind its initiatives, including the power of
being "the state." Hence, there was not the very necessary critical analysis
of the goals, intentions or outcomes of the process. Those critiques which
existed indicated a choice of mounting a boycott against the conference, going
to the conference and "taking it over," or acquiescing. Significantly, a boycott
was dismissed as wrong-headed. Taking over the conference was the more
popular strategy since acquiescence could not be seen in light of the class
interest of the "advisory." The second and third options would amount to the
same strategy but choosing the second was significant of the dynamic of the
class fraction among the petit bourgeoisie. This gave a visage of radicalness
to the choice. "Grassroots" thinking gave way to a new pragmatism and

"grassroots" organizers agonized their way through the pros and cons of this new pragmatism. As the conference drew closer, those who were not "in" were "out." The state was going to do the conference anyway.

Therefore, even people otherwise committed to working class struggle became involved in planning the conference because of their convictions that the larger outcomes of such a conference would be beneficial to the working class women who would be affected. Careful analysis, however, reveals that what actually happened was that the state's goals conflicted with and caused a reformulation of the issues. The ultimate result was a secondary status accorded to the issue of how some state-initiated and supported policies facilitated racism and sexism, because the notion of defining "visible minority" and forming a coalition of "visible minority" women took the forefront. An added result was the identification of a smaller constituency whom the state could call on for consultation and assistance when issues affecting Native, Black, South Asian and South East Asian women arise.

It is instructive to point out here that after the state-initiated, supported and staged the 1983 conference, the necessary follow-up resources were not forthcoming. This could result in the newly formed organization ultimately competing with all the other representative women's organizations for the small pool of state funds.[7] Perhaps more important, the Coalition spent the first year working on its constitution. This meant that the very much needed resourcefulness of the women involved was being refocused away from their groups, and onto drafting the constitution for this state-formed organization.

It also deserves to be mentioned that while the state did not provide the Coalition with funding it nevertheless in effect assigned to the organization the burden of all the problems of all women whom it considered to be in the category "visible minority." This required the Coalition to deal with language rights of South Asian and South East Asian women as well as issues around work. Similarly, it had to strategize to deal with the issue of racism in its varied forms and as it is experienced differently by women of each different group. Other issues, such as sexism and pay equity, were also passed on to the Coalition. Hence, all the aspirations of the affected groups of women were packed into what could only be an inadequate structure.

Because state-initiated or state-formed organizations are never in conflict with the state, any conflicts which arise within or among them puts them in a conflict mode with each other instead of with the state, although closer scrutiny of the issues reveals the latter to hold ultimate responsibility. For example, on the specific issue of pay equity the newly formed "Visible Minority" Women's groups and committees may find themselves responding to the National Action Committee on the Status of Women, since NAC, as the largest Canadian body representing all women's groups, has appeared unconcerned with the issue of pay equity for Native, Black, South Asian, and South East Asian women.

It is not within the scope of this paper to examine NAC in any detail but certainly it is worth observing that NAC is a government and state-funded and supported organization, and like any other such relationship in advanced capitalism it can be said to be a conduit of legitimation despite its "relative autonomy" from the state. It cannot help but be such. Precisely because of its vaunted representation of all women and precisely because of the political diversity of its member organizations, it typifies the liberal-democratic discourse within advanced capitalism of co-existence being possible despite opposing views. Notwithstanding the purposes for which NAC was formed, it is now clearly an organization in which influential sectors of its membership support state policy and belong to the class which holds state power. The most striking example of this was shown when during NAC's 1988 annual meeting in Ottawa a seemingly ideological split came about in the membership where the more and lesser conservative and liberal paths diverged. The leader of the Progressive Conservative women's caucus walked out of the conference stating that NAC was straying away from government policy and programs. The statement was made with such assurance that one cannot ascertain whether it was simply a ruling class *faux pas* or whether some women are obviously and genuinely under the impression that NAC's role is to carry out government policy. What is revealing, if not disturbing, about this comment is that NAC's policies have always been accomodated. It is not farfetched, therefore, to conclude that NAC represents an arm of the state and is expected to endorse mainstream government policies regarding women.

State policy around issues of race, class or sex can be characterized as policy of containment and control. It is not unusual for the state to move to contain a problem once it is identified. It is, therefore, not by accident that the state initiated organizations to contain "immigrant" and "visible minority" women and their political demands. In doing so the state signified these women's "immigrantness" and "visible minorityness" as the organizing principle. Their "womaness" was secondary. Had women themselves formulated the issue, the intersections between race and gender may have been more obvious. As it stood, Black, Native, South Asian and South East Asian women were cast as more interested in issues of race than gender, and white women were cast as more interested in issues of gender than race. And in the process the state took credit for taking care of both racism and sexism.

What actually happened, however, is that the "Visible Minority" organizations are seen to disregard issues like abortion, daycare and pay equity, because the implicit line of demarcation has made these the fight of NAC. It is understandable, then, why the "Visible Minority" organizations may not reach or help the working class constituency they expect to help, because the issues of daycare, abortion, and pay equity are primary concerns of Black, Native, South Asian and South East Asian women just as are racism and discrimination. It must be said that organizations such as NAC were forced, because of the Coalition, to look at issues of racism, which they had refused to examine.

It is not simply a reformulation of gender for these different racial groupings of women, including white women, which is taking place in these processes. It is also essentially the allocation of the material resources available to contain gender, race and class.

The Canadian state deflects its responsibilities for dealing with minority women onto agencies such as NAC and the Coalition. It often pretends interest in the issues, nevertheless, by becoming directly involved when absolutely necessary, though this involvement takes the form of royal commissions, advisory committees, race relations units and experts, and the big public relations pay-offs: conferences. These can all be seen to be strategies designed to ameliorate the problems, diffuse potential conflict, and ultimately placate offended parties. After all, the state is paying attention to the issue and cannot be accused of inaction. It is noteworthy that in the end, however, the results of the royal commissions, advisory committees and so on are an excessive number of reports which are directed to no one in particular, and to no specific action. It was not surprising, therefore, that while the state took responsibility for staging the 1983 conference it did nothing to implement the many recommendations which resulted from the conference.

It must be noted that all this activity has not occurred in isolation but amidst a growing atmosphere of political and economic conservatism of the state itself and undeniably even of the electorate. It has been occurring simultaneously with a growing immigrant petit bourgeoisie which has an awareness of itself as such. And it has been occurring with the burning out of working class advocates carried away for the time being in the undertow of class conflict. It cannot be overlooked either that this entire process has major political implications for the self-organizing of the specific racial groupings which seems to have been temporarily arrested.

Conclusion

We have tried to address a complex range of issues within the limited confines of this article. In so doing, we have only broken the surface. What we hope is clearly evident from our analysis is the way in which the state constructs race and class, then plays these important issues against each other around gender to its own advantage. The thesis here is that state-initiated, funded and supported organizations of any hue necessarily carry out state aims. That is not to dismiss the work or struggle of progressive sectors within them, it is merely to examine critically the workings of the state as regards women in advanced capitalism.

Sexism, Racism, Canadian Nationalism

Roxana Ng

My starting point

My concern about the dynamics of sexism and racism, and of the interrelation of gender, race/ethnicity, and class arose out of my experience as a "visible minority" immigrant woman and a member of the intelligentsia living in a white-dominated Canada. Working politically in the immigrant community, I and other women of colour frequently feel that our status as women does not have weight equal to our status as members of minority groups. Our interests and experiences are subsumed under the interests of immigrant men, expecially those of "community leaders." This situation is analogous to the classic position of the Left: women's issues are secondary to the class struggle. Women are often told that their interests can be taken up only after the revolution.

Working in the women's movement, on the other hand, women of colour also feel silenced from time to time. Our unique experiences as women of colour are frequently overlooked in discussions about women's oppression. At best, we are tokenized; at worst, we are told that our concerns, seem to be less advanced, have to go with a patriarchy characteristic of our indigenous cultures.[2] There is something missing in the women's movement which gives us an increasing sense of discomfort as we continue to participate in struggles in which only a part of our experiences as women of colour is or can be taken up.

Analytically, in standard social science debates (which filters to the Left and to the women's movement through people's multiple roles and locations in society), there is a tendency to treat gender, race and class as different analytic categories designating different domains of social life. While I continue to experience gender and race oppression as a totality, when I participate in academic and intellectual work I have to make a theoretical and analytical separation of my experience and translate it into variables of "sex," "ethnicity," and "class" in order for my work to be acceptable and understandable to my colleagues. It is not uncommon, when I present papers in conferences, to receive comments about the lack of definitional clarity in my use of concepts of gender, race/ethnicity, and class. I am asked to spell out clearly which category is more important in determining the position of, for example, immigrant women.

It is out of these experiences and concerns that I began, over ten years ago, to search for a way of thinking about the interrelation of categories of gender, race/ethnicity, and class, which would account for the lived experiences of people of colour; a way of understanding their experiences which does not fragment them into separate and at times opposing domains of social life.

Furthermore, as I continue to teach and do research in ethnic and women's studies, and especially since my two-year sojourn in New Brunswick, it became clear to me that we cannot understand gender and ethnic relations in Canada without attending to how these relations have been mediated by the Canadian state historically, and continues to be organized by state processes. (Let me remind the reader that Nova Scotia and New Brunswick are the oldest provinces in the colony of Canada, settled and dominated not only by Irish and Scottish immigrants, but also by Loyalists.) Thus, I would argue that it is not enough for feminist and ethnic historians to rewrite women's history and ethnic history. In order to understand how Canada came to be a nation with its present configuration, we have to rewrite the history of Canada.

This paper does not address problems of racism and sexism in the Left and of racism in the feminist movement directly. It is a methodological paper which calls for a different conceptualization of gender, race/ethnicity and class by grounding these relations in the development of the Canadian social formation. In so doing I challenge current theorizations of ethnicity and class, and show the interlocking relations of gender, race and class by means of historical examples. I make use of a method of work informed by Marx's analysis of capitalism in the nineteenth century[3] and feminist interpretations of Marx's method.[4] This method insists on locating the knower in a particular subject position in relation to her inquiry, and on situating contemporary realities in the historical development of nation states in a definite mode of production. It treats historical and contemporary moments and events, not as separate fields or areas of study, but as constituents of a society with its own internal logic and dynamic.

In developing the present analysis I asked myself: How do I account for the silencing I and other women experience in our diverse and different social locations? How do I have to understand history in order to understand my experience as a totality lodged in a particular social formation? I don't claim to put forward a complete or definitive theory or argument. This paper is an attempt to develop a method of thinking which illuminates sexual and racial oppression from the standpoint of women of colour -- standpoint in this context referring to the the relationship between the knower's experience and the social organization generating her experience. It is also an attempt to develop a praxis for eradicating sexism and racism, not merely in structures and institutions, but more fundamentally in our unconscious thoughts and action.

Before proceeding I want to make a couple of qualifications. First, I am using the concepts "ethnicity" and "race" interchangeably throughout this paper. Although I am aware of the technical differences between the two concepts, I want to draw attention here to their socially, ideologically, and politically constructed character. For instance, while the difference between people of Irish and Scottish descent in New Brunswick is seen as sub-cultural today, at one time they treated each other as people belonging to different races with distinct and distinguishable characteristics. Certainly, the Acadians were, and to an extent still are, treated as people from an inferior race, distinguishable from the Anglo-Saxons and the Celts by social and physical differences.

Today, the term "ethnic groups" is used primarily to refer to immigrants from non-British and non-French backgrounds, especially those from third world countries. In the past, immigrants were referred to as "Europeans," "Orientals," "Negros," etc., signifying their different racial origins. In this connection, we should remember that the change of studies in race relations to "ethnic relations" in the late 1960s and early 1970s was a political move on the part of the state to diffuse rising racial tensions among different groups in the U.S., notably between black and white Americans. This terminology was adopted in Canada to diffuse the antagonistic relations between Quebec and English Canada, and between the Native people, other minority groups, and the Canadian state. The reverse movement toward policy development in race relations in Ontario since the mid-1980s, as opposed to multiculturalism, signals the increasing militancy and political clout of minority groups in the changing political economy of that province.[5] Thus, it is important to bear in mind that definitions and meanings of ethnicity and race are social constuctions that shift constantly, reflecting the changing dynamics of gender, race/ethnic, and class relations over time.

Second, I am using the term "the Canadian state" as a short-hand for the multiplicity of institutions and departments which administer and coordinate the activities of ruling. It therefore includes the formal government and the various policies and programs which come under jurisdiction, and the functions performed therein. More importantly, I wish to advance the notion of the state as the central constituent in the developing relations of capitalism in Canada.[6] This set of relations didn't appear overnight. As Corrigan correctly points out, it was constructed through time, by complicated and extensive struggles of people grouped together by their differing relationships to the emerging dominant mode of production.[7] Indeed, as we shall see, the history of ethnic and gender relations is the history of Canadian state formation.

Ethnicity, class and gender — standard conceptual problems

In his latest book, *Ethnic Canada*, Leo Driedger distinguishes three views of the interrelationship of class and ethnicity. The first view states that ethnicity is a by-product of the class structure and reducible to class. The second view holds that ethnicity may or may not be reducible to class, but it certainly is a drawback to social mobility. The third view, held by Driedger himself, suggests that ethnicity and class are separate phenomena and should be examined separately.[8] Certainly, ethnicity and class are observable features of social life. Both have an objective reality outside of people's subjectivity. While orthodox Marxists contend that ethnicity is a product of the class structure,[9] Leo Depres maintains that ethnicity and class are different bases of sociality, although at times they overlap.[10]

I suggest that the difficulties encountered by these theorists in understanding the interrelationship between ethnicity and class has to do with the fact that they treat these phenomena as analytic categories whose relationship to each other can be established only abstractly, through the construction of clever analytic schema developed to discover correlations between variables. In this kind of approach, ethnicity and class are conceptualized as variables which have no actual relationship to one another in the everyday world. The indicators for "ethnicity" as an analytical category are descent, common religion, and a shared feeling of belonging to the same group. This list can be expanded and changed depending on the group the researcher is investigating; the criteria used do not change the procedures and conceptual schema adopted. Class, on the other hand, is an economic category which has to do with occupations, level of education, income, etc. Class is relevant to researchers of ethnic groups only if they wish to study the economic participation and social status of the groups. The question then becomes: how do particular groups rank in terms of this socio-economic classification (class)?[11]

Standard approaches to ethnicity, then, treat "the ethnic phenomenon"[12] as a separate ontological and epistemological domain, much like the way scholars of Orientalism treat the study of the Orient according to Edward Said.[13] What is considered as the ethnic phenomenon is severed from the relations which give rise to it. Its ontological domain is one whose relevance resides in race, kinship and — following from these two major attributes — a sense of belonging and a shared identity. Seen in this light, ethnicity can be considered apart from and as unrelated to the political and economic processes of any particular society; it is detached completely from the context within which the phenomenon arises. Similarly, the phenomenon of class, for these researchers, arises in terms of a person's relative position in a stratified society. Since class and ethnicity are seen to be different variables designating different social phenomena, their relationship has to be derived by examining their correlation (or the lack thereof) in a conceptual schema devised by the researcher. Their interconnection in the shaping of social life is left unexaminable.

Gender usually falls outside the realm of analytical relevance for ethnic theorists. Implicitly, like other areas of sociology, women's experiences are subsumed under those of men's. More often, the significance of gender (read woman) is overlooked or treated as a separate field of investigation. Thus, we find women being included in the study of the family or the domestic labour debate, for example, but political economy remains completely sex blind.[14] While efforts by feminists to incorporate women into the study of ethnicity and class are increasing, these efforts are only at a preliminary stage. Frequently, the similarities between racism and sexism are compared,[15] and parallels between the experiences of women and the experiences of ethnic

minorities are drawn.[16] Recently, feminists such as Roberts and Juteau Lee
have attempted to conceptualize the relationship between gender, ethnicity/
race, and class by suggesting that they are three different systems of domination which overlap.[17] Their inclusion of gender in ethnic studies is a major
breakthrough, but the question of the precise relationship between these
three systems of domination remains to be conceptualized and investigated.

Gender, race/ethnicity, and class as relations

This paper calls for a different conceptualization of ethnicity/race, gender, and class: they must be treated as social relations which have to do with
how people relate to each other through productive and reproductive activities. This conception is consistent with Marx and Engels' treatment of class,[18]
which refers to people's relations to the means of production, rather than as
an economic category. As Braverman eloquently explains, class — properly
understood — never precisely designates a group of people; rather, it is the
expression of a process which results in the transformation of sectors of
society.[19] When we speak of class, then, we are referring to a process which
indicates how people construct and alter their relation to the productive/
reproductive forces of society, using whatever means they have at their
disposal.

Reviewing the historical development of Canadian society we find that
family and kinship, perceived or real, are means people deploy to exert their
domination or overcome their subordination. The deployment of kin ties and
common descent is what theorists have identified as the salient condition for
the formation of ethnic groups. However, as Weber has pointed out, descent
itself is not sufficient condition for the formation of ethnic groups. He correctly observes:

> *it is primarily the political community, no matter how artifically organ-
> ized, that inspired the belief in common ethnicity. This belief tends to*

*persist even after the disintegration of the political community, unless
drastic differences in the custom, physical type, or above all, language
exist among its members.*[20]

In terms of gender relations, women's work within and outside the
family is taken for granted. It is deemed not worthy of consideration in ethnic
studies.

Weber's contribution lies in his identification of political and ideological
factors in the formation of ethnic groups. In particular, he draws attention to
the importance of colonization and emigration as an important basis for
group formation. In this sense, his conception of ethnicity coincides nicely
with Marx's conception of class: they both see these two phenomena as arising out of the struggles for domination and control, notably in colonization as
capitalism emerged as the dominant mode of production in the Western
world.

Similarly, gender relations are crucial and fundamental to the division
of labour in a given society — any society. In most societies, gender is the
basic way of organizing productive and reproductive activities. But gender
relations are not the same in all societies. Furthermore, like ethnic and class
relations, they change over time in response to changing social, political, and
economic relations. My investigation of immigrant women's domestic work,
for example, reveals the transformation of their domestic labour after immigration to Canada. Whereas in a less industrialized setting women's work is
organized organically in relation to farming and other subsistence activities,
in Canada it is organized industrially by the husband's waged work outside
the home, school schedules, the degree of mechanization of the household
(e.g., the use of vacuum cleaner and other appliances), public transportation
systems, distances to shopping facilities, and so on. The change in women's
domestic labour in turn creates new areas of contestation and conflict between immigrant women and their husbands; as well, it upsets the previous
balance of power among all family members.[21] Smith observes:

*In pre-capitalist societies, gender is basic to the "economic" division of labour and how labour resources are controlled. In other than capitalist forms, we take for granted that gender relations are included. In peasant societies for example, the full cycle of production and subsistence is organized by the household and family and presupposes gender relations. Indeed, we must look to capitalism as a mode of production to find how the notion of the separation of gender relations from economic relations could arise. It is only in capitalism that we find an economic process constituted independently from the daily and generational production of the lives of particular individuals and in **which therefore we can think economy apart from gender** (emphasis in original).[22]*

Thus, gender relations as well as ethnicity and race, are integral to the organization of productive activities. The theoretical and analytical separation of gender from the economy (productive relations) is itself the product of capitalist development, which creates a progressive separation between civil society, politics, and the economy in the first place, and renders relations of gender, race, and ethnicity more abstract and invisible to productive processes in the second place.[23]

When we treat class, ethnicity, and gender as relations arising out of the processes of domination and struggles over the means of production and reproduction over time, a very different picture of their interrelationship emerges. We find that we have not crystallized over time, as Canada developed from a colony of England and France, to a nation built on male supremacy. Indeed, we can trace ethnic group formation and gender relations in terms of the development of capitalism in Canada, firstly through its history of colonization, then subsequently through immigration policies which changed over time in response to the demands of nation-building. People were recruited firstly from Ireland, then the Ukraine and Scandinavia to lay an agrarian base for England and Canada; they were imported from China through an indentured labour system to build the railways for Canada's westward expansion; more recently, people from southern Europe were recruited to fill gaps in the construction industry. In the overall framework of immigration, men and women were/are treated differentially. For example, Chinese men were not allowed to bring their wives and families to Canada so they could not propagate and spread the "yellow menace."[24] Even today, men and women enter Canada under different terms and conditions. The majority of third world women enter the country either as domestic workers on temporary work permits or as "family class" immigrants whose livelihood is dependent on the head of the household or on the sponsor.[25]

Indeed, the emergence of the Native people as a group, not to mention the Metis sub-group, is the result of the colonization process which destroyed, re-organized, fragmented, and homogenized the myriad tribal groups across the continent. Until very recently, the differential and unequal status of Indian women was set down by law in the Indian Act.[26] Ethnicity and gender are the essential constituents in the formation of the Canadian class structure.

The treatment of gender and ethnicity as relations constituted through people's activities helps us to observe the differential work carried out by men and women in nation building. Barbara Roberts divides the work of national building during the period between 1880 and 1920 into two aspects. The first aspect had to do with developing the infrastructure of the economy: the building of a nation-wide transportation system, the development of a manufacturing base and a commodity market, and so forth. The development of this aspect of the economy was the domain of men. The second aspect had to do with the building of the human nation: the development of a population base in Canada. Women reformers (whom Roberts calls upper class "ladies") were the active organizers of this aspect of the nation building. To ensure the white character and guarantee Christian morality of the nation, upper class women from Britain worked relentlessly to organize the immigration of working class girls from that country to serve in the new world as domestics and wives.[27] These "ladies" thus established the first immigration societies in the major cities of Canada, attending to the plight of immigrants.

Similarly, Kari Dehli's research on school reforms in Toronto at the turn of the century shows how middle class mothers of (mainly) British background worked to enforce a particular version of motherhood on working class immigrant women. In the 1920s Toronto experienced a serious depression. Many working class immigrant women were forced to engage in waged work outside the home. Alarmed by the declining state of the family (many working class children attended school hungry and poorly dressed), middle class women worked hard to propagate and enforce "proper" mothering practices in working class families. It was in this period that the notion of "proper motherhood" gained prominence in the organization of family life through the school system.[28]

These examples point to the class-based work done by men and women to preserve Canada as a white nation and to enforce a particular ideology to guarantee white supremacy.

But as ruling class men consolidated their power in the state apparatus, they also began to take over and incorporate women's work into the state. Roberts found that, by 1920, control over immigration and the settlement of immigrants had shifted from the hands of women to the hands of state officials. As state power was consolidated, women's work was relegated more and more to the domestic sphere.[29] Similarly, community work has been incorporated into the local state — in boards of education. The central role played by middle class women in school reform was supplanted by the rise and development of an increasingly elaborate bureaucracy within different levels of the state. Interestingly, while the state consolidated its power, sexuality became legislated by law. During this time, homosexuality became a crime, and sexual intercourse was legitimized within legal marital relationship only.[30]

I am not arguing that gender and ethnicity are reducible to class. I maintain that the examination of gender, ethnicity, and class must be situated in the relations of a specific social formation, which have to do with struggles, by groups of people, over control of the means of production and reproduction over time. An examination of the history of Canada indicates that class cannot be understood without reference to ethnic and gender relations; similarly, gender and ethnicity cannot be understood without reference to class relations.

On the basis of the foregoing one can see why I maintain, at the beginning of this paper, that gender, race/ethnicity and class relations are inextricably linked to the formation of the Canadian state, if we see the state as the culmination and crystallization of struggles over the dominant -- in the case of Canada: capitalist--mode of production. The history of the Native people, from the fur trade period to their entrapment in reserves, is the most blatant example. (The expulsion of the Acadians — a primarily agrarian group with a subsistence economy — by the British colonizers, including the Loyalists, from the richer arable lands of the Atlantic region offers another historical testimony of consolidation of power and control by the Anglo-Saxons and the Scots.) The struggles of groups of Irish, Scottish and English descent in the Maritimes is yet another example.[31]

Although we don't have an encompassing picture of the detailed interplay of gender, ethnicity, class, and Canadian state formation--because few systematic studies making use of the above conceptualization have been carried out--we can begin to see the centrality of gender, ethnicity, and class in the formation of the Canadian state by reviewing selected historical studies. Armstrong's research on the Family Compact during the eighteenth and nineteenth centuries, for example, begins to pinpoint the genesis of the Ontario Establishment. He describes ways in which groups from Scottish and English origins consolidated their power through the acquisition of land and wealth, marriage, and connections in the officialdom in Britain, which eventually culminated in the formation of the Canadian elite. He ends his investigation by suggesting that, once in power, the elite tended to "de-ethnicize" themselves.[32]

The process that Armstrong describes becomes, in the twentieth century, what Porter has called "the vertical mosaic."[33] Although Porter's empirical study of the interrelationship between ethnicity and class is essentially correct, his positivism has prevented him from coming to grips with the actual connection between ethnicity, class, and the state. While he correctly points out that the upward mobility of certain groups tends to be curtailed by their ethnicity, he does not perceive ethnic relations as part of the organization of productive relations in Canada, nor does he see the state as the culmination of the struggles betweent the various groups over time. The framework proposed here, on the other hand, explains the emergence of what some researchers have called "ethnic nationalism,"[34] being played out in the present historical conjuncture when capital is undergoing global restructuring.

In sum, I have presented some historical sketches of gender, race/ethnicity, and class dynamics as relations which underpin the development of Canada as a nation-state. It is important to note that these historical events are not presented as instances to support a particular theoretical proposition. Rather, I made use of a way of understanding the world which does not splinter the different historical events and moments into compartmentalized fields or areas of study.[35] In the latter approach, what upper class women did would be seen as "women's history," which has little to do with the organization of the labour market, and as the continuance of Anglo supremacy in nation building, which would be treated as "imperial history." The framework I put forward enables us to put together a picture of the formation of Canada as a nation-state with strong racist and sexist assumptions and policies — out of the seemingly separate pieces of history which are in fact pieces of the same jigsaw. It is thus that we come to see racism and sexism as the very foundation of Canadian nationhood.

Political implications

On the basis of the above discussion I want to explore how we may work to eradicate sexism and racism from our praxis as feminists, as intellectuals, and as people of colour.

The first thing that needs to be said is that gender, race/ethnicity, and class are not fixed entities. They are socially constructed in and through productive and reproductive relations in which we all participate. Thus, what constitutes sexism, racism, as well as class oppression, changes over time as productive relations change. While racism today is seen in discriminatory practices directed mainly at coloured people (the Black, South Asians, Native people, for example), skin colour and overt physical differences were not always the criteria for determining racial differences. The racism directed towards the Acadians by the Scots and the Irish is no less abhorrent as that encountered by the Native people and today's ethnic and racial minorities. Within each racial and ethnic group, men and women, and people from different classes are subject to differential treatments. For example, while virtually no Chinese labourer or his family was allowed to enter Canada at the turn of the century through the imposition of the head tax, Chinese merchants and their families were permitted to immigrate during this period.[36]

Thus, it seems to me that our project is not to determine whether gender, race/ethnicity, class, or the economic system is the primary source of our oppression. The task is for us to discover how sexism and other forms of gender oppression (e.g., compulsory heterosexuality),[37] racism, and class opression are constituted in different historical conjuctures so that the dominant groups maintain their hegemony over the means of production and reproduction. Meanwhile, it is important to see that the state in modern society is a central site of the struggles among different groups. Recognizing the way in which the state divides us at each historical moment would enable us to better decide how alliances could be forged across groups of people to struggle against racial, sexual and class oppression.

Secondly, from the above analysis, it becomes clear that racism and sexism are not merely attitudes held by some members of society. I am beginning to think that they are not even just structural--in the sense that they are institutionalized in the judicial system, the educational system, the workplace, etc. — which of course they are. More fundamentally, they are systemic: they have crystallized over time in the ways we think and act regardless of our own gender, race, and class position. Indeed, sexist, racist and class assumptions are embodied in the way we "normally" conduct ourselves and our business in everday life.[38]

Thus, we cannot simply point our finger at, for example, the media or the school, and accuse them of gender and racial discrimination. While we begin from a recognition of the fundamental inequality between women and men, and between people from different racial and ethnic groups, at the everyday level we have to recognize that we are part of these institutions. We must pay attention to the manner in which our own practices create, sustain and reinforce racism, sexism, and class oppression. These practices include the mundane.

and unconscious ways in what and to whom we give credence, the space we take up in conversations with the result of silencing others, and the space we don't take up because we have learned to be submissive. We need to re-examine our history, as well as our own beliefs and actions, on a continual basis, so that we become better able to understand and confront ways in which we oppress others and participate in our own oppression. While this in itself will not liberate us completely from our own sexist, racist, and classist biases, it is a first step in working toward alternate forms of alliances and practices which will ultimately help us transform the society of which we are a part.

Speaking of Women's Lives and Imperialist Economics: Two Introductions from *Silenced*

Makeda Silvera

Introduction to the first edition

This is a book about the lives and struggles of West Indian women who are employed as domestic workers on Temporary Employment Visas in Canada. In it, ten women tell of their day to day struggles as Black working class women.

The women in the book come from the English-speaking Caribbean. Some of the women are from Jamaica while the others are from Trinidad, St. Vincent, Antigua, St. Lucia and Guyana. All of them have children who are left in the care of grandmothers or other relatives back home. These women came to Canada to work as domestic workers with the hopes that they will make enough money to feed, clothe and educate their families back in the Caribbean.

When I first came to this country, I came with three intentions - to help my kids, to go to school, to better myself, and to go to work and save some money. But now that I'm here, I find you can neither save money, go to school nor send for your kids.[1]

The misconception of Canada as the land of milk and honey is rein-
forced by airline advertisements, domestic agencies, weekly dramas on television which show North America as the land of plenty where happiness and
wealth can be bought on credit and where maids like those shown on the
weekly sit-coms are treated with respect and as a special part of the family.

What is never talked about, or made clear to many of these women, is
the widespread prejudice they will come up against in Canada and the racism
imbedded within a system which thrives on the labour of women of colour
from Third World countries, women who are brought to Canada to work
virtually as legal slaves in the homes of both wealthy and middle class Canadian families. In most cases, both their employers are themselves employed
and have an average combined income of $40,000 to $100,000 a year. Meanwhile, women who work in these homes as domestic servants get as little as
$200 a month for an eighteen hour day, seven days a week job.

*Right now my day begins at round 5 a.m . . . sometimes after 7 p.m. you
want to put on your sleep clothes, but it is not possible because sometimes
at 10 p.m. they calling you to feed the eight month-old baby if he wake
up. Then when the children sick, when they have the cold, it's me who
have to get up, not their mother and father.[2]*

The recruitment of female immigration labour for upper and middle
class Canadian families from outside Canada was, and remains, the most
effective means used for securing domestic labour. In the book *Women at
Work (Ontario 1850 - 1930): Domestic Service in Canada*, Genevieve Leslie
discusses this briefly:

*In 1911, for example, immigrant women formed thirty-five per cent of the
female work force in domestic and personal service, even though they
made up only twenty-four per cent of the female work force in all occupations including service jobs. Female domestics were "preferred immi-*

grants" long before 1880 but the drive to recruit immigrant domestics intensified as industrialization diverted (Canadian) women from service into other occupations.³

Many of these women were poor and came from families who could no longer support them; others were homeless and some were in fact children from workhouses in Britain.

The usual arrangement was that an employer applied for a servant and sent her passage money to the Superintendent of Immigration. An immigration agent would then choose a domestic in the Old Country, have her sign an agreement which bound her to service with her employer from six months to a year, advance her passage money, and arrange for her transportation, housing, and placement upon arrival. The amount advanced would later be deducted from the domestic's salary in monthly installments.⁴

On the job, they encountered many of the same problems that today's live-in domestic workers face, including sexual harassment, long hours and low pay. The general pattern of these immigrant women was that as soon as they completed their tenure agreement, they left domestic work and went on to other jobs with better working conditions.

An immigrant domestic complained in 1919 that the agent in London (England) . . .

Has so much to say about the good time maids have and how free you are, that you decide you will come... The lady meets you at Union Station, takes you to her house, where she has employers waiting to engage you. You have no choice of a place or work — just have to go where you are sent.⁵

There was a high turnover rate, since European immigrant women and girls did not stay long in these jobs. Because of this, the Canadian government attempted to take a look at some of the problems of this special group of women and became more involved in the recruitment of domestic servants from abroad.

In 1898, for example, a Mrs. Livingstone was commissioned by the Department of the Interior to travel to Scotland and select one hundred girls for service in the North West. Mrs. Livingstone attempted to match servant and employer when choosing women for immigration, by allowing servants to evaluate employers and decide where they would like to work — "actually realizing the oft laughed at idea of the kitchen demanding that the drawing room, like it, should give references." However, this arrangement was considered troublesome. It was soon discarded, while employers continued to specify age, physique, race, character, and experience of the servants they wanted.[6]

The problems between employer and employee continued, particularly in the case of the live-in domestic worker, who was on call twenty-four hours a day. As tenure was completed hundreds of women left domestic work. Many sought jobs in factories, dress shops and offices. These women quickly assimilated into Canadian society.

As the need for domestic workers grew, Canada began to look at Third World countries to supply domestic labour.

The first full-scale recruitment of West Indian women to Canada was initiated in 1955 by the Canadian government. These women came under a new organized program, known then as The Domestic Scheme. Hundreds of women from Jamaica, Trinidad, and Barbados came to Canada annually to work as domestic workers through this Scheme.

To qualify for the Scheme, applicants had to be between the ages of eighteen and thirty-five, single, with at least a grade eight education, and be able to pass a medical examination. Final applicants were interviewed by a team of Canadian immigration officials who visited the islands once a year specifically for this purpose.[7]

Many of these women were sole-support mothers. Upon arriving in Canada, they were granted landed immigrant status, and like their European sisters before them, they were required to work in a home for a period of one year. After a year's service, they had the option of finding work in another field or remaining in domestic labour.

Not much has been documented about this group of workers. "Hearsay and rumour stress the alienation and loneliness of these women and their difficulties in assimilating to the new Canadian scene."[8] But what is well known, though, is that like their European counterparts, they too found domestic work unrewarding, the hours long, and the salary inadequate. They, too, eventually left domestic work after their contracts had expired. Many went back to school to upgrade their education and move on to better jobs, but unlike European women, many Caribbean women experienced downward mobility, and because of their colour and the racism they experienced, found it much harder to assimilate into larger society. This did not stop the determination of many Caribbean women who opted out of domestic work after their tenure was completed; because of this pattern, the shortage of domestic workers continued to increase. The department of Employment and Immigration appeared not to be interested in improving the situation of many West Indians who decided to abandon domestic work. Instead of taking steps to improve the working conditions of domestic workers, the government stopped granting automatic landed immigrant status to domestics, thus putting an end to the Domestic Scheme, and instead issued Temporary Employment Visas.

Temporary employment visas

Temporary Employment Visas are, for the most part, issued to workers from Third World countries. The main purpose of the Temporary Employment Visa is to fill the labour shortage in certain jobs inside Canada: in particular, domestic labour, seasonal farmwork, and other non-union jobs,

201

where the wages are rock-bottom and the working conditions reminiscent of the 19th century. Each visa is issued for a particular kind of job, for a specific employer, and for a definite period of time. If any of these circumstances change, the holder of a visa must immediately report to the Employment and Immigration Commission or run the risk of being deported.

Unlike the Domestic Scheme of 1955 and the others before, the holder of a Temporary Employment Visa is not automatically entitled to landed immigrant status. The Canadian Employment and Immigration Commission considers employment visas a "temporary solution" to the domestic labour shortage, and thus feels quite justified in exploiting the labour of Third World women and turning a blind eye to the inhumane working conditions that have become synonymous with domestic work.

In *Union Sisters*, Rachel Epstein confirms the excessive use of cheap immigration labour, with figures obtained from Employment and Immigration Canada:

> In 1974 the number of landed immigrants admitted to Canada was two
> and half times as great as the number of employment visas issued. In
> 1978 the balance was reversed and there were more visas issued than
> landed immigrants admitted. Although in 1981 the numbers were al-
> most equal, this represented a substantial increase in the numbers of
> people entering the country on employment visas and a decrease in the
> numbers of landed immigrants from previous years.[9]

In 1978, 12,483 Temporary Employment Visas werre issued for domestic work in Canada. The bulk of these were issued in Ontario, Quebec, British Columbia and Alberta. In 1982, there were more than 16,000 visas issued, despite the fact that unemployment in Canada had been rising at an alarming rate.

The major reason for this increase in Temporary Employment Visas is that few Canadian workers are willing to do this work, which requires, in most cases, "living-in."

Living and working conditions

The living and working conditions of employment visa holders differs from home to home, depending on the individual employer, but, in general, the working conditions are poor and in some cases totally unacceptable.

Employment and Immigration Canada has established certain minimum standards to be used as guidelines by people who employ workers on the Temporary Employment Visas. According to Employment and Immigration, the worker should receive $710.00 per month (in Ontario), with a deduction of $210.00 per month for room and board. The worker must also pay Unemployment Insurance and Canada Pension. The guidelines also state that the domestic's working period is an eight hour day and provides for two days off each week.

The reality for domestic workers differs greatly from these departmental regulations. On the contrary, what is most common is that the employer does not follow these guidelines. Many employers view these guidelines as a mere bureaucratic formality. They have, in fact, a free hand in setting wages because Immigration does little to enforce its regulations. So, duties, hours of work, and salaries are often changed unilaterally by the employer. One worker complains:

The other day I was telling a friend of mine about Mrs. Smith and the meagre salary she was paying me. My friend was asking how she manage to get away with it from Manpower. But the thing is, Manpower don't know because she told Manpower she was paying me $100.00 a week. It's on the paper. It's written down in the contract . . . when I started working with her she told me she was paying me $85.00 a week.[10]

The Employment and Immigration Commission advises that if an employer does not adhere to these rules, the employee should contact a Canada Employment and Immigration Centre, where an officer will assist the permit holder in finding another job as a domestic. But there is a huge gap between stated policy and the real experience. Therefore, many women when faced with a breach of contract are afraid to make a formal complaint to an Immigration officer.

> *Right now I get $710.00 a month, which is what I am suppose to get as Manpower say, but when I took the job, I wasn't told that I was suppose to clean and wash clothes too for that money. I am afraid to go and complain to Manpower, because this is my third job . . . so maybe if I go and complain they might tell me to go home. They might think I am a troublemaker.*[11]

These sentiments are the norm. Employment visa holders who have had more than one employer have been forced to leave the country by Immigration officers. Many of the women in this book do not get two days off each week as stipulated in their contracts. Some are not even aware that they are entitled to statutory holidays. Many of the women complain that they must share their rooms with the younger children or babies in the family. Others reported that they were not given enough food, despite the fact that employers deduct money for room and board. Domestic workers also receive no overtime or vacation pay. They are not covered under the Canada Pension Plan and cannot collect Unemployment Insurance even though they pay into it. As stated earlier, the Employment and Immigration Commission has made attempts to set up some minimum standards for wages and working conditions, but have done nothing about employers who renege on their agreement. This policy clearly benefits certain sectors of Canadian society, by supplying substantial amounts of cheap imported labour to fill the domestic needs of upper and middle class Canadian families. It is also an effective way of controlling the permanent migration of Third World working class women to Canada.

Educational opportunities

Up until recently, women on the employment visa were prohibited by law from upgrading their education in Canada. Many of these women had been here for over nine years, working as live-in workers, paying into Unemployment Insurance and the Canada Pension Plan without having the right to vote and choose government representatives.

In the winter of 1980, a series of incidents concerning domestic workers on employment visas began to crop up in the media. One such incident that was widely reported was that of a domestic worker who took an Ontario Government minister to court for back wages.

There were countless other incidents that did not make the headlines or the 10 o'clock news, but which have been documented by community groups working with domestics. Many other cases appeared in court and through support of various community organizations, some women have been able to win their cases and collect back-pay. If it had been the intention of the established newspapers and the government in power to ignore the demands of these women for justice, it was in vain.

In November 1981, the government was forced to look at its Immigration policy concerning domestic workers on the Temporary Employment Visa:

Ottawa: Employment and Immigration Minister Lloyd Axworthy today announced new measures to assist foreign domestics working in Canada to gain permanent resident status . . . the measures follow an extensive review of the policy on domestic workers on the employment visa.[12]

Speaking about the change, the Minister said that domestic workers who have been in Canada for more than two years may apply for permanent resident status.

> *Domestic workers currently in Canada who have been here two years, and who wish to be considered for permanent resident status, will be given the opportunity of gaining that status from within the country when their employment authorisations are due for renewal. Assessment will be made by Immigration officers, and those who have been here for two years and who have achieved a potential for self-sufficiency will be advised that they can make application for permanent resident status from within Canada. Those not yet sufficiently established or who have been here for less than two years will be given the opportunity for upgrading their skills to the point where they also can be considered for permanent resident status.[13]*

But again, there is a gap between stated policy and practice. Though it is still too early to see the full implications of the new policy, one thing is certain and that is that it is much more complicated than it sounds. First, whether or not a woman qualifies for landed status is left up to the individual Immigration officer who must judge whether she has an "aptitude for learning," "an adaptability to Canadian lifestyle," and "personal suitability." Given that there is no clearly stated policy, this has already led to discriminatory practices. Already, older women who have been in Canada for nearly ten years, or women with more than four children, are worried that their applications will be rejected.

The new policy also stipulates that Canadian employers must provide a certain amount of free time each week for domestic workers to attend upgrading courses at night school. The new policy also states that employers must contribute towards the cost of training during the time of study. But many employers are not providing the token twenty dollars per month or the time off required. Again, and for obvious reasons, many women are afraid to bring this situation to the attention of Immigration officers.

The women in this book

These women have never been heard. Usually we know of them through cold, impersonalized statistics, or through the voices of others who speak for them, or when the media sensationalizes their plight and briefly forces us to acknowledge, if only temporarily, their existence.

I met most of the women in this book through my involvement in working and helping to organize domestic workers. It was through my experience as a working class woman and my involvement with poor people that I developed the anger and persistence that pushed me forward to work on this book. And it was the warmth, and courage of these women that gave me the inspiration to complete it.

We rarely hear about women like Molly, Irma, Myrtle, Hyacinth or Angel, and when and if we do learn about their hopes, struggles and vision, it is often heard through the words of others. It is not their lack of education and lack of writing skills that have served to silence many of these women. It is, rather, that their silence is the result of a society which uses power and powerlessness as weapons to exclude non-white and poor people from any real decision-making and participation.

This book hopes to help shatter this silence. Ten West Indian women talk about their lives as domestic workers in Canada, the bitter-sweet memories of family back home, the frustration of never having enough money, and the humiliation of being a legal slave. They tell of working overtime for no pay, of sharing their rooms usually with a baby or the family pet, of shaking off the sexual advances of their male employer, and in the case of Hyacinth, of being raped. They talk about the experience of being manipulated and degraded by female employers. Although their cries are usually ones of despair at their isolation, they also talk about their lives as mothers and daughters, and about continued visions of hope for the future.

Each chapter in this book represents a life story or part of one. Their experiences illustrate a wide range of issues that concern them as workers and as women: sexual harassment, alienation, atrocious working and living conditions, inadequate pay, and inevitably, discrimination and oppression because of race, class, and age.

All the women whose stories appear in this book are between the ages of twenty and fifty-four years old. Nine women are Black and one woman is East Indian from Guyana. All ten women are from poor and working class backgrounds. (This categorization is based on their previous occupation in the Caribbean and their educational background.) Seven of the ten women did not attend high school, while three attended but did not complete it. Four of the ten women were unemployed in the Caribbean, five were employed as domestic workers, and one as a secretary. Nine of the ten women have children back home, and of that nine, seven are solely responsible for their children's financial welfare. Only one of the ten women is married and her husband remains in the Caribbean.

Although the interviews were generally unstructured, I approached them with a few specific topics that I was interested in — their views on the role of women, their views on feminism, and the relationship between their female employers and themselves. But after much thought about silence and the silenced, I felt that it was better to leave it at whatever each individual woman wanted to focus on. Since working class women do not often have the opportunity or the resources to write about their lives, it was important that these women talk about whatever they wanted to, that they speak directly about the problems they face as domestic workers.

During the interviews, I respected each woman's decision on what were, for her, private areas. I did not want to drag painful memories out of people and then leave them to deal with the emotional aftermath alone. However, many of the women talked unabashedly and unguardedly, even about painful times. Some, like Molly, talked for hours on end; others cried in desperation and relief. Not one of us who participated were unmoved.

Although many of these women share the same feelings of loneliness, isolation, and hope, they remain isolated from each other in suburban

Canada, and will meet for the first time within the pages of this book.

Molly was one of the first people I interviewed for the book. It was a very warm and intimate interview - the kind every interviewer dreams about. We sat down in her one room apartment and talked for five hours, taping the conversations as we talked.

A number of the women, particularly those who work as live-in domestics, were interviewed at my house. These interviews followed much the same pattern as Molly's and were also taped.

Some interviews were easier than others. For example, when I first started to interview Primrose, I had a hard time trying to get her to talk about her feelings and her life in Canada as a domestic. It took a very long time to develop the trust that we now have. Nevertheless, it added an important sense of reality to our conversation, given the fear of many domestic workers of speaking out, the fear of being identified by their employers and, as a result, losing their jobs.

On the other hand, Angel's interview flowed quite smoothly and was very touching. She talked about her difficult relationship with her mother and the strains and anxieties that her mother also experienced as a domestic worker. But generally, the women were very eager to talk once trust and respect was established.

At the end of each interview, I took home the tapes, transcribed and then edited them. I then took the transcribed tapes back to the women, who read them over and sometimes suggested changes. Then I took them home again and re-typed them and gave them back to be read a final time.

If there were anxieties about parts of the interview, we talked it over and came to some amicable agreement. This was a very long and laborious process. The book took me three years to complete, juggled between my family, work, and academic and community activities. There were times when it was frustrating, and I felt like giving up, times when I didn't have enough money to buy tapes, to rent a typewriter, to buy paper or to pay for the other expenses that I incurred. At those times, I had to put the book on hold. Nonetheless, it was well worth the time and the money spent on typing and re-typing the manuscripts when the women wanted to change a paragraph or a page. I remember one woman being quite concerned about what she had said on tape about her family. She feared they might read the book and get angry with her. Upon reading the manuscript she felt that she had the power to change anything she wanted, and she did change it.

I hope the lives and struggles of these women will provide other domestic workers with a sense of power and a sense of their own history.

I hope it will serve, too, as a point of identity for all women who have been silenced. Here are ten stories of women who are silenced no longer. I say no more. Turn the pages and meet them.

January, 1983

Introduction to the second edition

This new introduction comes six years after the first publication of *Silenced* in 1983. The book was an immediate success and between 1983 and 1988 it was reprinted three times. It was the first of its kind; that is, the first account in Canadian history of Caribbean domestic workers talking about their work experiences and living conditions in Canada.

New introductions are supposed to introduce new findings, to update and shed new light on the subject of study, but the single most important statement that this new introduction can make is that there is nothing new; were this book written today about the collective experience of the women, their voices would say the same things because the situation has changed minimally since the first publication of *Silenced*. For example, in 1983 domestic workers on the work permit earned $3.50 per hour, in 1989, they earn $5.00 per hour. They are entitled to work no more than 44 hours per week, beyond that they are entitled to time and a half. They can now register complaints with the Ministry of Labour to claim for overtime wages if their employers refuse to acknowledge this. For many domestic workers, this entitlement is seen as bureaucratic jargon, the reality remains the same as it was in 1983, and that is, individual women remain afraid and intimidated, and complaints of any kind are rarely registered. The perception of domestic work and those who work as domestics have not changed, nor have the reasons for coming to Canada to do this kind of work.

Yet, despite this sense of frustrating stagnation, this new introduction offers reflective analysis of the historical/political climate in Toronto during the early and late 1970s; for it is the climate experienced by the Black community which helped set the stage for a book like *Silenced*. This new introduction also provides a further opportunity to discuss the process of writing the book and the importance of using oral history as a methodology to chart the experiences of Caribbean domestic workers.

The 1970s signalled both the birth and simultaneous coming of age of the Black community. The community built on the struggles of previous generations, who in organizations like the Universal African Improvement Association (UAIA), The Negro Citizenship Association, the Canadian Negro Women's Association, and with individuals like Harry Gairey, Don Moore, Violet Blackman, Carrie Best, fought the earlier battles for dignity and justice. In the 1970s the demographic expansion of the community facilitated the emergence and development of new talents, new organizations, new strategies. Much of this activism in Toronto's Black community was spearheaded by the student movement.

In responding to the political situation of Blacks in Canada, we were encouraged by our brothers and sisters south of the border, who were demanding equal rights and justice for Blacks in the United States. The situation demanded re-active and pro-active strategies and the community responded with numerous groups, committees, organizations which sought to confront the issues. The issues were numerous: discrimination in housing and employment, undeniable institutional bias in education, increasing police abuse of authority, and official harassment characterized by the random deportation of racially visible groups. Many Caribbean domestic workers were affected by all of these issues and in particular by random deportation. Although, because of their legal status, they were only tenuously connected to the wider Black community, our plight was theirs and their struggle for dignity ours.

The Black community newspaper often reported the heart-rending situations of some of these domestics, yet in retrospect it seemed as if there was no time for activists to record and to document this important and historic period for posterity. Many activists and leaders who participated in the political movements did not seem to realize how important it was to document and chronicle that period of history. My decision to work on *Silenced* was clearly informed by this gap in our cultural development. It became increasingly clear to me that, as the community matured and grew in strength, it required some kind of documentation of its past which would inform its present and be available for future generations in their struggle. The task of recording the total picture, that is, the struggles of the wider community, appeared overwhelming and to some extent remote. But because of my direct involvement in grassroots activism and my years of involvement in organizing and working with Caribbean domestic workers I took on the challenge of recording their experiences.

In 1977, I was working as a journalist for *Contrast* (a Black newspaper) and I was assigned to cover a demonstration which was in support of seven Jamaican women who were facing deportation by the Canadian government. The case was dubbed "The Seven Jamaican Mothers" although in fact there were more than seven women who were facing deportation. Many of these women had come to Canada in the early 1970s to work as domestics as part of a Jamaica-Canada agreement similar to the domestic scheme of 1955. Both arrangements sought to transfer surplus labour from stagnant Caribbean countries to satisfy the need for cheap domestic labour in an expanding Canadian economy. One of the "qualifications" for this kind of job was that the woman had to be single without children.

Many of the women claimed that on the advice of the Jamaican government and with the knowledge of the Canadian High Commission staff they omitted on their application forms the fact that they had children. Many of these women worked for years as domestics in Canada. Some had been in Canada since 1971 and had applied for landed status and received it. In 1975, the government arbitrarily decided to deport many of these women who had been granted landed status. The charge was that they had submitted fake immigration applications claiming they had no children, but were now attempting to apply for landed status for children they now acknowledged in Jamaica.

This was clearly sexist since single fathers were not routinely rounded up and deported. In fact, men were never asked about children. It was also clearly racist because it was only Black landed immigrants who were being deported. There were no known cases of non-black women who were harassed and deported during that period. It was only Caribbean women who, forced to emigrate as domestics as part of their strategy for economic survival, had to deny the existence of their children and were now paying for this indiscretion.

The attack against domestics had to be understood against a background of changing economic conditions in Canada and the consequent changing need for imported cheap labour. It was in the late 1970s, when the Canadian economic picture had changed and local unemployment had risen to a new high, that the government began to round up these women on charges of fraud. Many felt that the intent of the government was to intimidate these women and to send them home now that their services were no longer needed. It was the general opinion that this attack on domestics was part of a policy to appease those uninformed Canadians who erroneously believed that Black immigrants were denying jobs to the unemployed.

During the next two years while the women and their supporters continued to battle against the racist and sexist policy of the Canadian immigration department, I came to know and work with many of these women. We demonstrated in the harsh Canadian winter, we cried together, and when we finally won, we rejoiced together. I was touched deeply by their lives of struggle and whatever personal problems I had seemed trivial in the face of their continual fight for respect.

The success of the Seven Jamaican Mothers and their victory was in large measure due to many of them speaking for the first time at large rallies about their plight, the wide media coverage their case received and the public outcry from many Canadians. There were numerous demonstrations organized so that the general public could be sensitized to the plight of these women. The case was fought on many different levels, through mass organizing, media reports, demonstrations, leafletting, press conferences, and in the courts. It was clear that the case could not be won only in the court room. It required the active participation and agitation of supporters who demonstrated, picketed, and signed petitions. The plight of these unprotected domestics evoked responses from many organizations both within the Black community and other non-black progressive groups. These organizations and groups included The International Committee Against Racism, Canadians Against the Deportation of Immigrant Women, the Universal African Improvement Association, the Canadian Labour Party, teachers, trade unionists, church leaders, and the Sikh community. It was difficult for any government to ignore this widely based ground swell of opposition to this inhumane and discriminatory policy.

Oral history as methodology

Oral history is the lifeline of this book. It is a book about women talking directly to the reader about their lives and their experiences. It is a powerful and a living testimony of the voices of "the ordinary" and the "powerless." Oral historians can learn from these testimonies because the document brings into the forefront the lived experience of the voiceless. It forces

214

one to confront the imposed muteness which has silenced women for so long and it encourages the recognition of the revolutionary potential of women's oral history. As a Black feminist engaged in research, I have become more aware of the neglect of the contributions to the Canadian society of peoples of colour and in particular Black women. This oral documentation fills the gap in Canadian herstory and attempts to satisfy the need for a reference text that relates the politics of Caribbean domestic workers.

In 1980 when I began work on Caribbean domestic workers in Canada, I was relatively new to academia and to feminist research. But I was both optimistic and enthusiastic about beginning work in this area. Two things struck me: one, that there was little significant research in this area and consequently an absence of empirical data, and two, that the existing material was for the most part clinical, and devoid of a life or rhythm of the "subject." The only available work that provided a feel of the reality of the life of Caribbean domestics in Canada were the novels by West Indian author Austin Clarke. I wanted to find a sociological work that was similar to Clarke's novels. I wanted to find a herstory of Caribbean women that was real — a piece of work in the voices of the women. It was reading other oral herstories of working class women written mostly in the United States and examining the oral research of Black historians in the United States that established for me the value of oral history as a methodology.

One of the most striking and obvious things about *Silenced* is the use of language by the ten women. They speak in their own words, in their own language, filled with cultural nuance and innuendo. This is an act of empowerment, particularly for these women who work as live-in domestics and for the most part have not been able to speak in their own language on a daily basis but have had to speak in another "language" to communicate with their employer. Language is a powerful aspect of culture. When it is taken away from an individual, it is an act of disempowering that person. How does this affect them? How do they maintain family ties and traditions?

The traditional methodological instruments of the academic are inad-

215

equate to handle the complexities of recognizing the extent of powerlessness and engaging in the task of empowerment. Perhaps in their defense it may be said that they were not designed for the task of engaged scholarship which is the mandate of the committed feminist scholar, especially from the Third World. The questionnaire, the survey, have their value/role/importance for those who from a distance attempt what is described by some as disinterested and dispassionate observation and analysis. I have no quarrel with that. But my mandate is different. My task is not merely to observe and record, but it is to facilitate that entry into public scrutiny those who must be the makers of their own history rather than merely the subjects of the recorders of history. Yet this task is not without its own "rules," methodological dangers; the oral historian must be familiar with the language and other aspects of the culture. The interviewer should be aware of cultural taboos and customs. Unfamiliarity with the language and cultural sensibilities can seriously affect the content of the interview. By this I mean that it is important to know what areas are taboo in a particular cultural context. For example, a woman might discuss with the interviewer the number of children she has and her children's fathers. Depending on the degree of privacy she wishes to maintain, she might become silent if you then proceed to ask her about her marital status. This might well be an open secret, something she talks freely about to her friends, but face to face in an interview she might want to eliminate this point.

What I would like to get back to and to single out for some discussion is the interview process. When I started to work on *Silenced*, I was curious about the protocol for interviewing. I found there were not many examples available which spoke directly about interviewing women, or with a "female sensibility." The reference books spoke about appearing neutral in an interview, not giving any opinions, being professional and cool, being in control and not sharing information about oneself with the interviewee. In the book *Methods in Social Research*, Goode and Hatt maintained:

*Consequently, the interviewer cannot merely lose himself in being
friendly. He must introduce himself as though beginning a conversation
but from the beginning the additional element of respect, of professional
competence, should be maintained. Even the beginning student will
make this attempt, else he will find himself merely "maintaining rapport," while failing to penetrate the cliches of contradictions of the respondent. Further he will find that his own confidence is lessened, if the
only goal is to maintain friendliness. He is a professional researcher in
this situation and he must demand and obtain respect for the task he is
trying to perform.[14]*

C.A. Moser talks about the problems of becoming too talkative with the
interviewee.

*Some interviewers are no doubt better than others at establishing what
the psychologists call "rapport" and some may even be too good at it - the
National Opinion Research Centre Studies found slightly less satisfactory
results from the . . . sociable interviewers who are "fascinated by people".
. . there is something to be said for the interviewer who, while friendly
and interested does not get too emotionally involved with the respondent
and his problems . . . Pleasantness and a business-like nature is the ideal
combination.[15]*

It is clear from the techniques suggested here that the interviewer must
be duplicitous and that this formal deception ostensibly in the pursuit of
distance, or disinterestedness is a stock in trade of the interview. But perhaps this may be a male-centred approach. I suggest that in interviewing
women we may require less distance and more openness.

Let me state clearly, that in any situation where one is the interviewer,
a power dynamic already exists. The interviewer's knowledge of, and sensi-
tivity around, this issue is important. It is the sharing of information about

self, as much as is possible, that breaks the dominant/dominated dynamic. As feminists working in this area we have a responsibility to break down these traditional male-dominant ways of research and replace them with ones that speak to us from the standpoint of women.

The kind of interviewing techniques suggested would not have resulted in a book like *Silenced*. The very act of asking women to speak for themselves makes it clear that the interviewer has an opinion, that we are interested in their lives, and that we are departing from the traditional male-centred ways of interviewing.

There are vast numbers of topics and issues that can be explored through oral history, which would continue to build on the precious little documentation available on Black women. They include, among others, Caribbean women and ageing in Canada; young Black women who migrated to Canada as teenagers; recounting our grandmothers' lives; Black immigrants who came here in the 1940s; and there is still more work to be done on domestic labour.

Though private, hidden, and regarded as unimportant, it is an everyday experience of women, and who better to listen to, who better to learn from, but the women themselves, and in this case domestic workers. They can provide insight into the support network which operates in domestic workers' circles, the sexual exploitation of domestics, their affiliation with the church, concerns around ageing and their vision and hope for a better future.

These oral herstories with Caribbean domestic workers uncover a wealth of information about migration, about class, race, and gender, and present to us much information that has not been recorded. These interviews show clearly that Caribbean domestic workers have played and are playing an important historical role in Canadian economic development as cheap labour to fill Canada's labour shortage.

September 1989

The statistical information in this article is now out of date, though probably not significantly so since this stiutation of Black women has not changed very much. The value of the article lies, however, in the analytical and poltical crititque adopted by the author.

A Working Paper on Black Women in Toronto: Gender, Race, and Class

Dionne Brand

There is little, if any, comprehensive work on Black women in Canada. With the recent exception of Makeda Silvera's *Silenced*, there has been no serious attempt to analyse the role of Black women in migration, settlement, and the labour force, or in the struggles against racism which mark the everyday lives of Black peoples in Canada. Such analysis would necessarily show the race/class/sex construction which mediates the way in which Black women live and would focus on the areas in which they struggle. This dearth of literature has contributed to the invisibility of Black women's struggles, not only in the social sciences but also within the feminist project. Neither acknowledge racism as a minor variation in the analyses of the social and political condition of women. These analyses do not point out the specificity of Black women's lives and do not locate Black women's experiences as emerging through racially constructed gender roles.

The perception of Black peoples as existing in a state of migrancy further contributes to this construction of invisibility, a construction which legitimizes the racist underpinnings of Canadian society. This perception is only part of the dominant construction of Canada as white. Recent insulting and fruitless state-sponsored conferences such as the Immigrant Women's

Conference in 1980 and the Conference of Visible Minority Women held in 1983 attest to the way in which we are "organized" from the outside, even when these groups include Black women. Black women's reluctance to participate in the International Women's Day Committee or in other broad-based women's groups attests to the marginalization of Black women's struggles which have been addressed only weakly — either in deference to those whom we call brothers, or in reification of the "strong Black woman." This "strong Black woman" is coaxed on various occasions, to repeat Sojourner Truth speeches, to be the exemplar of patient motherhood/secret sexuality, and generally, to mannequin the role of deepest sufferer/strongest back. Thus, from within and without the community, the reality of Black women's experiences is systematically suppressed and evaded.

This article explores how Black women's lives/sexuality are constructed in Canada: where our oppression is located, and how to focus on these locations in struggling/organizing against oppression. What I hope to contribute in this working paper is an analysis toward an organizing tool for Black women, an organizing tool which would have as its basis the recognition of who we are and what we live. To that end, I will look at migration, labour, gender, and at the construction of Black women's sexuality.

Historically, work outside the home has been a crucial site of Black women's oppression, from the institution of slavery in the Americas to current exploitative work structures. Black women, along with other women of colour and immigrant women, rank as the lowest-paid waged workers. A look at the history of Black women outside the home demythologizes the claim that women are largely part-time workers and secondary family income earners.

Many Black women are heads of households; they are generally primary income earners, poor, and working class. These realities belie the claim that our wages are secondary, and the exploitation that this claim conceals. As I will show in the section on migration, labour, and gender, the experiences of Black women in Canada point even more sharply to the centrality of women's work outside the home. Moreover, this work for wages has been implicitly recognized in Canadian immigration policy. Black women immigrating from the Caribbean, more often than not, have come as independent immigrants or on work permits, rather than as spouses. A condition of Black women's migration has been/is the value of their work outside the home.

As class informs our lives, so racism too is a historical determinant in our lives. For us, the relevance of any socio-political theory, and of feminist theory especially, depends on its understanding of the role of slavery, of colonialism, and of the attendant racist culture in the development of capitalism. An understanding of slavery and colonialism reveals the ways in which institutions in the "new world" were fashioned — Canada not excepted. All one has to do is examine the genocide and exploitation of Native peoples here, the practise of slavery in Canada until its abolition by Lord Simcoe, and the imperialist adventures of the eighteenth and nineteenth centuries which resulted in the European settlement of Canada. These are the historical roots of this society. The contemporary manifestations of these practices are no less racist: immigration laws limiting Third World migration, the containment of Black populations and cultures, state intransigence on Native autonomy, the internment and disenfranchisement of Japanese Canadians, the images of non-white peoples in the media, the activities of Canadian banks and corporations in Third World countries, Canadian foreign policy - the list goes on.

Racism is a "common sense" notion within the set of relations that comprise our everyday activity; it is part of the structures that prescribe the power relations of production. Taking its historical metaphor from the justification for slavery, it ascribes "natural," "biological" inferiority to various groups at various times. As commonsensical quality. In the case of Black women, a complex construction, encompassing both racism and sexism, lays out the common sense notions addressed to them.

The construction of Black women's sexuality occurs within an historical moment where patriarchy, class, and race conjoin to produce oppression that is particular to Black women. Racist-sexist received opinion of Black women's sexuality needs especially to be investigated: from what does this stem? Where is it reproduced, and for what is it used, given the place of Black women in society?

Migration, labour and gender

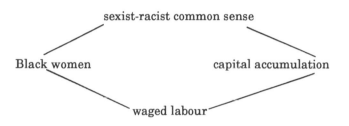

Two significant phases of migration account for Black people's presence in Canada: in the seventeenth and eighteenth centuries, the importation of slave labour into Upper and Lower Canada and the escape of Blacks from slavery in the United States and, in the last twenty to thirty years, the importation of cheap labour from the Caribbean. Black women figure prominently in these two periods. Freedom-fighter Harriet Tubman led some 300 Blacks escaping slavery to Canada. Risking her life time and time again she went back to lead to more freedom in Canada. Mary Ann Shadd, a free woman, set up a one-room school in London in the 1850s. She also set up a newspaper on King Street in Toronto. Black women worked in agriculture and domestic work in the 1800s in southern Ontario, Nova Scotia, on the Prairies, and as slaves prior to the abolition by Lord Simcoe.

Up until the 1930s, Black women worked as indentured labour. The contemporary version of this form of bondage includes domestic workers, primarily from Third World countries, who are brought here on work permits.

There is a historical characterization of Black women as fit for any kind of work — except for the jobs that white men want. We have always done

223

manual work, i.e., "non-traditional" work. Our history knows no category called "women's work": there is "white men's work," "white women's work," and "nigger work." "Nigger work" has its roots in slavery in the "new world," and in the ascriptions of less-than-human characteristics to Black peoples as a whole.

> *Subordinates are expected to make pleasant, orderly, or clean those parts of the body or things to do with the body that are perceived as unpleasant, uncontrollable, or dirty. (Providing clean laundry is one superficial example; providing a necessary sexual outlet is another, not so superficial example.)* (Baker, Miller, 22)

I will now examine the kind of work Black women are currently engaged in to show that the types of work ascribed to Black women have not changed significantly from the time that Black people landed in the Americas as enslaved labour.

Black women in Toronto are to be found mainly in service jobs (domestic work, nursing, nursing aides), in factory work, in food and service work, and, more recently, as telephone operators, hotel workers and clerks.

A 1981 study by Reitz et al shows Black women concentrated in segregated occupations: nursing aides and orderlies, personal service occupations, nursing, and electronic data processing equipment operators. (Reitz's study examines "West Indian" women. I have inferred "Black," given the similarities of experiences and the social placement of third and fourth generation Black women in Canada.) Many of the nurses in Toronto hospitals are Black or Filipino women. This trend is not unlike that in Britain, where during the early 1950s, Black women's socialization to become nurses can be seen as a trajectory from maid/servant/domestic help to helping, caring subordinates. Black women themselves saw nursing as an escape from domestic work. Teaching is also a profession which is looked upon this way.

The distinction established between men's and women's work, in so far as it exists, is found within the realm of "nigger work" and occurred after emancipation. It remains only partial. Prior to that, Black women worked in the fields picking cotton, cutting cane, and drawing oxen. Black women still work in these areas, but the distinction between pre- and post-emancipation work is important. Freedom meant not having to do the same kind of work as during slavery. It also meant setting up structures equal to those of white society. "White femininity" played a major role in slavery: "Miss Anne" — the southern belle, the pride and purity of the white race — could not have emerged in the absence of the image of Black carnality. Racism did and still does prevent Black women from acquiring positions which white women hold, so nursing and other jobs in the helping professions are seen as the most "decent" jobs which Black women may hold.

The current socialization of young Black women in schools in Toronto perpetuates these job trends. Many young Blacks, women and men, can be found in lower stream high schools around the city. In commercial and vocational high schools such as Eastern Commerce, Bickford Park, West Park Vocational, and Brockton, there are large numbers of young Black women who are studying typing, office practices, shorthand, and computer fundamentals. They can also be found in community colleges in the community worker and nursing aide programmes. (The proliferation of Blacks in sports - Angela Bailey, Angela Taylor, Marita Payne, and others on the Canadian women's track team — is also evidence of the prescribed social locations where Blacks are allowed to excel.)

White employers see the type of work that Black women do as "natural," as what they were born to do, and it is expected that Black women will "make do." In some nursing homes, notorious for their poor facilities and under-paid staff, Black nurses and nursing aides take the brunt of managing with inadequate staffing and supplies. This is, after all, what they are supposedly used to. Much extra work gets wrung out of Black women because of their designated place in society. A particularly cogent analysis of Black women's presence in domestic work is put forward by Hazel Carby. She reveals the white middle-class bias of that tendency within the women's movement which locates the focus of all women's oppression primarily within the reproduction of labour power in the home:

> *In using this (reproduction) concept in relation to the domestic labour of black women we find that in spite of its apparent simplicity it must be dismantled. What does the concept of reproduction mean in a situation where black women have done domestic labour outside of their own homes in the servicing of white families? In this example they lie outside of the industrial wage relation but in a situation where they are providing for the reproduction of black labour in their own domestic sphere, simultaneously ensuring the reproduction of white labour power in the "white" household.* (Carby, 218)

Carby suggests that a deeper look at the reproduction of labour power reveals how Black women's work effects first "the construction of ideologies of black female sexuality, and second how this role relates to the black woman's struggle for control over her own sexuality" (Carby, 218).

Black women do put forth resistance within the workplace, resistance which often costs them their jobs. In factories, Black women point out when the clock has been deliberately set back, won't stand at the machine to wait for their break to use the facilities, and are known to be intractable; they are, therefore, unpopular with factory owners. Thus, there are factories that have a policy of not hiring Black women. During a recent hotel strike in Toronto, I met several Black women who, dressed in their best to picket, were yelling at the management and scabs inside. The recent wave of strikes by largely Black and immigrant working class women and white working class women is more than a signal of general working-class militancy emerging anew; it is also a signal that during the crisis of capitalism, the women who are the most exploited are resisting bearing the brunt of cutbacks and layoffs. Employers see these women as the most easily dispensed with and dispensable workers. Support from other women during those strikes also points to the maturing of feminist practice.

The tradition from which such resistance springs is one which explicitly pinpoints racist culture: "I refuse to be treated like an animal; I'm doing your shit work; I'm not going to take shit from you too." For Black women, this resistance is rooted in slave rebellions, in the Black power movement, and in the ongoing struggle against racism. It also comes out of a history of labour strikes in the Caribbean where, beginning with the 1920s and 1930, labour struggles have been part of the struggle for political autonomy. In Canada, following the refusal of the white union to admit Blacks, the struggle of the sleeping car porters in the 1930s signalled the separate development of Black unions.

The history of women in the Caribbean reveals that sixty per cent of Black women there are heads of households. Where there has been industrialization and urbanization, men have had to leave rural areas for work in the towns, or leave the smaller islands for the larger ones where the level of industrialization is greater. The movement and access of men to export-oriented waged labour trap women in the subsistence agricultural economy.

Up and down the Caribbean, the traders in provisions and food stuffs are women. Women comprise forty per cent of the agricultural labour force in the region, are subsistence farmers, landless labourers, and trader/producers. They dominate the distribution and retailing of locally grown food crops. They work in excess of fifteen hours a day, taking care of domestic chores before heading for the fields for five to six hours. Inventory control, accounting, sewing, and family business make up late evening work. In addition, trader/producers have to find a day to set aside for marketing seventy to eighty per cent of their produce. When wage work is available women share poverty with men unequally as sex discrimination in wages is prevalent. Access to education is also a serious problem for rural Caribbean women on less urbanized islands or in rural areas of urbanized islands. This brief sketch shows the conditions under which Black women who migrated to Canada lived, and points out their major function in Caribbean societies.

Even though Canadian immigration policy has always had the need for cheap labour as its basis, the treatment of Black women immigrants during the last twenty to thirty years has also been mediated by racist-patriarchal assumptions. A look at the terms and conditions of Canadian immigration policy reveals how white patriarchy operates in the case of Black women. To begin with, Black women have always immigrated for the most part as unsponsored, i.e., independent immigrants.

> *The full scale recruitment of West Indian women to Canada was initiated in 1955 by the Canadian government . . . To qualify for the scheme, applicants had to be between the ages of eighteen and thirty-five, single, with at least a grade eight education, and be able to pass a medical examination . . . Upon arriving in Canada, they were granted landed immigrant status.* (Silvera, 13)

"Single" meant no dependents, no man, and no sex; by inference and in actuality, as Silvera points out, it meant coming to clean and to be sexual receptacles. The man, the employer, was the master of your labour and your sexuality. Working conditions offered Black women twenty-four hour shifts with but one day off per week to function as independent persons. Then, as now, Black women arrived in Canada to serve those who run things--those who own or manage. They were assumed to be docile, easily manageable, strong, and plodding. The basis of these assumptions was that Black women are chattel. The received wisdom of the employer was, and is, that this work is what these women do by nature, that they should be grateful for the work, and that they will neither leave it nor speak out on their own behalf.

But Black women coming to Canada under this scheme did not see themselves as permanently bound to this type of work. They quickly up-graded their skills and terminated their contracts. In response, Canadian immigration policy changed from the domestic worker scheme to the permit system which brought restrictions on the terms and conditions of Canadian residence; the intent of the new policy was to keep women in those domestic jobs. During roughly the same period in the 1970s, Canada's general immigration policy also changed to reduce the number of immigrants admitted from the Third World. Nonetheless, the percentage of Black women immigrating as independents remains high, in contrast to the immigration patterns of Portuguese, Greek, and Italian immigrants where men were followed by their families, with the women coming as dependents. At an earlier period, Chinese men who worked on the railroad were not allowed to bring their families or to marry. With the exceptions of this early immigration of Chinese men and of Black women, immigration policy has always certified men's control of women by ruling that women with spouses come as dependents. In the case of Black women, racist, patriarchal legislation has certified and continues to certify a particular social class of white men, the employers and the managers, as the controllers of Black women.

A 1979 study by Juliet Christianson et al on the ratio of Black female to male immigration to Canada shows that there were 1.8 Black women coming for every Black man, in the age group between twenty-five and thirty-nine years. Men came as students in the 1960s and early 1970s, or were sponsored by women. Women also sponsored their children. Eighty-one per cent of the women at the time of the study had been in Canada between three and ten years; only seventy per cent of the men fall into this category.

A look at the economic condition of Black women reveals that in 1979, the mean income of Black women was $8,000 as compared to that of white males' $16,600. Black women and Italian women (the latter averaging $8,500) were the lowest paid in the metro Toronto labour force (Reitz et al). The mean income for white women was $14,000.

We can deduce from current wages, and from the segregated occupations where Black women are still to be found, that the present mean income of Black women is an estimated $11,500. Consider that Black women may have to support, on average, two or three children on this income and the dire economic straits in which they live will become clear.

The Reitz study also goes on to note that job security is lowest among Portuguese and Black women (again, "Black" by inference, since their term is "West Indian"), though Black women had a mean educational level of 11.7 years.

The notion that "women should not be educated" is not part of Black women's culture. Women under slavery resorted to any available means to learn to read and write and then taught others. After emancipation, Black women continued to get as much education as they could, and have been prevented from study only by a lack of money. Many Black women, on arrival in Canada, immediately enrolled in night school in an attempt to better their economic prospects. It is not uncommon to find Black women who came to Canada twenty years ago on the domestic worker scheme working today as teachers or social workers. These exceptions notwithstanding, Black women in Toronto remain over-worked and underpaid. Many work at two jobs outside the home and are single parents.

Contrary to the theory that women can be defined primarily by their work in the home, that this is the main function of women in late capitalism, the historically repeated use of Black women's labour outside the home shows that production under capitalism presupposes an exploitable workforce. This is true not only of Canada, but also of South Africa where the exploitation of Black labour is pushed to the limit and where the so-called Black homelands reveal that the unprofitability of Black domestic life makes it superfluous to South African capitalism.

The reality is that wherever cheap labour outside the home is most required, Black women, women of colour and white working-class women are used, regardless of the family configuration. The common sense notions of white femininity that say women don't work are lodged in the experiences of white middle-class women and are used against all women. These notions obscure the real relations of working class women - Black, immigrant, white - to work outside the home. Thus the nominal privilege of white middle-class women merely holds the line against resistance by working-class women and the eventual fall of this system of exploitation.

For their part, Black women have always had to work as a condition of their race. It is not, then, a question of the right to work outside the home, but a matter of the economic imperative of waged work and a question of the kind of work available to them.

Wisdoms

The centrality of work is emphasized in the upbringing of Black women. Every Black woman has a mother or grandmother who has told her that she had to do it, probably alone, and that she had to continue to find ways of surviving, that she must be cognizant that no man would rescue her. This vision is reflected in the proportion of woman-headed households in the Black community (thirty-five per cent) and in our participation in waged work. Certainly, there are other historical and economic factors which influence our presence in these spheres, but what I wish to point out here is the creation of ways of living, thinking, and speaking which have developed in response to these conditions. Generations of Black women's creativity are contained in the philosophies handed down from grandmothers to mothers and grand-daughters. One woman says, "My grandmother told me never to save money with a man. When I was married, every Friday I would take my pay cheque to my grandmother's house. She would bank part of it and I'd take the rest home. My husband thought that I made a $65.00 per week instead of $75.00. My grandmother and I had a joint account. She said, 'You never know when things will go bad.'"

Grandmothers were also vigilant on education. They saw it as the way to freedom from dependency on men as well as upliftment from the oppression of racism. One woman remembers, "Every week when my grandfather gave my grandmother money for the house, she would say to me, 'You see how much money your grandfather gave me? You go to school and get an education so that no man would do this to you, you hear me girl?'"

A fifty year old woman says, "My mother said, 'Get yourself a profession before you get married.' My father said that, too."

For as long as I can remember, my grandmother used the threat of dependency on men to motivate the women in my family to pursue higher education, professions or trades. She would say, "If you don't go to school, you'll have to stay home and wash men's khaki pants for the rest of your life." Truancy from school elicited her most damning curse: "You have no ambition, you want to be a slave to a man?"

Implicit in these anecdotes is the knowledge that Black people's lives in general are economically unstable. It is not practical, and at times, is impossible, for Black women to depend on Black men's incomes, since Black men are too frequently found in the most marginal jobs.

Of course, male domination also exists in Black women's lives and exists despite the reality of the overall economic independence of Black women. But what is important to note is that it exists in an ongoing, antagonistic relation to the psychic map of self-sufficiency, the socialization of generations of Black women.

Woman-built systems

Other structures of support and solidarity bolster Black women's socialisation. When one examines the contemporary extended family in the Black community, one realizes that it is a woman-built system, resting on three social building blocks: (a) the imperative of waged work; (b) the stress of child bearing and rearing; (c) an understanding of children as grace. Emerging in some ways from African kinship systems, the contemporary extended family is basically matrilineal. It includes sisters, grandmothers, nieces, aunts, and older children, both male and female. It also includes some men: uncles, cousins and grandfathers. Its scope extends to women in the family of the child's father, depending on the levels of cordiality between the mother and the father of the child, sometimes all the more so in the absence of good relations between the parents. Friends and neighbours also play a role in looking after children. The responsibility of godmothers or godfathers may include financial support. There are, of course, other functions of this kinship system, but its central feature is the rearing of children. The system does come under a good deal of pressure in Canada, given that the human and material resources necessary to its operation are limited here. It depends on the family's having a bit of land in the country which produces food, on there being an unemployed grandmother, cousin, sister, grandfather, or friend living close by, and on neighbours who are also friends. Under more progressive conditions, free and easily accessible daycare might supplant the extended family.

The elaborate structure of the extended family also represents the importance of children to Black women. Children are grace. They are people with whom you imbue aspirations for the future. They are people who will not have to live the way you do.

But what does all this mean for the formulation that the family is one of the locations of women's oppression? Carby notes

We would not wish to deny that the family can be a source of oppression for us, but we also wish to examine how the black family has functioned as a prime source of resistance to oppression. We need to recognize that during slavery, periods of colonialism, and under the present authoritarian state, the black family has been a site of political and cultural resistance to racism. Furthermore, we cannot easily separate the two forms of oppression because racist theory and practice is frequently gender specific. Ideologies of black female sexuality do not stem primarily from the black family . . . The use of the concept of "dependency" is also a problem for black feminists. It has been argued that this concept provides the link between the "material organisation of the household, and the ideology of femininity." How then can we account for situations in which black women may be heads of households, or where, because of an economic

system which structures high black male unemployment, they are not
financially dependent upon a black man? (Carby, 214-215)

Overstating the matriarchy

It would not do to overstate the matriarchy, to say that Black women
are not exploited in relationships with Black men. Black men exhibit male-
dominant behaviour and exercise influence on the ways in which Black
women live, although they cannot be said to hold the same positions of power
or exercise the systemic male dominance of white men. Black men are not
now and never have been privy to the power structures established during
slavery, colonialism, or the current configuration of capitalism. These power
structures, because they are intrinsically racist, can only accommodate Black
men at the bottom.

Nonetheless, the sexist organization of the state ensures that the state
will approach Black males as the "natural" leaders in the Black community,
even though, for example, if we look at community agencies over the last
twenty or thirty years, we will find that women dominate therein. Black men
may benefit from male privilege by getting bank loans with less difficulty,
getting certain male-identified jobs, or getting the support of police in cases of
spouse assault/abuse. But these privileges operate only when they do not
conflict with state, corporate, or ideological interests.

There is a moment of experiential honesty between Black women and
Black men. Black women know they cannot expect from Black men that
which the dominant culture says must be expected from a man, Black women
know that Black men do not own, control, or run the world. Black men are
aware that Black women know these things. This accounts for the liberties
taken by the former and the tolerance shown by the latter. Internal discussions on black men are nevertheless a necessary part of Black women's organizing since Black women and men internalize the power structures so
that internally, as well as externally, these structures have a real and debili-

tating effect on their lives. A look must also be taken at the racist-sexist construction of Black men's sexuality.

One other point that overstating the matriarchy fails to take into account is the difference between intent and outcome. Black women did not get up one morning and say, "Let's create matrilineal systems." They worked with what they faced and often discovered incredibly creative structures to deal with it, hence the extended family. In Canada, this structure has to be recreated. It cannot continue as it did in another time and place. It may take other routes, (for example, the struggle for free universal daycare) and may look quite different in the next ten or twenty years.

Struggle for control

The struggle for Black women's control of their sexuality and for their reproductive rights is an old one. Marie Joseph Angelique, running away to live in freedom with her lover, escaped a slave owner in Montreal. She was recaptured and beaten, whereupon she escaped again, setting a fire which destroyed fifty buildings in Montreal. Marie Joseph was then hunted down, and burnt at the stake. Her refusal to be a broodmare, to have her sexuality determined by a white slave owner, defines a major theme in Black women's everyday lives from that time to the present.

During slavery, the breeding of children was the production of a commodity. It replenished the supply of enslaved labour. The free expression of sexuality was, at best, risky and usually virtually impossible. The situation of Black peoples in the Americas was not unlike that of animals caught and used for labour and breeding. Any attempt at family, at kinship, within this context was an act of resistance, of open rebellion.

In the post-emancipation period, women would still work as labourers and breeders. Women and children began to work at waged labour; former slaveholders extracted surplus value from their labour once slave labour became economically outmoded.

235

Beginning with the slave trade, the needs of capital accumulation have always been antagonistic to the sexuality and the reproductive rights of Black women. The slave trade was a key method of the primitive accumulation of capital for various emergent European capitalist countries. In England, it "rapidly carried (Liverpool) to its present state of prosperity; has occasioned vast employment for shipping and sailors, and greatly augmented the demand for the manufactures of the country" (Marx, 759).

It would appear, however, that we did not breed rapidly enough to meet the continuing demand for enslaved labour. This traffic in slaves went on long after it had been officially outlawed by international as well as national conventions.

From the days of slavery to the present, our sexuality and our reproductive rights have been systematically denied to meet the continuing need for the accumulation of capital. Where we once did not breed rapidly enough to meet the demand for enslaved labour, we are now told, along with other Third World peoples, that there are too many of us. Where we were once abused for not producing enough workers, we are now blamed when there are not enough jobs.

The testing of contraceptives in Latin America, the use of depoprovera on non-white women, the sterilization of Black women in the southern United States and in the U.S. colony of Puerto Rico, the cry that the world needs population control, all work to contain and to use the sexuality and reproductive rights of Black and other non-white women. The contradictions within this are endless. If we place the scientific experimentation with in vitro conception, frozen sperm banks, surrogate motherhood, cloning, genius sperm banks, etc., beside the experimentation on Black and Third World women, the racist-sexist underpinnings of capitalism are laid bare. The equal distribution of the world's wealth is never suggested as a solution to poverty. The powerful consortiums controlling the bulk of this wealth are not called to account. Both the use of contraception and access to abortion are important for Black women, but any external control, any exploitation of the sexuality

236

and reproductive rights of Black women is oppressive.

In 1978, ten Black women were threatened with deportation from Canada on the grounds that they had "lied" concerning their children on their entry forms. The women had come as domestic workers and were applying for landed immigrant status. They had been in Canada between five and ten years. Both the Canadian and Jamaican governments had tacitly indicated that the women should not declare their children on their entry forms. Now, they were being threatened with deportation because they wanted the children they had not declared to join them in Canada. This was one of the most publicized cases of the state's position on Black women. It shows that the state has no use for Black women outside of their function as cheap labour. That the state did not apply this rule to Back men, who just as surely had children back home whom they did not declare, reveals this case as the outcome of racist-sexist policy.

The case occurred during a time of high unemployment, a time when immigrants are usually blamed for the country's problems, rather than the blame being directed at bad economic policy and incompetent leadership. To scapegoat ten Black women in order to alleviate public pressure about the scarcity of jobs was to play up all the racist "common sense" notions which inform the culture. Another perception employed was that Black women did not have the right to have children, did not have the right to be sexual, and that punitive action would "justly" be taken if these rights were exercised. Raising the slogan "Good enough to work, good enough to stay," several groups, including the International Committee Against Racism and the Committee Against the Deportation of Immigrant Women, fought a successful campaign to have the women remain in Canada.

Socialisation and racist-sexist common sense

Black women have never been socialized to be women in the way that the dominant class and culture define women. The images and prescriptions of femininity which structure white women's lives structure Black women's lives in contradiction to their lived experience and in contradiction to white images of those Black experiences. The common sense idea of the "ultra feminine" or even of the "feminine" woman is not a construction directed at or meant to fashion only the behaviour of white women, even though they do not apply to the lived experiences of many white working-class women. "The way the gender of Black women is constructed differs from the construction of white femininity because it is also subject to racism" (Carby, 214)

"White femininity" is not only contradictory to the reality of Black women's lives, but also contradictory to white images of Black women's lives. The common sense notions about Black women's sexuality emanate from the justification for slavery and are reproduced in the workplace, in legislation and, in language.

Just as slave women were expected to sexually service the male slave owner, so too today's white male employer may feel he has the right to sexual service from "his" domestic worker. Black women employed as domestic workers on the work permit are tied to their jobs and thus reluctant to report sexual assault to either the police or immigration officials. Furthermore, the domestic worker may find herself confronted with an immigration officer who expects sexual service in payment for favourable attention to a permanent residence application. I know of a case where for a year and a half an immigration officer sexually harassed a Black woman, with the threat of deportation if she did not comply.

The state's welfare legislation also demands that Black and other working-class women must not act on their sexuality. Women living on social assistance must not only subsist on a pittance, but also must give up the right to sexual expression to receive it. Invariably, women who head single parent families and who also live in Ontario Housing projects are subject to social surveillance. This happens at Jane-Finch, at Regent Park, at Alexandra Park, and in other public housing developments. To live in public housing is to be seen to be in need of social control, to be attended by the social services, the Ontario Housing Corporation, the Children's Aid Society, the police. The emergence of the "female headed single parent family" as common coinage among white social workers came about as a result of their encounters with Black women who, in turn, woke up one day to find that they were a problem, but, it was to be hoped, one that could be solved. Redress was promptly sought for what was addressed as "the problem of single mothers," as though the mothers were the problem, and for the "problem of having children with more than one man," as though this, too, were somehow pathological. None of the institutions dealing with the "problems of single parenting" really wanted to look at the fact that working-class women in general, and Black women in particular, are paid the lowest wages, that unemployment is high among women, and that daycare costs are high and subsidies low in amount and number and granted only on a very restricted basis.

Other groups, including some that purport to be progressive, have also taken up the notion that the Black family structure is somehow deficient when compared to that of whites. As Carby points out:

> here ironically the Western nuclear family structures and related ideologies of "romantic love" formed under capitalism, are seen as more progressive than Black family structures. (Carby, 215-216)

Accommodating and supporting this denial of our right to determine our sexuality is the language of the dominant culture. This language had embedded within it the exploitation of Black peoples and the basic characterizations of Black women as chattel and thus inherently animal. These characterizations are consistently and constantly expressed and reconstructed in the media's treatment of Black women. We exist in the media primarily as objects of illicit pleasure; in advertisements for the Caribbean, "It's better in the Bahamas," in popular songs, "Down in Jamaica they got lots of pretty women, they steal you money and break your heart," in the coverage of government ministers' sybaritic visits to the Caribbean, in last summer's

Toronto Sun caricature of a busty Black woman strolling past a group of white men drooling, "Is that ever a visible minority!"

Meanwhile, within the Black community there are other and contradictory common sense notions operating. On the one hand, Black men see Black women as "stiff, unyielding, straightlaced," and "not wanting to give of the pussy"; on the other hand, sometimes because of these ascriptions, Black men embrace our strength, but believe it less valuable, because, having also been sexually characterized as animals, they do not value themselves.

Even more contradictory is Black women's socialization as "strong" when all about them "weakness" in women continues to be glorified. This particular contradiction is invariably resolved on the side of strength: its alternative can only be the destruction of one's well-being and that of one's children. Black women are also told by their socialization that they are inferior as women, that they are "unfeminine." Ironically, resistance to this perception has precipitated the copying of white women's exploitation: hence, the Miss Black Ontario, the Miss Black Quebec and the Miss Black America beauty pageants. Witness the community's unbridled joy at Miss America being Black in 1984. The preponderance of Black cosmetic, beauty and hairdressing shops, their windows full of Caucasian-looking Black woman, is further evidence of the white feminization of Black women.

Nonetheless, the internalization of white femininity is neither uniform nor without resistance. The cultural wing of the Black Power movement of the 1960s and 1970s addressed the self-hate implied in the white feminization of Black women. As a result, Black women began to wear their hair natural and stopped wearing cosmetics. They also began to speak out against the exploitation and belittling of Black women. Since that time, the cultural movement has undergone various convolutions. Once "Black is beautiful" was picked up by capitalist interests, Black beauty aids began to appear in the store, and the trend is back to the assiduous copying of white femininity. Now we have the "new natural." It requires the straightening of the hair, followed by a permanent, and then a plethora of moisturizers, conditioners, fixers and relaxers, along with frequent and costly trips to the hair-dresser.

But this can only teach us more about struggle. It teaches us that there is a co-opting character to advanced capitalism. As we organize, as we develop oppositional cultural forms, advanced capitalism is able to reshape those forms. It does this through its own cultural and material resources which manifest themselves in tokenism and other innovations. These attempts at co-optation leave the basic structures which oppress us intact while giving the appearance of change.

Black women in Toronto have a history of organizing against imperialism and racism and against class and gender oppression. As these sites of struggle are revealed, feminist theory and practice will be deepened and energized. Black community groups and organizations have developed under the leadership of women: the Black Heritage Programme, the Black Workers' Group, African Liberation Support Committees, the Rastafarian Cultural Workshop, the Immigrant Women's Job Placement Centre, and the Organization of Parents of Black Children, to name a very few. Women's groups and coalitions include the Congress of Black Women, the African Sisterhood Organisation, Black Working Women, the Committee Against the Deportation of Immigrant Women and the Coalition of Visible Minority Women. Most Black women who are political activists in Canada had their grounding in the African Liberation and other anti-imperialist movements and were part of the Black Power movement.

That Black women will continue to organize against racism and sexism is certain. We cannot afford to pull back. But we have to do more or risk losing the little ground we hold. We have to build on existing analyses, to strategize, to draw out of our culture, as Black women, the instruments of political struggle. We cannot live under the present system; it exploits and degrades us. Given the locations of our oppression, our struggle is by nature working-class, anti-sexist, anti-racist, and anti-imperialist. It is to be fought in the factories and the offices, in the houses we clean for a living, in our homes, and against state legislation, and capitalism.

Endnotes and References

Returning the Gaze: An Introduction
Himani Bannerji

Endnotes

[1] Smith, D.E. Smith. "Feminist Reflections on Political Economy", *Studies in Political Economy*, vol. 30, Autumn 89, 37-59.

[2] Minh-ha, Trinh T. *Women, Native, Other*, (Indiana, University Press), Bloomington, Indiana U.S. 1989, 4-6.

[3] Smith, Dorothy E. "Introduction", *Conceptual Practices of Power. A Feminist Sociology of Knowledge*, University of Toronto Press, Toronto, Canada, 1990,

[4] Smith, D. E. "Everyday World As Problematic: A Feminist Methodology" in *The Everyday World as Problematic: A Feminist Sociology*, University of Toronto Press, Toronto, Canada, 105-145.

[5] Jordon, June. "Black Studies: Bringing Back the Person" in *Moving Towards Home; Political Essays*, (U.K., Virago), 1989, 25.

[6] Mohanty, Chandra T. "Introduction" in *Third World Women and Politics Of Feminism*, C.T. Mohanty, A. Russo and L. Torres, eds., Indiana University Press, Bloomington and Indianapolis, U.S., 1991, 1-47.

[7] Hamilton, Roberta and Michele Barrett. eds., see "Introduction" to *The Politics of Diversity*, (London, Verso), 1989.

[8] Mohanty, Chandra T. "Under Western Eyes Feminist Scholarship and Colonial Discourses", in *Third World Women and the Politics of Feminism*, 51-80.

Finding The Way Home Through Issues of Gender, Race and Class
May Yee

Endnotes

[1] The "Chinese Exclusion Act" refers to the immigration law enacted by the

Canadian government from 1923 to 1947, which effectively halted Chinese immigration to Canada. This had followed the racist Head Tax Laws which were started after 1885 (the year the national railway, built by Chinese workers, was completed), which required only Chinese immigrants to pay a head tax on entry. By 1904 Chinese Head Tax was $500, about two years' wages. Since 1985 a campaign for redress for the Chinese Exclusion Act and Head Tax has been led by the Chinese Canadian National Council (CCNC). For general information on Chinese Canadian history, a good book is Anthony Chan's (Vancouver: New Star Books, 1983).

[2] *Jin Guo: Voices of Chinese Canadian Women* (Toronto, Women's Press) 1992 is an oral history book edited by the CCNC's Women's Book Committee. The title "Jin Guo" is from a traditional Chinese proverb, a reference that women are no less strong than men.

[3] Ibid.

[4] "Who Killed Vincent Chin?" is a powerful Asian American documentary film by Christina Choi, about a Chinese American autoworker who was murdered in Detroit by two laid-off white auto-workers, who blamed the Japanese for losing their jobs. The two men, a father and son, were eventually acquitted by U.S. courts.

A Jewel in the Frown: Striking Accord Between India/n Feminists
Anita Sheth and Amita Handa

Endnotes

[1] This title was suggested by Punam Khosla.

[2] We have printed the term "India/n" in this way to avoid confusion with First Nations people of North America who are frequently referred to as "Indian" in the Canadian lexicon. The slash in the term is used to highlight reference to people from both the country "India" and the diaspora.

[3] The difference between "racism" and "racialism" as Sivanandan notes is that the latter "refers to attitudes, behavior, `race relations'; [while the former] is the systematization of these into an explicit ideology of racial superiority and their institutionalization in the state apparatus" (1987, p.170). The material differential power exercised by the white group over non-white groups justified either on the grounds of genetic science, capitalism, Catholicism, and/or Euro-

American socio-cultural value systems produces everyday racism - daily fueling the ideology of white supremacy and its practices of exploitation by racial discrimination. In internalizing the relations that serve to exploit and racially rate us to maintain the racist white supremacist ideology, non-white groups unwittingly assist in the very practices that are designed by whites to exclude, exploit, harass and demean all non-white people. Racialism then, though not having the same material differential power relations of white racism, carries its own discriminatory procedures wherein "not so coloured non-whites" exploit the "unmistakably coloured non-whites." We maintain that racism is the (white) ideology and racialism the attitude; that racism is the (white) action that drives the practices of racialism.

[4] This point was made by Punam Khosla, personal communication, Toronto 1992

[5] This point was made by Rinaldo Walcott, personal communication, Toronto, 1992

[6] The crucial difference between the caste system of India and the colour system of South Africa, for example, is that the former is "legitimized by cultural-religious criteria," while the latter is "legitimized by so-called `racial' criteria" (Sivanandan, 1987 (164). To characterize the two systems as if they were one and the same is misleading, not to mention historically false. As Sivanandan argues, "caste relations in India grew organically out of caste functions of labour [in pre-capitalist formations]. They were relations of production predicated by the level of the productive forces but determined by Hindu ideology and polity...South Africa, however, has caste relations without ever having had a caste function. Such relations have not grown out of a pre-capitalist mode; nor are they relations of production stemming from the capitalist mode. They are, instead, social relations enforced by the state to demarcate racial groups with a view of differential exploitation within a capitalist system" (165). He expands, "[South Africa's] caste system bears an uncanny resemblence to the Hindu caste system of medieval India, though we know them to be inspired by Calvinism, the religion capital. It combines...the Afrikaners' fundamentalist racialism with the instrumentalist racism of British imperialism", (167).

[7] Sherene Razack, professor in Adult Education, in conversation, Toronto, Ontario Institute for Studies in Education, 1992.

[8] This song was one of eight that made it to the calypso music festival finals, competing for a first prize of Bds $15,000. This competition was presented by CBC TV Barbados in association with the National Cultural Foundation.

References

Uma Chakravarti. "Whatever Happened to the Vedic Dasi? Orientalism, Nationalism and a Script for the Past", Kum Kum Sangari and Sudesh Vaid, eds., *Recasting Women: Essays in Colonial History*. New Delhi: Kali for Women, 1989.

Linda Carty. "Black Women in Academia.", Himani Bannerji, Linda Carty, Susan Heald, Kari Dehli and Kate McKenna, eds., *Unsettling Relations: The University as a Site of Feminist Struggles*. (Toronto, Women's Press), 1991.

Robert Blauner. "The Ambiguities of Racial Change.", Margaret Anderson and Patricia Hill Collins eds., *Race, Class and Gender: An Anthology*, (California, Wadsworth Publishing), 1992.

Frantz Fanon. "The Fact of Blackness" ed. David Theo Goldberg. *Anatomy of Racism*, (Minneapolis, University of Minnesota Press), 1990.

bell hooks (Gloria Watkins). "Sisterhood: Political Solidarity Between Women" Sneja Gunew, ed., *A Reader in Feminist Knowledge*, (London, Routledge), 1991.

Hanif Kureshi. *The Buddha of Suburbia*, (London, Penguin Books), 1991.

Audre Lorde. *Sister/Outsider* , (New York, The Crossing Press), 1984.

Biddy Martin and Chandra Talpade Mohanty. "Feminist Politics: What's Home Got to Do With It?" Teresa de Lauretis ed., *Feminist Studies, Cultural Studies*, (Bloomington, Indiana University Press), 1986.

Trinh Minh-ha. *Woman, Native, Other: Writing Post-Coloniality and Feminism*, (Bloomington, Indiana University Press), 1989.

Cherrie Moraga. "La Guera." Margaret Anderson and Patricia Hill Collins, ed., *Race, Class and Gender: An Anthology*. (California, Wadsworth Publishing), 1992.

Minnie Bruce Pratt. "Identity: Skin, Blood, Heart." Elly Bulkin, Minnie Bruce Pratt and Barbara Smith, eds.. *Yours in Struggle: Three Feminist Perspectives on Anti-Semitism and Racism*, (New York, Firebrand), 1984.

Gayatri Chakravorty Spivak. *The Post-Colonial Critic: Interviews, Strategies, Dialogues*, Sarah Harasym ed., (New York, Routledge), 1990.

A. Sivanandan. *A Different Hunger: Writings on Black Resistance*, (London, Pluto Press), 1987, 2nd edition.

Alice Walker. *In Search of Our Mother's Gardens*, (New York, Harcourt Brace Jovanovich), 1983.

Storytelling for Social Change
Sherene Razack

Endnotes

[1] I have used the word ethnical to describe a collective reflection on the moral values we each hold. An ethical vision informs our politics in the sense that it is a shared sense of what is right and wrong.

References

Norma Alarcon. "The Thoretical Subject(s) of This Bridge Called My Back and Anglo-American Feminism" in *Making Face Making Soul*, Gloria Anzaldua, ed., 1990.

Gloria Anzaldua. ed., *Making Face, Making Soul. Haciendo Caras*, (San Francisco, C.A. Aunt Lute Foundation Books), 1990.

Gloria Anzaldua. *Borderlands/La Frontera* (San Francisco, Spinsters/Aunt Lute), 1987.

Bettina Aptiieker. *Tapestries of Life*, (Amherst, University of Massachusetts Press), 1989.

Richard Brosio. "Teaching and learning for democratic empowerment: A critical evaluation", *Educational Theory* 40(1), 68-81.

Kimberle Crenshaw. "Whose story is it anyway?" in *Race-ing Justice Engendering Power*, Toni Morrison ed., "Essay on Anita Hill, Clarence Thomas, and The Construction of Social Reality", 402-440, (New York, Pantheon), 1992.

Richard Delgado. "When a story is just a story: Does voice really matter?" *Virginia Law Review*, 76(9), 1990, 95-111.

Elizabeth Ellsworth. "Why doesn't this feel empowering? Working through the repressive myths of critical pedagogy", *Harvard Educational Review*, 59(3), 1989, 297-324.

Paulo Freire. *Pedagogy of the Oppressed*, (New York, The Continuum Publishing Corp.), 1970, republished 1984.

Gayle Green and Copelia Kahn. "Feminist Scholarship and the Social Construction of Woman", in *Making a Difference*, Feminist Literary Criticism, (London, Routledge), 1985, 1-36.

Methcild Hart. "Critical theory and beyond: further perspectives on emancipatory education", *Adult Education Quarterly*, 40(3), 1990, 125-138.

Maria Lugones. "Hablano cara a cara/Speaking face to face" in *Making Face, Making Soul*, (1989), 46-54.

Salomon Magendzo. "Popular education in non-governmental organizations: Education for social mobilization", *Harvard Educational Review*, 60(1), 1990, 49-61.

Toni M. Massaro. "Empathy, legal story-telling, and the rule of law: New words, Old wounds", *Michigan Law Review*, 89, 1989, 2099-2127.

Mari J. Matsuda. "Looking to the bottom: Critical legal studies and reparations", *Harvard Civil Rights-Civil Liberties Law Review*, 22, 1987, 322-399.

Mari J. Matsuda. "Public response to racist speech: Considering the victim's story", *Michigan Law Review*, 87, 1989, 2320-2381.

Carrie Meadow Menkel. "Portia in a different voice: Speculations on a woman's lawyering process", *Berkeley Woman's Law Journal*, 1, 1985, 39-63.

Uma Narayan, "Working Across Differences", *Hypatia*, 3(2), 1988, 31-47

Charles Paine. "Relativism, Radical Pedagogy and the Ideology of Paralysis", *College English*, 50, 6, 1989, 557-570.

Sherene Razack. *Canadian Feminism and the Law: The Women's Legal Education and Action Fund and the Pursuit of Equality*, (Toronto, Second Story Press), 1991.

Kim Lane Scheppele. "Foreword: Telling Stories", *Michigan Law Review* 87, 1989, 2073-2098.

Gayatri Chakravorty Spivak. *The Post-Colonial Critic. Interviews, Strategies,*

Dialogues, Sarah Harasym ed., (New York & London, Routledge), 1990.

Carolyn Steedman. *Landscape For a Good Woman*, (London, Virago), 1986.

Minh-Ha T. Trinh. *Woman, Native, Other*, (Bloomington, Indiana University Press), 1989.

Minh-Ha T. Trinh. "Not You/Like You: Post-colonial women and the interlocking questions of identity and difference", in *Making Face, Making Soul*, 1989, 371-375.

Lynet Uttal. "Nods that silence", in *Making Face, Making Soul*, 1989, 317-320.

Valerie Walkerdine. "On the regulation of speaking and silence.Subjectively, class and gender" in *Contemporary Schooling, Language, Gender and Childhood* Carolyn Steedman, ed., (London, Routledge & Kegan Paul), 1985, 203-341.

Kathleen Weiler. *Women, Teaching for Change, Gender Class and Power* (New York, Bergin & Garvey), 1988.

Robin West. "Jurisprudence and gender", *University of Chicago Law Review*, 55(1), 1988, 1-72.

Iris Marion Young. *Justice and the Politics of Difference* (Princeton, Princeton University Press), 1990.

Ricardo Zuniga. "La Gestion Amphibie", *Revue internationale d'action communautaire*, 19, 1988, 157-167.

Re-imaging Racism: South Asian Canadian Women Writers
Aruna Srivastava

References

Meena Alexander. "The Poem's Second Life: Writing and Self-Identity," *Toronto South Asian Review*, Fall-Winter 1987-88, 77-85.

Himani Bannerji. "doing time", *Doing Time: Poems*. (Toronto, Sister Vision Press), 1986, 9-11

Himani Bannerji. "Paki Go Home." *Doing Time: Poems*. (Toronto, Sister Vision Press), 1986, 15.

Himani Bannerji. "A Savage Aesthetic." *In A Separate Sky*. (Toronto, Domestic Bliss), 1982, 46-47.

Madeline Coopsammy. "The Second Migration." *Kunapipi* 8, 2, 1986, 72-73.

Diana Fuss. *Essentially Speaking: Feminism, Nature & Difference*, (London, Routledge), 1989.

Lakshmi Gill. "Song". *Her First Cleaning (an immigrant's tour of life): poems*, (Maria Estaniel Press), 1972, 6.

Nila Gupta. "So She Could Walk." Silvera, Makeda. ed. *Best of Fireweed*. (Toronto, The Women's Press), 1986.

Jamila Ismail.. *From the Diction Air*. Unpublished chapboo, 1989.

Surjeet Kalsey. "Farm Worker Women". *Footprints of Silence: Poems*. (London, Third Eye), 1988.

Trinh T. Minh-ha. "Introduction." *Discourse* 11, 2, Spring-Summer 1989, 5,18.

Arun Mukherjee. "South Asian Poetry in Canada: In Search of a Place". *Towards a Aesthetic of Opposition*. (Stratford, Williams-Wallace), 1988.

Bharati Mukherjee and Clark Blaise. *Days and Nights in Calcutta*. (Garden City, Doubleday), 1977.

Bharati Mukherjee. "Introduction." *Darkness*. (Markham, Penguin), 1985.

Bharati Mukherjee."An Invisible Woman." *Saturday Night*, March 1981, 36-40.

Bharati Mukherjee."Tamurlane." *Darkness*. (Markham, Penguin), 1985.

Suniti Namjoshi. "How to be a Foreigner." *More Poems*. (Calcutta, Winters Workshop), 1971.

Uma Parameswaran. Untitled poem. *Toronto South Asian Review* 1,3 1982,15.

Gayatri Chakravorty Spivak. *In Other Worlds*. New York: Methuen, 1987.

Right Out of "Herstory": Racism in Charlotte Perkins Gilman's *Herland* and Feminist Literary Theory
Arun P. Mukherjee

Endnotes

[1] Gilbert, Susan M. and Sandra Gubar. "Introduction: The Female Imagination and the Modern Aesthetic," *Women's Studies*, 13, 1986, 10.

[2] Gilbert and Gubar. "The Man on the Dump Versus the United Dames of America or What Does Frank Lentricchia Want?", *Critical Inquiry*, 14, 2, 1988, 389.

[3] Mulvey, Laura Mulvey. "Visual Pleasure and Narrative Cinema," *Screen* 16, 3, 6-18 Annette Kuhn, *Women's Pictures: Feminism and Cinema*, (London, Routledge and Kegan Paul), 1982; Judith Fetterley, *The Resisting Reader: A Feminist Approach to American Fiction* (Bloomington, Indiana University Press) 1977, reprinted 1978.

[4] Burke, Kenneth. *Counter Statement*, (Berkeley and Los Angeles, University of California Press) 1931, 1968 147.

[5] Freibert, Lucy M., "World Views in Utopian Novels by Women", in *Women from Utopia: Critical Interpretations*, Marlene Barr and Nicholas D. Smith eds., (Lanham, University Press of America), 1983, 67.

[6] Gilman, Perkins Charlotte. *Herland*, with an Introduction by Ann J. Lane, (New York, Pantheon Books), 1979, 48.

[7] Spivak, Gayatri Chakravorty, "Three Women's Texts and a Critique of Imperialism" in *Race Writing and Difference* ed. Henry Louis Gattes Jr. ed., (Chicago, University of Chicago Press), 1986, 27. The same volume also includes Abdul R. JanMohamed's "The Economy of Manichean Allegory: The function of racial difference in colonialist literature", 78-106. "Imaginary texts," says JanMohamed, "like fantasies which provide naive solutions to the subjects basic problems, tend to centre themselves on plots that end with the elimination of the offending natives." (86). I might note here that I arrived at a similar reading of the Western popular cinema in the "Third World Viewer" in my *Towards an Aesthetic of Opposition: Essays on Literature Criticism and*

Cultural Imperialism (Stratford, Williams-Wallace Publishers), 1988, 100-8.

[8] In Peter Abrahams', *The View From Coyaba*, (London, Faber & Faber), 1985, 117; David Drown the black pastor, says: "It is not enough to take what is mine. You want me to tell you it is right for you to do it."

[9] hooks, bell. *Ain't I A Woman: Black Women and Feminism*, (Boston, South End Press), 1981, 1984, 85.

[10] Gilman, "Women, And Economics: A Study of the Economic Relation Between Men and Women as a Factor" in *Social Evolution*, (London, G.P. Putnam's Sons), 1899, 1920, 134.

[11] Ibid., 136.

[12] Gilman, "With Her In Ourland", serialized in *Forerunner*, 7 1916:42.

[13] Flexner, Eleanor. *Century of Struggle the Women's Rights Movement in the United States*, 1959, revised ed. (Cambridge, Belknap Press of Harvard University Press) 1975, 1982, 239.

[14] Gilman, *Women and Economics*, 147.

[15] Ibid., 169.

[16] Showalter, Elaine. *A Literature of Their Own: British Women Novelists from Bronte to Lessing*, (Princeton, Princeton University Press), 1977, 4.

[17] Davis, Angela Y. *Women, Race and Class*. (New York, Vintage Books), 1983, See chapters 3 and 4.

[18] Hewitt, Nancy A. "Beyond The Search For Sisterhoood American Women's History in the 1980s" *Social History*, 10:3, October, 1985, 302.

[19] Ibid., 301.

[20] hooks, *Ain't I A Woman*, 121.

[21] Although the subtitle of Gilbert and Gubar's *No Man's Land* (New Haven and London, Yale University Press), 1988, purports to be the place of the women writer in the twentieth century, the book devotes only a few paragraphs to Zora Neale Hurston and Ann Petry, just as their Norton Anthology of literature by

women marginalizes non-white women by devoting only token space to them. However, since they discuss these non-white women only in terms of gender conflict, they fail to note the anti-racist, anti-colonial and anti-capitalist stance of these writers. I agree with Frank Lentricchia's assessment of Gilbert and Gubar being authors of Manichean sexual allegory because they completely ignore these other, fundamentally important aspects of texts of non-white women. See Lentricchia, Andiamo. *Critical Inquiry*, 14:2, Winter, 1988:409.

22 Showalter, Elaine. "Mr. Horse and Mrs. Eohippus", *London Review of Books*, 30, January, 1992, 20.

23 Baca Zinn, Maxine, Lynn Weber Canon, Elizabeth Higginbotham, and Bonnie Thornton Dill, "The Cost of Exclusionary Practices in Women's Studies", *Signs*, 11, 21 Winter, 1986, 295.

Popular Images of South Asian Women
Himani Bannerji

Endnotes

1See Ernesto LaClau, *Politics and Ideology in Marxist Theory*, (London, Verso,) 1979, for discussions of the articulation process.

2The name of the ship which carried Sikhs to Vancouver in 1914. The Canadian government would not allow them to disembark, and prevented water and supplies from reaching the ship.

Thinking through Angela Y. Davis's *Women, Race & Class*
Cecilia Green

Endnotes

1 Flexner, Eleanor. *A Century of Struggle: The Woman's Rights Movement in the United States.* (Massachusetts, Belknap Press of Harvard University Press), 1959.

2 Wallace, Michele. *Black Macho and the Myth of the Superwoman.* (New York,

Dial Press), 1979.

[3] Genovese, Eugene. *Roll, Jordan, Roll: The World Slaves Made.* (New York, Pantheon Books), 1974. Genovese also seems to be arguing that the white Southern planters made fanatastic and heroic masters.

[4] Gutman, Herbert. *The Black Family in Slavery and Freedom, 1750-1925.* (New York, Pantheon Books), 1976. Gutman's thesis has more grassroots and radical appeal than Genovese's.

[5] Hare, Nathan. "Revolution Without Revolution: The Psychosociology of Sex and Race." *The Black Scholar* 7, April 1978, 2-7.

[6] Sudarkasa, Niara Sudarkasa. "African and Afro-American Family Structure: A Comparison." *The Black Scholar* 8, Nov./Dec. 1980, 37-60.

"Visible Minority" Women A Creation of the Canadian State
Linda Carty and Dionne Brand

Endnotes

[1] Miliband, Ralph. *The State in Capitalist Society,* (London, Quartet Books), 1969, 50.

[2] Therborn, Goran. *What Does the Ruling Class Do When It Rules?* (London:, Verso), 1980 150.

[3] Ralph Miliband, 64.

[4] This class fraction, while it has cleavages with the working class, cannot be said to be of the working class. It is more easily discernible by its role in capitalist production. While not actively involved in productive labour, it is situated within the rationalization of labour through administrative processes. See N. Poulantzas, *Classes in Contemporary Capitalism* (London, Verso), 1978, Part Two.

[5] Ironically, it is through these "grassroots" organizations that the state became aware of the needs of immigrants and racial groupings. Many of these organizations became victims of bureaucratization and many suffered divisions among their membership during the process and eventually folded.
[6] Three years later, at the planning meeting for the founding conference of

[6] Three years later, at the planning meeting for the founding conference of NOIMVM, the "Visible Minority" women had to fight for inclusion into this national immigrant women's organization. By now, "Immigrant" meant white immigrant and "Visible Minority" meant everyone else.

[7] It is not inconceivable that in the future, state-initiated organizations such as NOIMVM and OCVMW would receive much state funding since their aims and objectives would be tailored to those expected of them by the state.

Sexism, Racism, Canadian Nationalism
Roxana Ng

Endnotes

[1] See, for example, the charge of racism by native and black women of Toronto's International Women's Day Committee IWDC in 1986 and the subsequent debates in socialist feminist publications such as *Cayenne* in 1986 and 1987.

[2] See Karl Marx *Das Capital*, vol. 1 (Moscow, Progress publishers), 1954 and *The Metaphysics of Political Economy: The Method, Writings of the young Marx on Philosophy and Society*, Lloyd Easton and Kurt Guddat eds., (New York, Anchor Books), 1967 475-495. For a critique of contemporary Marxists and a concise discussion of Marx's method see Derek Sayer, *Marx's Method, Ideology, Science and Critique in Capital*, (Sussex, The Harvester Press), 1979; (New Jersey, Humanities Press), 1983.

[3] Sandra Harding has called this the standpoint approach in her book *The Science Question in Feminism*, (Ithaca, Cornell University Press), 1986. The major proponents of this approach according to Harding are Nancy Hartsock and Dorothy Smith. See Nancy C. M. Hartsock, *Money, Sex and Power:Toward a Feminist Historical Materialism*, (Boston, Northeastern University Press), 1983 and 1985 and Dorothy Smith, *The Everyday World as Problematic. A Feminist Sociology* (Toronto, University of Toronto Press) 1987. While both Hartsock and Smith insist on the primacy of women's standpoint in social analysis, their theories differ in important ways. The way I make use of their work is to begin from the experiences of women of colour and to situate their experiences in the social organization of Canadian society. I make no claim to follow their theories exegetically. See Roxana Ng, "Immigrant Housewives in Canada: A Methodological Note," *Atlantis* 8:1 1982 111-118.

[4] See various Ontario Ministry of Education documents released since the mid-

Ethnocultural Equity," Report of the Provincial Advisory Committee on Race Relations, September 1987.

[5] See Mary Mcintosh, "The State and the Oppression of Women" in *Feminism and Materialism. Women and Modes of Production*, Annette Kuhn and Annmarie Wolpe, eds. (London, Routledge and Kegan Paul), 1978, 254-289.

[6] Corrigan, Philip., ed., *Ethnic Canada: Identities and Inequalities* (Toronto, Copp Clark Pitman), 1987, 6.

[7] Driedger, Leo., ed., *Ethnic Canada. Identities and Inequalities* (Toronto, Copp Clark Pitman), 1987, 6.

[8] For example, Oliver C. Cox, *Caste, Class and Race: A Study in Social Dynamics* (Garden City, Doubleday), 1948.

[9] Depres, Leo., ed. Ethnicity and Resource Competition (The Hague, Mouton) 1975.

[10] See, for example, Peter C. Pineo, "The Social Standing of Ethnic and Racial Groupings," *Canadian Review of Sociology and Anthropology*, 12:2, 1977, 147-157; Peter C. Pineo and John Porter, "Ethnic Origin and Occupational Attainment" in *Ascription and Achievement: Studies in Mobility and Status Attainment in Canada*, M. Boyd, J. Goyder, F.E. Jones, P.C. Pineo and J. Porter, eds. (Ottawa, Carleton University Press), 1985.

[11] This term is borrowed from Pierre L. Vanderberghe, *The Ethnic Phenomenon* (New York, Elsevier), 1981.

[12] See Edward Said, *Orientalism* (New York, Vintage Books), 1979, 2.

[13] For a critique see Dorothy E. Smith, "Feminist Reflections on Political Economy Paper presented at the annual meeting of Political Science and Political Economy, Learned Societies Meetings, Hamilton, June 1987.

[14] See Roxana Ng, "Sex, Ethnicity or Class: Some Methodological Consideration Studies" in *Sexual Politics* 1 1984, endnotes 1 and 3 for a discussion on the exclusion of gender from ethnic studies.

[15] For a review, see Danielle Juteau-Lee and Barbara Roberts, "Ethnicity and Femininity (D') Apres nos experiences", *Canadian Ethnic Studies* 13:1 1981 1-23.

[16] Ibid.

[17] See Karl Marx and F. Engels, *The Communist Manifesto*, (Penguin Books), 1967 translated by Samuel Moore, first published 1888, and *The German Ideology*, (New York, International Publishers), 1970.

[18] Braverman, Harry. *Labour and Monopoly Capital the Degradation of Work in the Twentieth Century*, (New York and London, Monthly Review Press), 1974, 24.

[19] Weber, Max. *Economy and Society*, (New York, Bedminister), 1968 first published in 1922, 389.

[20] Ng, Roxana and Judith Ramirez. *Immigrant Housewives in Canada*, (Toronto, Immigrant Women's Centre), 1981.

[21] Smith, Dorothy E. "Women, Class and Family" in Women, Class, Family and the State" by Varda Burstyn and Dorothy E. Smith, (Toronto, Garamond Press), 1985.

[22] See the works of Dorothy E. Smith cited in this paper; lectures given by David Mole in the Dept. of Sociology Ontario Institute for Studies in Education 1979-80; and Derek Sayer Marx's *Method*.

[23] See for example Anthony B. Chan *The Gold Mountain: The Chinese in the New World*, (Vancouver, New Star Books), 1983.

[24] See Alma Estable, "Immigrant Women in Canada: Current Issues" (A background paper prepared for the Canadian Advisory Council on the Status of Women), March 1986. Angela W. Djao and Roxana Ng, *Structured Isolation Immigrant Women in Saskatchewan* in Women Isolation and Bonding the Ecology of Gender Kathleen Storrie, ed. (Toronto, Methuen) 1987, 141-158.

[25] See Kathleen Jamieson, *Indian Women and the Law in Canada Citizens Minus*, (Ottawa, Advisory Council on the Status of Women and Indian Rights for Indian Women), April 1978.

[26] See Barbara Roberts, "Ladies Women and the State: Managing Female Immigration, 1880-1920" in *Community Organization and the Canadian State*, Roxana Ng, Gillian Walker and Jacob Muller eds. (Toronto, Garamond Press, forthcoming); Jackie Lay, "To Columbia on the Tynemouth: The Emigration of Single Women and Girls in 1862" in *In Her Own Right: Selected Essays on Women's History in B.C.*, Barbara Latham and Cathy Kess, eds., (Victoria, Camosum College), 1980, 19-42.

[27] See Karl Dehli, "Women in the Community Reform of Schooling and Motherhood" in *Toronto, Community Organization and the Canadian State*, Anna Davin, "Imperialism and Motherhood", *History Workshop* 5, 1978, 9-65 for discussion on a similar phenomenon in Britain.

[28] See Barbara Roberts, "Ladies Women and the State"; Dorothy E. Smith, "Women's Inequality and the Family" in *Inequality Essays on the Political Economy of Social Welfare*, Allan Moscovitch and Glenn Drover eds., (Toronto, University of Toronto Press), 1985, 156-198.

[29] Kinsmen, Gary. *The Regulation of Desire Sexuality in Canada* (Montreal, Black Rose Books), 1987.

[30] See T.W. Acheson *Saint John: The Making of a Colonial Urban Community* (Toronto, University of Toronto Press), 1985.

[31] Armstrong, Frederick H. "Ethnicity and the Formation of the Ontario Establishment", *Ethnic Canada*, p 290.

[32] Porter, John. *The Vertical Mosaic*, (Toronto, University of Toronto Press), 1967.

[33] For example, Anthony Richmond, "Ethnic Nationalism and Postindustrialism" in *Two Nations, Many Cultures: Ethnic Groups in Canada*, (Second edition), Jean Leonard Elliot, ed., (Scarborough, Prentice-Hall Canada), 1983; Joan Nagel, "The Ethnic Revolution: Emergence of Ethnic Nationalism" in *Ethnic Canada*.

[34] For a critique of sociology see Dorothy E. Smith, 'Women's Perspective as a Radical Critique of Sociology", *Sociological Inquiry*, 44:1, 1974, 7-13; for a critique of political economy, see Dorothy E. Smith, "Feminist Reflections on Political Economy".

[35] Chan, Anthony B., *Gold Mountain*.

[36] This term is used by Adrienne Rich to describe the institution of heterosexuality which discourages and stifles intimate relationships among women. See Adrienne Rich, "Compulsory Heterosexuality and Lesbian Existence in *The Signs Reader - Women, Gender and Scholarship*, Elizabeth Abel and Emily K. Abel, eds., (Chicago, University of Chicago Press), 1983, 139-168.

[37] In examining racism embodied in feminist praxis, Himani Bannerji calls this form of racism "common sense racism." See Himani Bannerji, "Introducing Racism: Notes Towards and Anti-Racist feminism", *Resources for Feminist Research*, 16:1, 1987, 10-12.

References

T.W. Acheson, *Saint John: The Making of a Colonial Urban Community*. (Toronto, University of Toronto Press), 1985.

Frederick H. Armstrong "Ethnicity and the Formation of the Ontario Establishment." *Ethnic Canada: Identities and Inequalities*. Leo Driedger, ed. (Toronto, Copp Clark Pittman), 1987.

Himani Bannerji. "Introducing Racism: Notes Towards and Anti-Racist Feminism", *Resources for Feminist Research* 16/1 (1987): 10-12.

Harry Braverman. *Labor and Monopoly Capital: The Degradation of Work in the Twentieth Century*. (New York and London, Monthly Review Press), 1974.

Anthony B. Chan. *The Gold Mountain: The Chinese in the New World*. (Vancouver, New Star Books), 1983.

Philip Corrigan. ed. *Capitalism, State Formation and Marxist Theory*. (London, Quarter Books), 1980.

Oliver C. Cox. *Caste, Class and Race: A Study in Social Dynamics*. (Garden City, Doubleday), 1948.

Anna Davin. "Imperialism and Motherhood." *History Workshop* 5 (1978): 9-65.

Kari Dehli. "Women in the Community: Reform of Schooling and Motherhood in Toronto." *Community Organization and the Canadian State*. Roxana Ng, Gillian Walker and Jacob Muller, eds. (Toronto, Garamond Press) forthcoming.

Leo Depre. ed. *Ethnicity and Resource Competition*. The Hague: Mouton, 1975.

Angela W. Djao and Roxana Ng. "Structured Isolation: Immigrant Women in Saskatchewan." *Women, Isolation and Bonding: The Ecology of Gender*. Kathleen Storrie, ed. (Toronto, Methuen), 1987, 141-158.

Leo Driedger. ed. *Ethnic Canada: Identities and Inequalities*. (Toronto, Copp Clark Pittman), 1987.

Alma Estable. "Immigrant Women in Canada, Current Issues." A

Background Paper prepared for the Canadian Advisory Council on the Status of Women, March 1986.

Sandra Harding.*The Science Question in Feminism.* (Ithaca, Cornell University Press), 1986.

Nancy C.M. Hartsock. *Money, Sex and Power: Toward a Feminist Historical Materialism.* (Boston, Northeastern University Press), 1983 and 1985.

Kathleen Jamieson. *Indian Women and the Law in Canada: Citizens Minus.* Ottawa: Advisory Council on the Status of Women and Indian Rights for Indian Women, April 1978.

Danielle Juteau-Lee and Barbara Roberts. "Ethnicity and Femininity (d') apres non experiences." *Canadian Ethnic Studies* 13/1 (1981): 1-23.

Gary Kinsmen. *The Regulation of Desire: Sexuality in Canada.* (Montreal, Black Rose Books), 1987.

Jackie Lay. "To Columbia on the Tynemouth: The Emigration of Single Women and Girls in 1862." *In In Her Own Right: Selected Essays on Women's History in B.C.* Barbara Latham and Cathy Kess, eds. (Victoria, Camosum College), 1980, 19-42.

Karl Marx. *Das Capital.* Vol.1. (Moscow, Progress Publishers), 1954.

Karl Marx. "The Metaphysics of Political Economy: The Method". *Writings of the Young Marx on Philosophy and Society.* Lloyd Easton and Kurt Guddat, eds. (New York, Anchor Books), 1967: 475-495.

Karl Marx and F. Engels. *The Communist Manifesto,* translated by Samuel Moore. (Penguin Books), 1967.

Karl Marx and F. Engels. *The German Ideology.* (New York: International Publishers), 1970.

Mary McIntosh. "The State and the Oppression of Women", *Feminism and Materialism: Women and Modes of Production.* Annette Kuhn and AnnMarie Wolpe, eds. (London, Routledge and Kegan Paul), 1978, 254-289.

Joan Nagel. "The Ethnic Revolution: Emergence of Ethnic Nationalism." *Ethnic Canada: Identities and Inequalities.* Leo Driedger, ed. (Toronto, Copp Clark Pittman, 1987.

Roxana Ng. "Immigrant Housewives in Canada: A Methodological Note", *Atlantis* 8/1, 1982, 111-118.

Roxanna Ng. "Sex, Ethnicity or Class: Some Methodological Consideration." *Studies in Sexual Politics* 1, 1984.

Roxanna Ng and Judith Ramirez. *Immigrant Housewives in Canada.* Toronto: Immigrant Women's Centre, 1981.

Ontario Ministry of Education. "The Development of a Policy on Race and Ethnocultural Equity." Report of the Provincial Advisory Committee on Race Relations, September 1987.

Peter C. Pineo. "The Social Standing of Ethnic and Racial Groupings." *Canadian Review of Sociology and Anthropology* 12/2 (1977): 147-157

Peter C. Pineo and John Porter. "Ethnic Origin and Occupational Attainment." *Ascripition and Achievement: Studies in Mobility and Status Attainment in Canada.* M. Boyd, J. Goyder, F.E. Jones, P.C. Pineo and J. Porter, eds. (Ottawa, Carleton University Press), 1985.

John Porter. *The Vertical Mosaic.* (Toronto, University of Toronto Press), 1965.

Adrienne Rich. "Compulsory Heterosexuality and Lesbian Existence". *The Signs Reader — Women, Gender and Scholarship,* Elizabeth Abel and Emily K. Abel, eds. (Chicago, University of Chicago Press), 1983, 139-168.

Anthony Richmond. "Ethnic Nationalism and Postindustrialism." *Two Nations, Many Cultures: Ethnic Groups in Canada.* Second Edition. Jean Leonard Elliot, ed. (Scarborough, Prentice-Hall Canada) 1983.

Barbara Roberts. "Ladies, Women and the State: Managing Female Immigration, 1880-1920." *Community Organization and the Canadian State.* Roxana Ng, Gillian Walker and Jacob Muller, eds. (Toronto, Garamond Press), forthcoming.

Edward Said. *Orientalism.* (New York, Vintage Books), 1979.

Derek Sayer. *Marx's Method: Ideology, Science and Critique in 'Capital'.* (Sussex, The Harvester Press), 1979.

Dorothy E. Smith *The Everyday World as Problematic: A Feminist Sociology.* (Toronto, University of Toronto Press), 1987.

Dorothy E. Smith "Feminist Reflections on Political Economy." Paper Presented at the annual meeting of Political Science and Political Economy, Learned Societies Meetings, Hamilton, June 1987.

Dorothy E. Smith "Women, Class and Family." *Women, Class, Family and the State.* Varda Burstyn and Dorothy E. Smith, eds., (Toronto, Garamond Press), 1985.

Dorothy E. Smith. "Women's Equality and the Family." *Inequality: Essays on the Political Economy of Social Welfare,* Allan Moscovitch and Glenn Drover, eds. (Toronto, University of Toronto Press), 1985, 156-198.

Dorothy E. Smith. "Women's Perspective as a Radical Critique of Sociology", *Sociological Inquiry* 44/1 (1974): 7-13.

Pierre L. VanderBerghe. *The Ethnic Phenomenon.*, (New York, Elsevier), 1981.

Max Weber. *Economy and Society.* (New York, Bedminister), 1978.

Speaking of Women's Lives and Imperialist Economics: Two Introductions from *Silenced*
Makeda Silvera

Endnotes

[1] Silvera, Makeda. *Silenced,* (Toronto, Sister Vision Press), 1983, 87.

[2] Ibid., 17.

[3] Leslie, Genevieve. *Women at Work Ontario 1850-1930 Domestic Services in Canada* (Toronto, The Women's Press), 1974, 95.

[4] Ibid., 99.

[5] Ibid., 99.

[6] Ibid., 99.

[7] Henry, Frances. The West Indian Domestic Scheme in Canada", *Social and Economic Studies*, March 1968, 83-91.

[8] Ibid.

[9] Epstein, Rachel, "Domestic Workers: The Experience in B.C.", *Union Sisters*, (Toronto, The Women's Press), 1983, 223.

[10] Silvera, Makeda, *Silenced*, 67.

[11] Ibid., 59.

[12] Guidelines and Procedures - Foreign Domestic Movement, (Canada Employment and Immigration Commission), Ontario Region Directive, December 6, 1981.

[13] Ibid.

[14] Oakley, A., "Interviewing Women", ed. H. Roberts *Doing Feminist Research*, 191.

[15] Ibid., 187-8, 195.

A Working Paper on Black Women in Toronto: Gender, Race, and Class
Dionne Brand

References

Hazel Carby. "Black Feminism and the Boundaries of Sisterhood." *The Empire Strikes Back*. (Birmingham, Centre for Contemporary Cultural Studies, University of Birmingham and Hutchinson), 1983.

Jeffery Reitz, Liviana Calzavara and Donna Dasko. *Ethnic Inequality and Segregation in Jobs*. (Toronto, Centre for Urban and Community Studies, University of Toronto), 1981.

Jean Baker Miller. *Toward a New Psychology of Women*. (Boston, Beacon Press), 1976.

Karl Marx. *Das Capital*. Volume 1 (Moscow, Progress Press), 1958.

Makeda Silvera, *Silenced* (Toronto, Sister Vision Press), 1983, 1989.

The Contributors

Himani Bannerji was born in India in 1942 and migrated to Canada in 1969. She currently teaches in the department of Sociology, York University, Canada. She has published two books of poetry, *Separate Sky, Doing Time*, a children's novel *Coloured pictures*, and short stories. A book of essays on cultural politics is forthcoming from *Toronto South African Review* publication, entitled *Writing on the Wall*. She reaches writers in the areas of feminist theory, gender and colonialism, theories of class and race. She has also co-authored and edited *Unsettling Relations: The University as a Site of Feminist Struggle*, (Toronto, The Women's Press)

Dionne Brand is a poet and writer living in Toronto. She has published six books of poetry. One of her collections of poetry, *No Language is Neutral*, was nominated for a Governor General's Award in 1990. She has also published a book of short stories, *Sans Souci and other stories*. She co-authored a work in non-fiction, *Rivers Have Sources Trees Have Roots-Speaking of Racism*. Her latest non-fiction book, *No Burden To Carry* is an oral history of Black women in Ontario. Brand also works in documentary film. She is currently working on her third film, A Long Time Comin'. She is also Assistant Professor in the English Department at the University of Guelph .

Linda Carty is Assistant Professor of Sociology at the University of Michigan-Flint, Michigan. She is a feminist theorist and her main concern is exploring the relationship between gender, race and class. She has written essays for journals and magazines such as, *Resources for Feminist Research*, and books including, *Unsettling Relations: The University as a site of Feminist Struggle*, (Toronto, The Women's Press).

Cecilia Green, a native of Dominica, has taught Caribbean, Women's and Diaspora Studies at the University of Michigan and Eastern Michigan University. She has authored a study on 'Export Processing' and women workers in Eastern Caribbean. Her research interests include Caribbean women's history and the Caribbean role in the transnationalization of certain industry. She currently lives in Ann Arbor, Michigan, where she is active in Haitian solidarity work.

Amita Handa is a South Asian woman living and struggling in Toronto, Canada. She has a love-hate relationship with academia. Handa is currently working on her thesis at the Ontario Institute of Studies in Education which will attempt to document the voices and struggles of South Asian teenage girls in Toronto.

Lee Maracle is a feminist Native author who is currently working on a Canada Council writing grant. She has a number of publications to her credit while remaining active in the Native Women's Movement in her new home of Toronto.

Arun P. Mukherjee was born in 1946 in Lahore in the pre-partition India. She came to Canada in 1971 on a Commonwealth Scholarship to do graduate work in English at the University of Toronto. She is an Assistant Professor in the Department of English at York University, North York, Ontario and teaches Post-colonial Literature. She is the author of *The Gospel of Wealth in the American Novel: The Rhetoric of Dreiser and this Contemporaries* (1987), and *Towards an Aesthetic of Opposition: Essays on Literature, Criticism & Cultural* Imperialism (1988). She recently finished editing *Sharing Our Experience: An Anthology of Letters by Aboriginal Women & Women of Colour* for the Canadian Advisory Council on the Status of Women.

Roxana Ng received her Ph.D from the University of Toronto in 1984, specializing in the area of immigrant women and the state. Following teaching stints at various universities (Saskatchewan, Queen's, New Brunswick), she is now a Professor at the Ontario Institute for the Studies in Education. Roxana's research interests lie with the history of immigrant women's organizing in Canada, along with race relations and multiculturalism. Principal publications are: *Immigrant Housewives in Canada*, with Judith Ramirez. Toronto: Immigrant Women's Centre, 1981; *The Politics of Community Services. Immigrant Women, Class and State*, (Toronto, Garamond Press), 1988; *Community Organization and the Canadian State*, Roxana Ng, Gillian Walker and Jacob Muller, eds., (Toronto, Garamond Press), 1989. Roxana has been active in the immigrant women's movement since 1976. She is currently working, with practitioners in the field, on the development of anti-racist and anti-sexist teaching methods.

Sherene Razack is an educator and an assistant professor at the Ontario Institute for Studies in Education. She teaches graduate courses on education for social change, race issue in law and education and feminist theory. Her publications include *Canadian Feminism and the Law* (Toronto, Second Story Press), 1991, articles on radical pedagogy and on women, race, culture and disability in law. She is currently researching Gender, Race and Culture in Canadian Courts with the assistance of a grant from SSHRC. As an educator in the area of human rights and social change, she has designed and facilitated workshops for trade unionists and community activists for the past twelve years. Sherene Razack has a Ph.D in education.

Anita Sheth came to Canada from India in 1982 to undertake a M.A. programme at Queen's University and has lived here as a foreign student ever since. She is currently a Ph.D student on visa permit at the Department of Sociology, Ontario Institute for Studies in Education. Her thesis work is on academic feminists as consumers of television. Sheth is an editorial Board Member of "Resources for Feminist Research (DRF)" and has co-guest edited the issue, "Transforming Knowledge and Politics". She also co-guest edited the issue, "South Asian Women" for *Canadian Women Studies Journal.* She has been active in student anti-racist, feminist politics at Ontario Institute for Studies in Education (OISE).

Makeda Silvera has been involved in community activism in Toronto since 1972, and spent over five years working with Toronto's black community newspapers. She is the author of *Silenced,* a book of interviews with Caribbean domestic workers in Canada. She has also published a book of short stories, *Remembering G and other stories,* and anthologized *Piece of My Heart,* the first lesbian of colour anthology in North America. She is the editor at Sister Vision Press. She is currently working on another collection of short stories.

Aruna Srivastava is a writer, cultural worker and a Professor of Post-Colonial Literature at the University of Calgary.

May Yee was born and raised in Canada. She studied political economy and political theory at Carlton University in Ottawa. She has worked as an "English as a Second Language" teacher to working people, and is an activist in anti-racist feminist organizing. She helped to set up and worked actively in Women's Action Against Racist Policing (WAARP). She is a poet, a writer and is currently residing in China where she is pursuing Chinese language training and other studies.